India Briefing, 1990

India Briefing, 1990

edited by
Marshall M. Bouton
and Philip Oldenburg

Published in cooperation with
The Asia Society

Deborah Field Washburn,
Series Editor

Westview Press
Boulder • San Francisco • Oxford

Copyright © 1990 by The Asia Society

Published in 1990 in the United States of America by Westview Press, Inc., 5500 Central Avenue, Boulder, Colorado 80301, and in the United Kingdom by Westview Press, 36 Lonsdale Road, Summertown, Oxford OX2 7EW

Library of Congress ISSN: 0894-5136
ISBN: 0-8133-1073-3
ISBN: 0-8133-1072-5 (pbk.)

Printed and bound in the United States of America

The paper used in this publication meets the requirements of the American National Standard for Permanence of Paper for Printed Library Materials Z39.48-1984.

10   9   8   7   6   5   4   3   2   1

Contents

Preface

Nineteen eighty-nine was a year of transition in India. After a heated campaign that culminated in India's ninth general election in November, Rajiv Gandhi's Congress(I) government stepped down and a government headed by V. P. Singh was installed in December. The new government, which depends upon the support of widely divergent groups in parliament, faces major challenges, among them the rise of communal tensions in Kashmir and Punjab state and an economic growth rate that, after an unprecedented surge in the 1980s, appeared to be tapering off at the end of the decade.

India enters the 1990s committed to decentralizing its politics and administration, enhancing its economic growth, and further improving the lot of its masses in poverty—an agenda on which significant progress has already been made. As it faces the future, the country must also find the will and the means to conserve its rich heritage of monuments, art, and artistic traditions.

In foreign relations, the new government has moved to improve its relations with neighboring states. Indian troops were withdrawn from Sri Lanka in March 1990, and revived economic and security agreements with Nepal appear to be in the offing. The dispute with Pakistan over Kashmir has flared again, however, with no solution in sight. *India Briefing, 1990* aims to bring to readers an understanding of these and other important developments in Indian affairs.

India Briefing, 1990 is the fourth in a series of annual assessments prepared by the Education and Contemporary Affairs Division of The Asia Society. The division also prepares *China Briefing* and, this year for the first time, *Korea Briefing*. All three books are copublished by The Asia Society and Westview Press. The Asia Society is a nonprofit, nonpartisan educational organization dedicated to increasing U.S. understanding of Asia and its importance to the United States and the world at large.

The editors wish to express their appreciation to the authors for their hard work in preparing and revising chapters, and to Susan McEachern and her colleagues at Westview Press for their unflagging support and enthusiasm for the series. Carolyn Kreuger did a fine job of preparing the chronology. Interns Salma Hasan Ali and Puneet Talwar provided excellent research and editorial assistance, and Patricia Farr and Steve Tuemmler were extremely helpful in the editing of particular chapters. The superb editing effort by Asia Society Senior Editor Deborah Field Washburn, with the able assistance of Andrea Sokerka, has made the individual contributions into a book.

Marshall M. Bouton
The Asia Society

Philip Oldenburg
Columbia University

June 1990

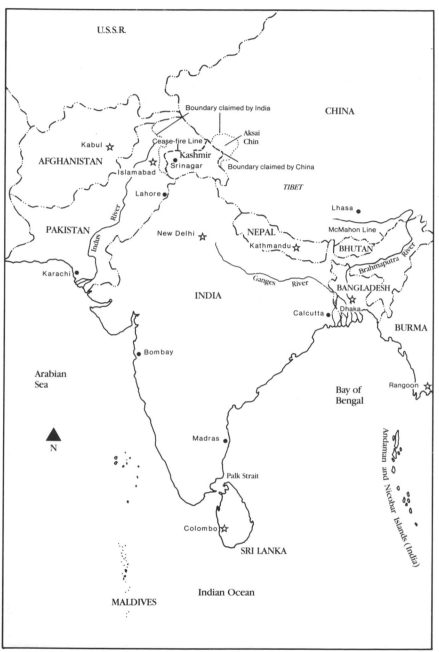

U.S.S.R.

CHINA

Boundary claimed by India

Aksai Chin

Kabul ☆

Cease-fire Line

AFGHANISTAN

Kashmir

Islamabad ☆

Srinagar ●

Boundary claimed by China

Lahore ●

TIBET

Lhasa ●

PAKISTAN

New Delhi ☆

NEPAL

McMahon Line

Kathmandu ☆

BHUTAN

Karachi ●

Indus River

INDIA

Ganges River

Brahmaputra River

BANGLADESH

Dhaka ●

Calcutta ●

BURMA

Bombay ●

Arabian Sea

Rangoon ●☆

Bay of Bengal

N

Madras ●

Palk Strait

Andaman and Nicobar Islands (India)

Colombo ☆

SRI LANKA

Indian Ocean

MALDIVES

South Asia

India

1
From Majority to Minority Rule: Making Sense of the "New" Indian Politics

Atul Kohli*

India held its ninth general election in 1989, and it failed to produce a majority government. Although India's premier political party, the Congress(I), remains the single largest group in parliament, its control of 197 of the 545 seats was insufficient to enable it to form a government. Instead, the second-largest group in parliament, the National Front, formed India's first minority government in four decades. Led by V. P. Singh, a former Congress(I) leader, the new government has fewer than 150 seats and rests on the tacit support of two ideologically distinct groups, the avowedly secular but essentially communal and pro-Hindu Bharatiya Janata Party (BJP), which controls 86 seats, and the Left Front, a group of allied communist and left-leaning parties that won more than 50 seats.

How does one explain this political shift from majority to minority rule, and what are the future implications for India of minority government? In this chapter I propose that the national election of 1989 confirmed and finally brought to the surface three long-term trends in Indian politics: the declining hold of the Congress Party; the growing activism of various political groups and their mobilization of support; and the attempts, albeit halting, to forge a national alternative to the Congress(I). A 1989 development representing change rather than continuity was the emergence of a religious party, the pro-Hindu BJP, as a significant political force.

The near future of Indian politics looks uncertain. Good democratic government requires that activism of the citizenry be channeled

*I would like to acknowledge the research assistance of Devesh Kapur and Arijit Sen and the helpful comments of Pratap Mehta on an earlier draft.

through coherent institutions. Demands by India's various socioeconomic groups are likely to increase, but it is far from certain that political institutions will be able to accommodate them. In view of recent trends, it is likely that both government and politics will be more unstable in the near future than in the past.

The Long-Term Trends

The election and related political issues will dominate any attempt to make sense of Indian politics in 1989. All other major domestic political developments had to do with sociopolitical conflicts: continuing terrorism in Punjab and growing tension in Kashmir, Hindu-Muslim conflicts in various parts of India, and demonstrations and agitation by various, often privileged, groups against the government's attempts to "reserve" jobs and educational opportunities for selected underprivileged groups (India's version of affirmative action). Before analyzing the elections and other political events of 1989, however, it is important to explore the political background.

The Changing Position of the Congress Party

Although the Congress Party has been India's ruling party for most of the past 40 years, electoral victories since 1967 have not come easily. As the major nationalist party, the party that had led a successful struggle against British colonialism, the Congress was India's "natural" ruling party in the 1950s. During the 1960s, however, opposition to the Congress grew in various parts of India. Like India itself, this opposition was quite diverse: it was led by a regional nationalist party in the southern state of Tamil Nadu; by a religious party, the pro-Sikh Akali Dal, in the Punjab; by various communist parties in West Bengal and Kerala; and by parties resting on the support of rural "backward" castes in the populous heartland state of Uttar Pradesh. (These castes are predominantly composed of landowning family farmers situated between high castes, such as Brahmins, and the lowest, or Scheduled, castes, also known as Untouchables.) The result was that the Congress Party nearly lost its majority in the national election of 1967.

Ever since that crucial election, the Congress has had difficulty maintaining a stable majority coalition.[1] Indira Gandhi, who inherited

---

[1] For a good overview of the Congress's changing electoral fortunes, see Paul Brass, "Political Parties and Electoral Politics," in Marshall M. Bouton and Philip Oldenburg, eds., *India Briefing, 1989* (Boulder, CO: Westview Press, 1989), pp. 61–106; see also My-

power from her father, Jawaharlal Nehru, won the 1971 election handsomely, but by then the political situation in India had changed quite sharply. The old Congress Party had split in two, and the segment led by Indira Gandhi never developed the hallmarks of an organized party: regular membership, internal party elections, or a second and third tier of leaders with support from the grass roots. Instead, Indira Gandhi adopted a populist slogan, *garibi hatao* ("away with poverty"), and used her considerable leadership skills to establish direct links with the majority of Indians, those living in poverty. Having risen to power in 1971 on a wave of populism and socialism, she fought and won the 1972 state elections in the shadow of a regional war that India had "won" and that had led to the dismemberment of Pakistan and the emergence of Bangladesh.

The rise of a populist Indira Gandhi had several major political consequences; especially important was the organizational decline of the Congress(I) Party.[2] The more Indira Gandhi's power came to be derived from a mass following, the more she bypassed established intermediate leaders and sought to appoint new party officers herself. Over the short run, as long as Indira Gandhi's popularity was unchallenged, this strategy of top-down political appointments helped consolidate her power. The strategy, however, had long-term costs. First, it tended to alienate from the Congress many who had independent power bases. Over time, these individuals have sought to combine their oppositional energies. And second, the system of top-down appointments often put in powerful positions individuals who would not necessarily have been the choice of the Congress's grass-roots membership. This development also weakened the Congress by diminishing the legitimacy of its lower-level leadership.

The electoral euphoria of 1971 and 1972 was short-lived. Opposition to Indira Gandhi, which had been there all along, reorganized, and it resurfaced with a vengeance in the mid-1970s. The political style in India had also become more activist. Indira Gandhi's populism and mobilization of support from the mass of Indians came to be matched by the opposition's militancy. States like Gujarat and Bihar became

---

ron Weiner, *India at the Polls, 1980* (Washington, DC: American Enterprise Institute, 1980).

[2] More detailed discussion of Congress's organizational decline is to be found in James Manor, "Parties and Party System," in Atul Kohli, ed., *India's Democracy: An Analysis of Changing State-Society Relations* (Princeton: Princeton University Press, 1988), pp. 62–98; Lloyd I. and Susanne Hoeber Rudolph, *In Pursuit of Lakshmi: The Political Economy of the Indian State* (Chicago: University of Chicago Press, 1987), chaps. 4–6; and Atul Kohli, *Democracy and Disorder: India's Growing Crisis of Governability* (New York: Cambridge University Press, forthcoming).

battlegrounds between Indira Gandhi and the opposition, by this time led by an old follower of Mahatma Gandhi, Jayaprakash Narayan. Labor and peasant militancy added to the turmoil. When Indira Gandhi's power was threatened, she imposed a nationwide Emergency, in which democratic rights were curtailed for nearly two years.

Indira Gandhi and her Congress Party lost the 1977 election. This defeat reflected both popular anger over her imposition of the Emergency and the fact that the diverse opposition to her party had managed to unite, if only momentarily. Factionalism within the opposition, however, resurfaced, and the opposition Janata Party government could not function. This failure, in turn, created a sense that there might not be a viable national alternative to the Congress. Indira Gandhi benefited from this shift in national mood and won the election once again in 1980.

There was a growing realization in India in the early 1980s that Indira Gandhi might not come back to power in 1985. Her attempts to alleviate poverty had not been very successful. As a result, she had failed to consolidate her populist support into a stable coalition. She was thus increasingly in search of new strategies for securing electoral majorities. Since Hindus are by far the majority in India, Indira Gandhi sought to mobilize support around the issue of Hindus versus Indian minorities. For the first time since independence and partition in the late 1940s, religious themes resurfaced in Indian politics at the national level. While complicated in origin, the government's failure to deal with the demands of Sikhs in Punjab state for religious and political autonomy, which resulted in political turmoil and terrorism, was in part rooted in Congress's political need to win the support of Hindus. Growing Hindu-Muslim problems, though quite complex and variable in origin, can also be traced to the need to build political majorities around religious appeals.

Indira Gandhi's tragic assassination in 1984 by two Sikh bodyguards turned out to be a great political dividend for the Congress(I) Party and for its new leader, Indira's son Rajiv. Rajiv Gandhi won by a large majority—nearly 48 percent of the popular vote and 77 percent, or 415, of the parliamentary seats. This was mainly a result of Indira Gandhi's assassination, which created sympathy for her son across India. Moreover, the fear of impending political turmoil was skillfully utilized by the Congress leaders to mobilize political support.

The important point is that, ever since 1967, the Congress has won elections under unusual circumstances, whether the leadership actually created those circumstances or simply took advantage of them. These victories were more the result of popular mood swings than of stable social support for the Congress(I) Party. What was significant about the 1989 election, therefore, was that it was probably the first "usual" election since 1967 in that it was not conducted in the shadow of mood-generating euphorias or crises. What looks like a major decline in the Congress's position is in part explained simply by the return to political normality.

Growing Political Activism

The unquestioned dominance of the Congress Party in the 1950s and the early 1960s rested in part on the legitimacy it inherited from its role in India's independence struggle and in part on a patronage network that stretched from New Delhi to India's numerous villages. The patronage system worked because the relations between social "superiors" and "inferiors," especially in the villages, were characterized in this period by the latter's relative acquiescence. As a result, rural elites were periodically able to sway the votes of the lower strata toward the Congress in exchange for resources that Congress governments controlled.

The spread of democratic ideas and competitive politics has over time helped transform the acquiescence of lower social groups into political activism in many parts of India. These changes started in the 1960s, and their significance has grown ever since. The more active and demanding various groups have become, the less successful has become the old Congress system of patronage networks. If rural elites cannot readily sway the votes of the lower rural strata, what is the political utility of channeling governmental largesse to them? These changing political patterns in the villages have, in turn, contributed to important changes at the top of the political pyramid.

Indira Gandhi was among the first to sense this important political change. It is clear in retrospect that her populist slogan *garibi hatao* was aimed at capturing the support of the new groups that were emerging from under the sway of traditional rural elites. Her populism, in turn, further contributed to mobilizing India's lower rural strata.

As noted above, the failure to implement anti-poverty programs in the 1970s made it difficult for Indira Gandhi to consolidate her position with her new supporters. The dissatisfied rural poor of India thus became susceptible to new forms of political mobilization in the 1980s. Their dissatisfaction has found diverse expressions, often varying from region to region. One disconcerting nationwide trend, however, has been the attempt by leaders to create new electoral majorities along religious lines. Whether the poorest of the poor support this appeal is not clear. What is clearer is that a failure of the Congress's populism has created a fluid political situation that can now be manipulated by demagogues for other purposes.

In addition to the poor, the somewhat better-off middle groups of rural India have become politically active over the last two decades. Two movements of national significance are worthy of note. First, there is the "reservation" movement of the "backward" castes, which demands that government-controlled jobs and educational opportunities be allocated—that is, reserved—according to such ascriptive criteria as caste. Demands of this sort have generally had a top-down quality in the sense that leaders, rather than social groups, have brought the issues to the fore in the hope of gaining the electoral support of the numerically significant "backward" castes. The more the champions of these castes have succeeded, the more resistance has been put up by elite castes. Some of the political turmoil of the 1980s in states like Gujarat and Bihar can be traced to this type of conflict.

The other movement among the middle rural groups has demanded higher prices for agricultural products and lower prices for such production inputs as fertilizer, electricity, and credit. Such initiatives have often attracted the support of those peasants who have done rather well for themselves by taking advantage of the government's "green-revolution" policies. These groups now seek to transform their newly acquired wealth into political clout, especially because they feel that the urban rich have done much better than they. The present government is more representative of both the "backward" castes and the better-off green-revolution farmers, especially those of North-Central India, than was Rajiv Gandhi's Congress(I) government.

India's urban middle-income groups are not politically well organized. Their political significance is considerable, however, much greater than their numbers (about 10 percent of India's total population) would suggest. This is because men and women of letters generally come from this stratum and tend to be society's opinion makers. Rajiv Gandhi benefited greatly from the positive evaluation of these groups in 1985 and 1986, in part because of the pro-urban consumer policies that he pursued and in part because of his initial image as an incorrupt "Mr. Clean." Between 1987 and 1989, however, many among India's urban educated groups became increasingly disturbed by revelations of corruption at the highest levels of government. The theme of clean government, which India's new prime minister, V. P. Singh, has also adopted, is aimed primarily at these groups.

In a country as diverse as India, a discussion at the national level can hide more than it reveals. The patterns of growing activism vary considerably from region to region. The following brief examples are provided to give the flavor of India's regional complexities.[3]

Punjab state is mired in a violent and fratricidal ethnic conflict involving Sikh militants in a confrontation with New Delhi as they seek greater political control. (Sikhs are a religious minority constituting nearly half of Punjab's population.) While complex in origin, the "Sikh crisis" is rooted in such factors as the growing wealth of the area's middle peasants, many of whom are Sikhs, issues of ethnic nationalism, and competitive political mobilization by both the Akali Dal (the party of the Sikhs) and the Congress Party.

The pattern of conflict in the state of Gujarat is different. Throughout the 1980s, elite and "backward" castes of the area fought, often violently, for control of state power and over issues of affirmative action for the "backward" castes. This caste conflict is quickly being transformed into Hindu-Muslim conflict as parties like the BJP succeed in mobilizing support across caste, but along religious, lines.

The government of yet another state, Bihar, has simply stopped functioning. The levels of mobilization along both caste and class lines are so high that nearly all of the groups are fighting each other, often with their own private armies. By contrast, highly mobilized labor, peasant, and student groups have provided the power base of a reform-oriented ruling communist party in the state of West Bengal. However, the resulting political stalemate between the property-owning groups and the communist rulers there has also generated economic stagnation.

In South India, themes of regional nationalism have declined in the state of Tamil Nadu. As a result, while the conflict between Tamil Nadu and New Delhi has receded, it has also become increasingly difficult to carve out a new majority coalition in the state. The new political situation is thus fluid, with wide swings in electoral behavior likely. The same is true in the state of Andhra Pradesh. The seven-year personalistic rule of the film-actor-turned-politician N. T. Rama Rao has left behind a highly deinstitutionalized political system. Weakness of both political parties and bureaucracy has, in turn, contributed to growing caste and class conflict.

In general, the levels of political activity in India are much higher today than they were in the past. This growing activism reflects, in part, the changing socioeconomic conditions that development neces-

---

[3] For one study that explores this diversity in great detail, see my forthcoming book, *Democracy and Disorder, op. cit.* For details of political changes in various states, see also Francine Frankel and M. S. A. Rao, eds., *Dominance and State Power in Modern India: Decline of a Social Order*, 2 vols. (New Delhi: Oxford University Press, 1989, 1990).

sarily produces, but, more important, it indicates the spread of democratic values and competitive politics. Egalitarian ideas have eroded the subservient relationships of social "inferiors" to "superiors." Political elites have, in turn, sought to mobilize the hitherto "inferiors" for their own political purposes. The Indian government controls a great many resources in a very poor society. As the realization has spread that this government, or parts of it, can be controlled by the mobilization of support among new groups, such efforts have spread. High levels of mobilization among diverse groups have made it difficult for governmental consensus to emerge.

Alternatives to the Congress

The organizational and electoral decline of the Congress Party and the growing activism of various political groups have been important political trends. If a well-organized alternative to the Congress had successfully accommodated the newly mobilized groups, India might well have had a more effective democratic government than it has in recent years. Unfortunately, the political record of the opposition to the Congress at the national level—certainly up until 1989—has been fairly poor.

The major problem of the centrist political parties opposing the Congress has been their inability to act in unity. In India's electoral system, the candidate who wins the most votes in a constituency wins a seat in the lower house of the national parliament, the Lok Sabha. If more than one candidate opposes the Congress candidate, the typical outcome is that the opposition candidates split the vote and the Congress candidate wins, usually with well under 50 percent of the total vote. In spite of this situation, in which it would be highly rational for those opposing the Congress to run a single candidate, it has repeatedly proven difficult for the opposition to unify.

A number of factors have inhibited the ability of the centrist opposition parties to unify, the most important of which is probably the ambitions of leaders competing for senior positions. Leaders have often pursued their short-term interests, at the expense of their larger goal of defeating the Congress. This has been true in nearly all of the elections in India except for two: the 1977 election after the Emergency and the most recent one. The Emergency created an intense, though temporary, horror of an authoritarian regime led by Indira Gandhi, thereby uniting the opposition parties under the umbrella of the Janata Party. This temporary unity, however, lasted for no more than two years before conflicting leadership ambitions led to the dissolution of the fragile coalition government.

What is true for the centrist opposition is not so true for opposition parties on the left and the right, whose ideology and superior organization have enabled them to tame leadership factionalism and act in relative unity. Both the BJP and the Communist Party of India (Marxist) [CPI(M)] reflect these tendencies. These parties, however, have until recently enjoyed only a limited power base. The CPI(M) has been confined to certain regions of India, and the BJP, to certain segments of the urban population, especially trading groups, in western and central India. The electoral position of the BJP, however, has changed quite sharply over the last two to three years.

Many of the non-Congress parties, whether centrist or ideological, have had some experience of being in power during the last decade, and some political learning has occurred in the parties over this time period. For example, the CPI(M)'s continuing stint in power in the state of West Bengal definitely transformed it from a revolutionary party in the 1970s into a reformist and a pragmatic party in the 1980s. While the BJP has not had an equivalent prolonged experience in running a state government, some of its prominent leaders, such as Atal Bihari Vajpayee, did serve as senior ministers during the Janata government (1977–79). Some of these leaders are also considered pragmatic, not deeply communal, in their management of everyday politics.

Other non-Congress leaders, for example, Ramakrishna Hegde, Devi Lal, and N. T. Rama Rao, also ran state governments (Karnataka, Haryana, and Andhra Pradesh respectively) during the 1980s. Among their experiences, a particularly valuable one was the attempt to collectively bargain with New Delhi for more state resources and greater political control. The non-Congress chief ministers met periodically to chart out their political strategies, and this provided them with experience in working together.[4]

Despite this shared political experience, one should not overstate the capacity of India's non-Congress parties and leaders to generate a unified opposition to the Congress(I) Party. While many leaders are pragmatic, there remain policy differences among them. More important, there is the ever-present danger of competing leadership ambitions. Leaders like Haryana's Devi Lal are especially troublesome because they come from a tradition of mercurial politics in which "power first" is the main goal. Moreover, the attempts to carve out a unified electoral force during much of the period leading up to the 1989 election were tortuous. Given the history of Janata rule and of numerous failed attempts to create a non-Congress political force, one

---

[4] I owe this insight to Philip Oldenburg.

cannot be too optimistic about the prospects of a unified non-Congress government in India.

The 1989 National Election

The significant political developments in 1989 were nearly all influenced by the imminence of the national election. The first half of the year was dominated by the on-again, off-again efforts of various opposition parties to forge a united front against the Congress. It would have been difficult to predict, say in February or March, whether the opposition parties would be able to work together. The Janata Dal, an aggregation of several smaller parties and now the main constituent of the National Front and thus of the government, was not formally recognized as a party in the Lok Sabha until April. Under the tacit leadership of V. P. Singh, the opposition then went on the political offensive and remained so until Congress's eventual defeat in November.

The opposition parties chose to focus their political energies on the issue of corruption. V. P. Singh and his cronies thus made much of the Bofors scandal: Bofors, a Swedish armaments company, allegedly made payments to high officials of Rajiv Gandhi's government to secure a contract to supply guns to the Indian armed forces. New revelations in July concerning payoffs led 73 non-Congress(I) members of parliament to quit the Lok Sabha en masse, demanding the resignation of Rajiv Gandhi. The opposition thus captured the moral high ground on the popular issue of "cleanliness" in government.

Rajiv Gandhi responded to the opposition's challenge by downplaying the issue of corruption and focusing political attention instead on decentralization of power. The Congress(I)-controlled Lok Sabha passed constitutional amendments in August that would have transferred a significant share of governmental resources directly from New Delhi to local governments. (The amendments failed to get the necessary two-thirds majority for passage in the Rajya Sabha, the upper house of parliament.) This political ploy was intended to simultaneously weaken the patronage powers of opposition-controlled state governments and enhance those of the Congress. It also aimed to counteract the image of Rajiv's government as elitist and removed from the people.

November's election was not announced until October, giving the opposition little time to formalize electoral agreements. Much to the Congress's chagrin, the National Front, the BJP, and the CPI(M) quickly managed to reach an arrangement to put up only one opposition candidate per constituency. Once these electoral agreements were

Table 1

Results of the Lok Sabha Elections, 1989*

	Number of seats won	(Percent)	Percentage of popular vote
Congress(I)	197	(37)	40.3
National Front			
Janata Dal	141	(27)	18.3
Telugu Desam	2	(1)	3.4
Congress(S)	1	(–)	–
BJP	86	(16)	11.8
Left Parties			
CPI(M)	32	(6)	6.5
CPI	12	(2)	2.7
Other Left	8	(2)	1.1
Others			
AIADMK	11	(2)	1.6
Akali Dal (Mann)	6	(1)	—
Bahujan Samaj Party	3	(1)	—
Small Parties and Independents	30	(6)	—

Source: Richard Sisson, "India in 1989: A Year of Elections in a Culture of Change," *Asian Survey*, Vol. 30 (February 1990), p. 122.

*No elections were held for 16 of the 545 seats in the Lok Sabha: the 14 seats for Assam state and the 2 seats reserved for Anglo-Indians. The total of 529 seats includes seats filled through by-elections held after November on account of vacancies due to resignations and deaths of candidates or incumbents.

reached, the Congress was in serious political trouble. While the magnitude of the Congress's defeat came as a surprise to many observers, part of the reason for this reaction was simply that the opposition parties had come together such a short time before the elections.

Below the national level, the electoral outcomes provided a mixed picture. One fairly consistent result was that nearly all parties in power before the election lost power. As a result, Congress and Congress-supported parties came to dominate much of South India, whereas opposition parties like the BJP, the Janata Dal, and the CPI(M) won power in much of North India, in both western and eastern states.

The elections proved a major setback to Rajiv Gandhi's Congress(I) Party. The decline in the number of seats that the Congress won in 1989 was dramatic—it won 197 seats, in comparison with 415 and 353 seats in the 1984 and 1980 elections respectively. The Congress's share of the popular vote, however, did not decline as dramatically (see Table 1); the Congress secured 40 percent of the vote, a drop of some 8 percent from the 1984 election. One needs to keep in mind, however, that Rajiv Gandhi's spectacular victory in 1984 was something of an exception; the voter turnout in 1989 was 10 percent lower than in 1984, suggesting that the extra level of politicization engendered by the sense of crisis in 1984 may have disappeared. The Congress's share of the popular vote in the 1980 elections, when the party also secured a comfortable majority in parliament, provides a different, and possibly more appropriate, point of comparison; its share that year was 43 percent. The decline in popular support for the Congress(I) Party between 1980 and 1989 was thus only 3 percent.

The juxtaposition of the dramatic decline in the number of Congress's parliamentary seats and the much less dramatic decline in its popular vote indicates that the Congress remains a significant political force in India, although its days of unquestioned dominance are clearly over. Even without dramatic changes in Indian politics, it could come back to power in the near future. The shift in India from a majority Congress national government to a minority non-Congress one is due to a small but significant decline in the Congress's popularity and to the changing nature of India's non-Congress parties, including their increased capacity to work together against the Congress.

Rajiv Gandhi's Loss of Support

One should not look for dramatic failures of Rajiv Gandhi to explain the Congress's defeat in 1989. However, his five years in power were not marked by any great successes.[5] When he established his leadership position in early 1985, he had specified the liberalization of the economy, the settlement of regional disputes, and the rebuilding of the Congress(I) Party as his political priorities. In retrospect, his performance in each of these areas was at best incomplete and at worst dismal. Even when his performance was relatively satisfactory Rajiv Gandhi never became a real leader, that is, someone who could persuade his detractors, as well as his followers, of the correctness of his actions.

---

[5] Two relatively brief assessments of Rajiv Gandhi's performance are Myron Weiner, "Rajiv Gandhi: A Mid-Term Assessment," in Marshall M. Bouton, ed., *India Briefing, 1987* (Boulder, CO: Westview Press, 1987), pp. 1–24; and the Epilogue in the paperback edition of Atul Kohli, ed., *India's Democracy: An Analysis of Changing State-Society Relations*, rev. ed. (Princeton: Princeton University Press, forthcoming).

Rajiv's attempts to liberalize India's economy had some success. India's macroeconomic performance under his rule was also relatively good: the economy grew by nearly 5 percent; agricultural growth was satisfactory; industrial growth picked up; and export performance was impressive. To the extent that his liberalization measures were responsible for the improved economic growth, Rajiv deserves credit.

Unfortunately for Rajiv, it proved difficult to translate economic performance into political dividends. First, his attempts at liberalization came to be interpreted as an abandonment of socialism. Rajiv's own party, the Congress(I), fearing that such policy shifts would cost the party electoral support, opposed many of his attempts to raise prices, trim public expenditures, and provide incentives to private producers. Other political parties took advantage of the opening that Rajiv's new economic orientation provided; they attempted to mobilize the people against the Congress(I) Party government, often successfully, and made the image of Rajiv as a pro-rich leader stick. The second reason for Rajiv's difficulty in getting political mileage from his economic successes was that his economic strategy rested, at least in part, on a boom in durable consumer goods purchased primarily by the better-off urban population. This created a sense, right or wrong, that the government was pro-city and less sympathetic to inhabitants of the countryside. The support of landowning peasant farmers may have been decisive in the electoral success of non-Congress parties, especially in such Hindi heartland states as Haryana and Uttar Pradesh.

In addition, for a series of complex reasons, the gap between the government's revenues and its expenditures grew, fueling inflation throughout 1988 and 1989. Since India's low-income democracy tends to be sensitive to inflation, there is no reason to doubt that dissatisfaction on this score cost Rajiv Gandhi political support. Thus, although India's economic performance—judged by international macroindicators—was relatively good, there was little in this performance to help mobilize the support of its electoral majorities, the peasant farmers and the poor.

Rajiv's attempts to solve such regional disputes as the Sikh crisis in Punjab state did not make much headway. After some initial successes in 1985 and 1986, he abandoned the attempt to find a political compromise between the demands of the Sikhs and the position of the national government. Part of the problem in this area was that the Sikhs are deeply divided among themselves. Equally important, however, was Rajiv's growing fear that such concessions to the Sikhs as the transfer of the city of Chandigarh—currently the joint capital of Haryana and Punjab—to Punjab would cost him political support, both in states like Haryana and within his own party. The failure to find a political solution, in turn, led to a "law and order" approach that exacerbated both terrorism and governmental repression.

It is not clear whether Rajiv's failures to solve regional disputes like that in Punjab had direct consequences in the 1989 election. It is hard to imagine a poor peasant in Tamil Nadu or West Bengal choosing to vote against the Congress on the basis of what was happening in Punjab. But what is likely is that such policy failures created a more general doubt about Rajiv's leadership qualities, especially in the eyes of India's urban middle classes. Since the opinions of these groups probably have some trickle-down effect, failures such as that in Punjab may have had an indirect negative electoral impact on Rajiv.

The failure that probably cost Rajiv the most in electoral terms was his inability to rebuild the Congress(I) Party. Internal party elections were announced, but, after considerable intraparty struggle, they were abandoned. The structure of the Congress(I) Party consists of a chain of officials appointed from the top. Replacement of this top-down hierarchy with a bottom-up structure would have reinvigorated the party, but it could also have posed a real threat to the existing party structure, including Rajiv's leadership. Because the effort to re-build the party was abandoned, however, Rajiv found himself without a dynamic organization to help him through the elections.

The opposition to Rajiv Gandhi, led by V. P. Singh, mobilized primarily around issues of corruption, rising prices, and, most important, the ineffectiveness of Rajiv as a leader—especially around the charge that he was not a man of the people, that he was too westernized to understand the plight of the ordinary Indian. Without detailed public opinion surveys, it is not easy to assess the electoral significance of such a political posture. However, although he stressed his own populist tinge, V. P. Singh did not emphasize any major policy differences with Rajiv Gandhi.

In addition, there were regional variations within this larger national picture. The fact that the Congress did rather well in several South Indian states requires explanation. Regional variations also suggest that local issues may have been as important as, if not more important than, national issues in influencing electoral outcomes. These phenomena are discussed further below.

The Coming Together of the Non-Congress Parties

The arithmetic of India's elections since 1967 has been such that a unified opposition could have kept the Congress out of office for nearly half of the last 22 years. How did India's significant non-

Congress parties manage to work together in the 1989 election? The simple and powerful answer is that they realized that the rewards of working together would be much higher than those of working separately. However, the inability of these same parties to work together in the past—and possibly again in the future—requires a further probing of the conditions that facilitated the working unity. Three factors were important: the nature of the main participants, the significant role of a new leadership, and a changing political situation in which the Congress's declining popularity bolstered the prospect of a non-Congress victory.

The parties that form and support the new minority government in India are diverse. Their separate identities, histories, and respective bases of support are difficult even for specialists in Indian politics to master. Fortunately, not all of the details are necessary for an understanding of the three major constituents: the National Front and its main component, the Janata Dal, which have now formed the government; the Left Front, dominated by the CPI(M), which supports but is not part of the government; and the BJP, which is in a similar position to the Left Front vis-à-vis the government.

The party that is at the heart of the new government is the Janata Dal, which was itself put together from other parties and groups in early 1989. The three main components of the Janata Dal were the Jan Morcha, the Lok Dal, and the Janata Party. The Jan Morcha was not a party; rather, it consisted of a group of senior former Congress(I) leaders like V. P. Singh, Arun Nehru, and Arif Mohammed Khan, who had at one time or another served under Rajiv Gandhi but who had later parted company with him and joined the opposition. The Lok Dal was the old party of the late Charan Singh and was itself by the mid-1980s divided into two factions, one led by Charan Singh's son, Ajit Singh, with a base in western Uttar Pradesh, and the other by Devi Lal, with a base in Haryana. As the party of the green-revolution farmers and "backward" castes, which had always opposed the Brahmin-dominated Congress, the Lok Dal also enjoyed the support of the middle peasantry in other northern and central states like Bihar. The third group, the Janata Party, was an offshoot of the old Janata that had ruled India from 1977 to 1979. Entering into the 1989 election, this group consisted of the remnants of the old Congress Party of Morarji Desai from states like Gujarat and Karnataka—identified with individuals like Ramakrishna Hegde, the former chief minister of Karnataka and the present head of India's Planning Commission—and socialist and other parties from eastern Uttar Pradesh and Bihar, represented by individuals like Chandrashekhar.

These groups and parties came together under the tacit leadership of V. P. Singh to form the Janata Dal. The process of party formation went on throughout 1989 and was not easy. The possibility that the group would come apart was alive all year, and it remains an issue. The problems of unity revolved mainly around personalities and leadership ambitions; there were no major ideological or policy divides within this group. What facilitated the eventual unity was the emergence of V. P. Singh as a seemingly reluctant but tacit leader. The members of this group understood that, in policy terms, they were not all that different from the Congress, certainly not enough so to create a distinct coalition. It must also have been clear to them that they needed a leader who could appear to be a viable alternative to Rajiv Gandhi. The only way to overcome the difficulties of working together was to be led by another popular national leader.

V. P. Singh was in a good position to occupy this spot. As a former *raja* (prince) from Uttar Pradesh, who had supposedly renounced his principality and associated lands, V. P. Singh is in the mainstream of Indian politics, much more so than other former challengers to the Congress like Morarji Desai and Charan Singh. A trained lawyer and student of physics at Allahabad University, V. P. Singh rose to prominence under the tutelage of Indira Gandhi. Before being made Rajiv Gandhi's finance minister, he had already had a couple of brief stints in the national cabinet and had served as chief minister of Uttar Pradesh. Under Rajiv, V. P. Singh had initiated the liberalization of the economy and had later led corruption raids on prominent businesspeople.

V. P. Singh's parting of the ways with Rajiv Gandhi was widely interpreted in India as a result of pressure from unhappy and possibly corrupt businesspeople. This gave V. P. Singh the aura of an anti-corruption champion from the very beginning of his independent rise to power. Having been closely associated with the Congress all along, V. P. Singh wisely chose not to disassociate himself sharply from the Congress's policy positions. Instead he harped more and more on themes of anti-corruption, respect for norms and values in the conduct of democratic politics, and the need to decentralize power in India. The more his popularity rose, the more it must have become clear to the motley coalition that is now the Janata Dal that it could not do without him as its leader. The less contentious the issue of who was likely to lead the opposition to the Congress became, the more likely it became that a new party could be formed.

The only representation the Janata Dal had in the south was in Karnataka. This lacuna was filled by a working alliance forged under the umbrella of the National Front. The Front brought together such

South Indian parties as the ruling party in Tamil Nadu, the Dravida Munnetra Kazhagam (DMK), and the former ruling party of Andhra Pradesh, the Telugu Desam. Although both the DMK and the Telugu Desam did poorly in the 1989 election, the fact remains that this alliance gave the Janata Dal a semblance of popular support in the south as well as in the north.

Both the communists and the BJP have their own reasons to support the Janata Dal in power. As parties on the left and the right of the political spectrum, they are likely to have important policy differences with the centrist Janata Dal. It is important to note, however, that on crucial basics, policy differences among these coalition constituents are not totally irreconcilable. The CPI(M), for example, is in practice more a social-democratic than a communist party. It is committed to a democratic system, it believes in multiclass alliances, it promotes reform rather than revolution, and it has come around to the view that in a private economy, if economic growth is to be facilitated, then private producers need government protection and support. Similarly, the BJP, while pro-Hindu in its overall orientation, is often willing to soften its religious militancy, especially when it is in a ruling position.

The power base of the CPI(M) is essentially regional. West Bengal remains its stronghold, although it also has considerable bases in both Tripura and Kerala. Besides an antipathy toward the Congress and Rajiv Gandhi, the CPI(M)'s main reason for supporting the Janata Dal government is that it views this as an opportunity to broaden its regional power base. Whether the CPI(M) continues to support the Janata Dal government or not will rest primarily on its assessment of whether or not this goal is being met. The CPI(M)'s main differences, in any case, are not with the Janata Dal but rather with the BJP over the issue of communalism, that is, over the appropriateness of religion as a tool of political mobilization. If the prospects of the BJP joining the government grow, this could lead to the withdrawal of CPI(M) support. That, in turn, could mean the end of the experiment in minority government.

The BJP has in the past actually worked fairly closely with several constituents of the Janata Dal, though not always with happy results. The BJP, which is the old Jan Sangh, was part of the Janata Party that ruled India from 1977 to 1979. Its electoral fortunes have fluctuated over the last few decades. Its present strength is in states like Rajasthan, Himachal Pradesh, and Madhya Pradesh. These states were at one time Congress strongholds. As there were no other major opposition parties in these states, the BJP utilized its superior organization to piece together a multicaste coalition that used fundamentalist sentiments to unify Hindus around political issues. For example, the BJP or religious organizations loosely allied with it are often alleged to be behind religious riots, especially anti-Muslim riots, that consolidate Hindu support for the party.

Over the last several years the BJP has expanded its political activities, and it has also benefited from Hindu revivalism. In states like Gujarat, for example, the BJP has slowly chipped away at the Congress alliance of lower-middle castes, lower castes, and Muslims against the dominant castes, by trying to unite Hindus against Muslims. Muslim communal violence such as that in Ahmedabad, which the BJP may itself have instigated, have contributed to the BJP's growing popularity. In other states, for example Uttar Pradesh, religious organizations such as the Vishwa Hindu Parishad were active throughout 1989, conducting *puja* (religious ceremonies) in villages and collecting money for the building of a Hindu temple on a controversial site in the holy city of Ayodhya, controversial because it overlaps the site of a revered mosque. Such activities also enabled these groups to mobilize religious sentiments of Hindus against Muslims. Political parties like the BJP, in turn, were well positioned to take advantage of such shifting sentiments, although, to be fair, it must be added that even Rajiv Gandhi attempted to capitalize on such mood shifts by declaring that his main goal in power was to create a *Ram Rajya*, or a kingdom of peace and prosperity such as that associated in Hindu mythology with the revered Lord Rama.

The BJP, more than the CPI(M), would like to join the Janata Dal government. Having won 86 seats in the national parliament, the BJP considers itself deserving of such a role. The arithmetic of the present situation, however, is such that no non-Congress government can be formed without the help of the left. The left, in turn, is deeply suspicious of the BJP. It is not likely that the two can join the same government. Hence has arisen the precarious situation in which the current government has assured support from only 144 seats in a parliament of 529 elected members (and worse, only 22 percent of the popular vote) and must count on the tacit support of another 138 seats from two ideologically distinct groups.

The Janata Dal, the BJP, and the CPI(M)-led Left Front are united mainly by their antipathy to Rajiv Gandhi and their calculation that a stint in power, or near power, will bolster their future electoral prospects. The unity is thus fragile at best.

Regional Patterns

The diversity of regional patterns underlines the significance of opposition unity and enables a further analysis of the reasons behind the decline in support for the Congress(I) Party. While the common impression that the Congress did better in the south than in the north is essentially correct, the related generalization that the 1989 vote was a vote against all those in power requires qualification.

To begin with an example from the Hindi heartland, the Congress(I) Party did poorly in Uttar Pradesh. Its share of the popular vote there declined by nearly 20 percent, from 51 percent in 1984 to 31 percent in 1989. Even discounting the "Rajiv wave" of 1984, this represents a substantial shift. What happened? The Congress's traditional power base in Uttar Pradesh had been an alliance of the upper castes, especially the Brahmins; the lowest, or Scheduled, castes; and religious minorities, such as the Muslims. The support for the opposition parties that now constitute the Janata Dal, by contrast, had been from the middle castes: the productive farmers of western Uttar Pradesh, like the peasant castes, had supported the former Lok Dal; and the "backward" castes of eastern Uttar Pradesh had been behind the old Janata Party. The BJP, the third important party of the region, generally cuts across caste groups; its core support has always been from urban traders, but it has in recent years successfully mobilized support around religious appeals in specific parts of the state.

What happened in the 1989 election was that the Congress lost some of its established vote banks. One remarkable, though relatively unheralded, change was the emergence of a new party, the Bahujan Samaj Party (BSP), which caters to the underprivileged groups, especially to the Scheduled Castes but also to the Muslims. This party received nearly 13 percent of the total vote. While the figure is not all that dramatic, the results were, because the entire 13 percent probably came out of the Congress's base, supporting the hypothesis that the Congress's failure to follow through on promises to alleviate poverty, and the subsequent abandonment under Rajiv Gandhi of an attitude favoring the poor, may have ended up costing it dearly in electoral support.

The Congress also lost some Muslim support in Uttar Pradesh. While evidence of this is sketchy, Rajiv's flirtation with pro-Hindu themes, and especially his tacit support for the building of the controversial temple in Ayodhya, led important Muslim leaders to announce their opposition to the Congress. The Congress(I) Party lost elections in several Muslim-dominated constituencies. V. P. Singh's firm secular stand probably attracted some Muslim support, although the Janata Dal's tacit alignment with the BJP suggests that such a stance may prove to be temporary.

In contrast to the Congress, both the Janata Dal and the BJP not only maintained their traditional power bases but were also able to broaden them. The Janata Dal benefited from the vote of the Thakurs, a significant elite caste of Uttar Pradesh to which V. P. Singh himself belongs. The BJP, as one would expect, used pro-Hindu themes to expand its base. Equally or possibly even more important was the simple fact of opposition unity: the BJP and the Janata Dal posed one-on-one contests with the Congress for nearly all of the Lok Sabha seats. Add to this the fact that the scheduled-caste vote for the Congress declined, and the puzzle of why the Congress lost a state like Uttar Pradesh becomes less of a puzzle.

In states like West Bengal in the northeast and Gujarat in the northwest, the pattern was somewhat different. West Bengal was one of the few states in which the incumbents increased their popularity, with the CPI(M) gaining both votes and seats in the Lok Sabha. This continued hold on power by the CPI(M) in West Bengal is in part due to the fact that the Congress is deeply factionalized in the region, but it also reflects the moderately effective performance of the CPI(M) in power: a well-disciplined party has consolidated an alliance between the middle and lower rural strata by implementing mild reforms, and at the same time it has maintained a fairly pragmatic attitude toward businesspeople. In Gujarat, by contrast, the Congress, which had put together a fairly similar ruling coalition of the middle and lower strata, made a mess of it. The Congress failed to consolidate the ruling coalition, both because the party organization was nonexistent and because reforms were not implemented. The resulting power vacuum in Gujarat has increasingly been filled by the BJP, which has successfully transformed caste conflicts into communal issues, mobilized Hindus as a bloc, and chipped away at the Congress's traditional alliance. The result was that the Congress's share of the popular vote in this traditional stronghold declined by nearly 16 percent between 1984 and 1989. The Congress won only 3 Lok Sabha seats to the BJP's 12 and the Janata Dal's 11 in the 1989 election.

The south does not present an undifferentiated picture either. The Congress, for example, did well in both Andhra Pradesh and Karnataka, but the underlying dynamics in the two states were quite different. The Congress's share of the popular vote in Karnataka declined by some 3 percent, whereas the number of seats that it controls in the Lok Sabha went from 24 to 27 (out of a total of 28). The main reason for this outcome was that the opposition to the Congress fought as two parties rather than as one. Andhra Pradesh, by contrast, provides a much starker picture of a vote against the incumbents. N. T. Rama Rao and his Telugu Desam Party lost nearly 10 percent of the popular vote between 1984 and 1989. While some of this decline was caused by growing caste conflict within the Telugu Desam coalition, it was mainly a result of Rama Rao's inept and arbitrary rule. After several years of empty promises, the film-actor-turned-politician lost some of his electoral magic.

The Prospects for the New Government

The transfer of power from Rajiv Gandhi and his Congress(I) Party to V. P. Singh's coalition government was relatively smooth, emphasizing once again the strength of India's democracy. No sooner were the election results known than Rajiv Gandhi accepted the defeat gracefully and resigned. Even though the Congress(I) Party remained the largest group in parliament, it was clear that it could not muster enough support from other parties to form a government. India's president thus called upon the leader of the next-largest party in parliament, V. P. Singh of the Janata Dal, to form a government and to demonstrate within 30 days that he controlled a majority in parliament. With BJP and CPI(M)-led Left Front support, he did so on December 21, 1989.

How well India will be governed by this minority government is a question that many would like to have answered. While predictions of political trends are at best hazardous, some tendencies are easier to discern than others. The answer can be separated into three components: the deeper political trends; the prospects of stability of the new government; and, assuming some stability, the minority government's likely performance.

As already discussed, the underlying political trends in India have been the steady weakening of well-established institutions and the increased mobilization of diverse political groups. Most political analysts understand that such trends do not augur well for long-term stability. This is not to suggest that threats to India's political stability are imminent. Several factors suggest that the Indian polity has considerable resilience: democracy has been practiced for nearly 40 years, and the more it is practiced, the firmer tend to be its roots; there is considerable talent in India's ruling circles, both in the bureaucracy and among the political elite; protest and violence in one part of India do not readily spread to other parts; the macroeconomic performance continues to be satisfactory; and the last line of defense, the armed forces, remains efficient, coherent, and largely apolitical. At the same time, however, it would be foolish to be too sanguine about India's growing political problems: major centrist parties are not really political parties in terms of organization, discipline, and programs; there is growing politicization of the bureaucracy, the judiciary, and even the armed forces; instances of caste, class, religious, and ethnic conflict are growing; and the use of force and violence in politics has become common.

These problematic long-term trends will be difficult to reverse, especially for a minority government. It is hard to visualize either the Congress(I) or the Janata Dal becoming a coherent and well-organized party in the near future. Without parties and programs, the capacity of leaders to create durable ruling coalitions will remain weak, as will their capacity to translate electoral mandates into specific policy outcomes. It is also difficult to imagine that political groups in India will somehow become less active. Mobilization is only in part fueled by economics; what really fuels political activism in India is competitive politics aimed at securing access to the state and to state resources. Chances are, therefore, that levels of mobilized political activity will remain high, major political institutions like parties will remain weak, and, as more and more groups make demands, the polity will be characterized by a fair amount of turbulence.

The hardest thing to predict in India's new political situation is how long the minority government will last. Many observers, including some of the Janata Dal's senior advisers, feel that a mid-term poll is likely; they expect that V. P. Singh will call elections sometime in 1992 with the hope of enlarging his power base. Whether this comes to pass or not, such anticipations help put boundaries on the likely range of political fluctuations. The new government does seem to have staying power, for several reasons: V. P. Singh has emerged as the preeminent leader within the Janata Dal; the antipathy to the Congress will facilitate unity, at least for a short while; both the CPI(M) and the BJP want to use this opportunity to secure their own political goals; and all the parties are exhausted from the recent elections and would just as soon wait, regroup, and get ready to fight in the near, rather than the immediate, future.

In its early actions the new government has sought to build on the minimal consensus that can be found among its diverse supporters. An important example of this is the partial freeing of television and radio from direct government control by establishing them as autonomous public corporations. The elections in several states in February 1990 further confirmed the popularity of non-Congress parties, especially the BJP, and thus generally strengthened the government vis-à-vis the Congress. And the budget for 1990–91 definitely reflects the capacity of the government and its supporters to work together on important issues.

Against these positive tendencies, however, must be set a number of destabilizing possibilities. At the time of this writing, in early 1990, very few observers think it likely that the minority government will last the full five-year term. A number of conditions militate against such an outcome: the BJP and the CPI(M) are likely to find it very difficult to publicly agree on such major and pressing policy issues as how to deal with political conflicts involving religious divisions, such as the conflicts in Kashmir and Punjab; it is not in the interest of either the BJP or the CPI(M) to sit calmly by and support the Janata Dal while V. P. Singh uses his stint in power primarily as a vehicle to improve his own and his party's position of power; the BJP's impressive performance in the state elections of February 1990 is likely to lead it to want more from the central government, thus pushing the CPI(M) farther from the ruling coalition; and the arithmetic of the current Lok Sabha is such that the Congress can form an alternative government with the help of the BJP, the CPI(M), or even a rump of the Janata Dal—one led, for example, by Devi Lal and Chandrashekhar.

The minority government in power is not likely to be a very effective performer. If Rajiv Gandhi, with his huge electoral majority in late 1984, was unable to translate popularity into effective policies, how likely is it that a minority government will perform better? The actions that the new government undertakes are likely to be those on which not only the government but also the CPI(M) and the BJP agree. Such policies as depoliticizing television and radio, decentralizing some power to the states, and minimizing political interference in the bureaucracy will find broad support. Beyond these, however, the real problem of the new government is likely to be inaction, born of the underlying absence of agreement on policy preferences.

As one looks ahead, therefore, there is no reason to expect crises and breakdown, but there are a fair number of reasons to be concerned about India's political future. The best possible outcome would be if—with the decline of the Congress's hegemony and the beginning of a period of alignments and realignments—the new arrangement that emerges were more truly democratic than past governments in the sense of being more truly representative of India's political heterogeneity. Before one gets from here to there, however, the prognosis for the near future is not good: the minority government is not very stable; even if it survives, its performance is not likely to be impressive; and the long-term political trends are toward institutional fragmentation and growing levels of mobilization of political activity. The most likely near future, therefore, is that India will remain a lively democracy but that this democracy, in terms both of absorbing conflict and of generating effective policies, will continue to muddle through at a low level of efficacy.

2
The Gathering Storm

Shekhar Gupta

Relations among the different religious communities in secular India, particularly between its majority Hindus and its largest minority, the Muslims, have always been uneasy. But by the end of 1989 they had slid to their worst state since partition. The year was not only one of India's worst in terms of the incidence of communal riots and the resulting loss of lives and property, it also marked the beginning of a dangerous phase in which religion had come to be accepted as a part of electoral politics and religious issues played a decisive role in political events. Political leaders from all the major national parties expressed concern, but there was no concerted national or regional effort to find a solution.

While the problems created by militant Sikh fundamentalists in Punjab state continued, belying the hopes briefly raised by the successful and peaceful conduct there of the elections to the Lok Sabha, fresh pressures arose elsewhere. The sensitive border state of Kashmir was convulsed under the impact of a religiously charged separatist movement. The controversial shrine of Ramjanmabhoomi–Babri Masjid[1] near Ayodhya in Uttar Pradesh became the epicenter of communal upheavals from which shock waves radiated throughout the Hindi speaking belt. And finally, riding these waves, the Hindu revivalist political groups, led by a rejuvenated Bharatiya Janata Party (BJP), arrived firmly at the center stage of national politics.

In a development that could have far-reaching consequences for Indian politics, the BJP won 86 seats in the Lok Sabha and emerged as the third force in parliament, after the Congress(I) and the National Front. While the party received roughly the same percentage of the national vote as it had in the past (about 11 percent), it won a much larger percentage of the seats it contested. More significantly, since

---

[1] Literally, Ram's Birthplace–Babur's Mosque, a name that embodies the controversy: one site claimed by two religions.

the ruling Janata Dal was still a cumbersome mix of individuals of conflicting ideologies and competing ambitions, the BJP was showing every sign of becoming the second force in parliament. The improvement it had made over its performance in the 1984 elections—when it was routed, winning just two seats in the Lok Sabha—was stupendous. Its 86 seats are now crucial for the survival of the National Front coalition government, which it supports from outside.

The subsequent elections to the nine state assemblies showed how quickly the party was progressing from the launching pad it had created for itself in the national election. As compared to a total of 152 seats won in all these assemblies in 1985, it now had 498, a gain of nearly 230 percent at the expense not merely of the Congress(I) but also of the other centrist groups. It returned with a clear majority in the large Hindi-speaking state of Madhya Pradesh and is the largest single party in Rajasthan. It made a virtually clean sweep in the northern hill state of Himachal Pradesh. In Bihar and Gujarat too, where it supported the local Janata Dal governments, the gains were impressive: from 17 to 39 percent and 16 to 67 percent respectively.

The significance of the figures becomes clearer when we consider that the BJP won its 498 seats out of 1,005 contested seats, a victory record of nearly 50 percent. The Congress(I), in comparison, won only 417 seats out of the 1,559 it contested. The only surprise was the state of Maharashtra, usually considered the bastion of orthodox Hindu fundamentalism, where despite its alliance with the even more right-wing Shiv Sena, the BJP was left behind by the Congress(I) in the Lok Sabha as well as in the assembly polls.

The year also saw a further decline in whatever moderate Muslim leadership there had been in India. In addition, the Sikh situation had, if anything, become more complicated, with some of the newly elected Akali Dal members of parliament—including former police officer Simranjit Singh Mann—even refusing to take the parliamentary oath of membership unless they were allowed to wear three-foot kirpans (a curved sword that is among the five essentials a Sikh is supposed to carry on his person) inside the House.

The outlook for 1990 and subsequent years is clouded by the fear of deepening divide and increasing bitterness among the various communities. None of the major issues that brought communalism to the forefront of national politics by the end of 1989—the disputed Ramjanmabhoomi–Babri Masjid, Muslim separatism in Kashmir, or Sikh separatism in Punjab—is likely to be resolved soon. And even though so far the new V. P. Singh government has shown remarkable tact and ability to compromise, the best it can do is to buy time. It is still too early to say whether Singh will follow the path of his predecessor, who promised much in his initial months but delivered little. But within its first three months in power, the government was confronted with communal riots as Hindu and Muslim mobs clashed in New Delhi's Nizamuddin neighborhood and in Bihar's steel town of Jamshedpur, and it gave no indication that it had a long-term plan for tackling issues of communalism.

The Expanding Territorial Reach of Communalism

In 1989 alone more than 500 persons were killed—almost twice the toll for the preceding year—in a series of communal riots that erupted in several parts of the country, notably Uttar Pradesh, Karnataka, Bihar, Madhya Pradesh, Gujarat, Maharashtra, and Rajasthan. Riots broke out in towns with no history of communal disharmony and in remote rural areas, marking the beginning of a new trend. In the past communal tensions had been confined mainly to mixed-population cities where communal differences were exacerbated by business and trading rivalries. The worst phase of rioting in 1989 came toward the end of the year as the election approached. According to credible estimates more than 150 persons were killed in Hindu-Muslim riots in Bhagalpur, a town in Bihar state, in violence directly related to *shilapujan*, the nationwide process of consecrating the bricks contributed by Hindu organizations for the reconstruction of the temple in Ayodhya. This was preceded by another particularly ugly and bloody round of rioting in a part of Uttar Pradesh that had so far remained immune from communal killings. The small district town of Badayun erupted in communal frenzy as Hindu organizations demonstrated against the introduction of Urdu, which they consider to be the language of the Muslims, in the state assembly. More than 30 persons were killed, and large parts of the town were laid waste.

Figures from the Indian Home Ministry underlined dangerous portents: in 1988 a total of 611 communal incidents were registered nationwide. Of these, 55 percent were reported from rural areas. And in 1989 the situation worsened: whereas in 1988 the Home Ministry had classified 88 districts of the country's 452 as hypersensitive, that number exceeded 110 in 1989 and is likely to grow substantially in 1990.

Why are communal riots increasing? There may be some validity in the argument that better communication results in better reporting of incidents. While that argument could apply to a comparison between riot figures for 1969 and 1989, it does not apply to a comparison between 1987 and 1989. There is also substance to the argument that increased communal violence is a consequence of significant economic changes over the past decade or so. The single most significant factor has been the Persian Gulf job boom. A much larger number of Muslim than of Hindu artisans, craftsmen, and workmen have gone to the Gulf and sent funds back to India. The result is economic tension in areas where Hindu domination was previously unchallenged. In the Uttar Pradesh city of Moradabad, known for its exquisite brassware, Muslims have for centuries been craftsmen who depended on Hindu traders and middlemen to sell their wares. Now many are setting up businesses of their own. In Badayun, again in Uttar Pradesh and approximately 300 kilometers from Delhi, tensions have arisen over the traditional Muslim shoemakers' entry into the shoe selling and export businesses, which were previously dominated by Hindu traders. Economic tensions such as these have contributed to the explosive situation already created by political issues.

The figures on communal violence cited above do not take into account the situation in Punjab, where approximately 40 percent of the 3,000-odd killings during the year were communal in nature. Nor do they include religiously oriented riots, notably the nearly 30 dead in riots in Bombay and Kashmir in protest against Salman Rushdie's *Satanic Verses*. Not surprisingly, the Indian state found itself under unprecedented pressure to control the situation. Throughout 1989 the central Home Ministry was engaged in fighting communal fires, switching the approximately 300,000 paramilitary troops at its command from one trouble spot to another. On March 1, 1990, V. P. Singh presided over the annual-day celebrations of the Central Reserve Police Force, the Indian Home Ministry's mainstay, at Jharoda Kalan on the outskirts of Delhi, and was told about a company (150 men) of the force that had been moved 51 times during 1989. There could hardly be a more telling commentary on the extent of civil strife during the year, which was mainly caused by communal tension.

Communal Divisions in India

India is one of the very few developing countries to have enshrined the principle of secularism in its constitution. But the roots of communal tension lie in India's demographic and ethnic makeup as well as in its history. Hindus constitute 82 percent of India's population, Muslims about 12 percent, and the rest is divided among Sikhs, Christians, and relatively microscopic communities such as Buddhists, Jews, and Zoroastrians (Parsis). The figure of 82 percent for the Hindus, however, is a census fallacy because it includes a large number of tribal groups, many of whom are animists or at best only nominally Hindus. There are also numerous subdivisions of caste and ethnicity among the Hindus. Even stronger are linguistic divisions. For example, equally devout Hindus in the north and the south often claim different identities because they speak different languages.

The situation is further complicated because the Hindu revivalist groups, notably the BJP and the Rashtriya Swayamsevak Sangh (RSS), consider several minorities, including Jains, Buddhists, and Sikhs, as part of the Hindu spectrum. Sikh fundamentalists, who seek a distinct constitutional status and a separate personal law from that of the Hindus, resent this unsolicited embrace.

Even within the Brahmanical Hindu orthodoxy there are different streams of thought. There is the old, puritanical Sanatani school that still believes in aggressive adherence to the caste system and in the supremacy of the upper "twice-born" castes. Four *shankaracharyas*, head priests of the four seats of Hindu religious power in different parts of the country, represent this school. The other stream emanates from the Arya Samajist movement that emerged in the 19th century as a reformist campaign to rid Hinduism of cumbersome rituals, superstition, and the caste system. The Arya Samaj too was an aggressive movement, aiming not merely to prevent large-scale conversions of Hindus, particularly those of the lower castes, to Islam and Christianity, but also to bring previous converts to those religions back to the Hindu fold. It is adherents of this school who dominate the Hindu revivalist groups now.

Historical Roots of the Hindu Revivalist Movement

Hindu insecurities began to find articulation in the earlier part of this century soon after the Muslims of the Subcontinent formed the Muslim League on December 30, 1906, in Dhaka (now the capital of Bangladesh). Within months the United Bengal Hindu movement emerged in the state of Bengal. Another reaction to the formation of the Muslim League came from faraway Punjab, with the formation of Punjab Hindu Sabha. Similar organizations sprang up elsewhere in the country, and in December 1913 a majority of them coalesced into one group, the All-India Hindu Mahasabha, which held its first session in the Hindu holy city of Hardwar on the banks of the Ganges. Eleven years later, the Rashtriya Swayamsevak Sangh, now the most important Hindu revivalist organization, emerged out of the Hindu Mahasabha. K. B. Hedgewar, a well-known Mahasabha functionary, decided to form a more activist organization, combining physical exercise and militaristic organization with revivalist thought. The first martial training classes for the RSS volunteers were organized in 1926 in Nagpur under the direction of Martandra Jog, a retired officer in the army of the Maharajah of Gwalior.

Slowly but steadily the RSS grew in strength under Hedgewar and gained in popularity. Hordes of new members joined during the Hindu-Muslim riots at the time of partition. The organization portrayed itself as the savior of Hindus but soon came under pressure because Nathu Ram Godse, Mahatma Gandhi's assassin, was alleged to have had links with it. The government imposed a ban on the RSS that lasted nearly two years. By 1950, however, it was active again, first making its reappearance in Assam with a substantial contribution to relief work following a major earthquake there.

In subsequent years the RSS, along with other Hindu revivalist groups, found several campaign causes. First there was a nationwide campaign to seek a ban on the slaughter of cows, considered holy by the Hindus. Then there was opposition to the Hindu Code Bill, a clutch of legislation that aimed to codify traditional Hindu personal law. The revivalists demanded a common personal law for all citizens of India irrespective of their religion and called the government's decision to enact the bills "nonsecular."

By 1952, however, as the RSS was finally recovering from the shock of the ban and charges of involvement in Gandhi's assassination, India saw the growth of yet another Hindu revivalist party, Ramrajya Parishad, which was formed in 1948 by the religious leader Swami Karpatri. As the name indicates, the party purportedly aimed to bring back the "pristine" glory of the days when Lord Rama ruled India. The party, consisting mainly of former rulers, landlords, and upper-caste feudal elements, was rabidly casteist, orthodox, and xenophobic. Yet for more than a decade it remained in the vanguard of Hindu revivalism along with the RSS and Hindu Mahasabha. The 1960s saw large-scale desertions from Ramrajya Parishad's ranks to the maharajah-dominated Swatantra party.

In the 1950s and 1960s the Hindu revivalist groups found causes that grew into nationwide movements. In the fifties the agitation against the Hindu Code Bill found conservative support, but this did not translate into votes, for the revivalist groups continued to do poorly in the elections. In 1966, however, a joint movement by all the Hindu revivalist groups demanding legislation against cow-slaughter built up into a major agitation. On September 5, 1966, a massive demonstration outside the Parliament in Delhi became violent, resulting in police firing on the demonstrators and seven deaths. The revivalists now made the demand for the legislation a major election issue. Meanwhile, to coordinate efforts on issues facing the Hindu communities, the Hindu organizations created an umbrella organization called the Vishwa Hindu Parishad (VHP) in April 1964. One of the first activities coordinated by the VHP was the opposition to proselytization by Christian missionaries, particularly in northeastern tribal India.

In the sixties, however, it was clear that all groups other than the RSS had become marginal to the Hindu fundamentalist stream. The political front of the RSS was the Bharatiya Jana Sangh (BJS), founded in 1951 in response to pressure from RSS supporters to enter the political fray. Initially the Jana Sangh was led by Shyama Prasad Mookerji, who resigned from Nehru's cabinet after becoming disillusioned with his policies, particularly his soft line on Kashmir. Later, the BJS grew into a major political party, less doctrinaire than the RSS but dependent on it for both ideological and physical sustenance. Its leadership, though almost entirely drawn from the RSS ranks, tried to veer a bit more to the center than the RSS and other Hindu revivalist groups. In the words of Craig Baxter, "The Jana Sangh is not so rigidly Hindu as the Mahasabha or the Ramrajya Parishad, nor does it stand solely for the interests of its community as does the Muslim League or the Akali Dal. There is a fine line between a communal party and a national party. The Jana Sangh appears to straddle that line."[2] This could also apply to the Bharatiya Janata Party, the latest incarnation of the Jana Sangh.

The Paradox of a Majority's Minority Complex

The history of communal tensions in India is also a history of how a community that constitutes more than 80 percent of the population has come to acquire a minority complex. On the surface, this is by far the most intriguing aspect of the communal problem in India. Hindu organizations and spokespersons claim that the Hindus are being discriminated against—being denied their share of power by minorities voting as blocs, witnessing a dilution of their religious values by a liberalization that has spared other religious faiths, and being ill-treated in those parts of the country where they are themselves a minority or close to becoming one. The litany of complaints is unending: the Hindus are the only community to have accepted family planning, so while their numbers are diminishing, those of the minorities, notably Muslims, are increasing; Hindu places of worship and religious institutions are starved for funds while the Muslims and the Christians get loads of foreign money; finally, and most devastating of all, the Hindus and perhaps the mainstream Sikhs are the only truly patriotic Indians with a stake in India. While there may or may not be a grain

---

[2] Craig Baxter, *The Jana Sangh: The Biography of an Indian Political Party* (Philadelphia: University of Pennsylvania, 1969), p. 312.

of truth in some of these complaints, there is at least an explanation for them.

The Hindu groups today draw strength mainly from the community's resentment over centuries of subjugation by Muslim invaders in the pre-British period. There is a fear of militant Islam that goes back 1,000 years. Partition and the riots accompanying it served to cement that fear for many more generations. As a matter of fact, the Hindu religious groups active today found their feet in the wake of the prepartition clamor by Pakistan. They feel that if there was ever any justification for a secular India, it was taken away by partition.

The Hindu organizations saw partition as a major defeat. Further, they believed that the creation of Pakistan was merely the first step in the Muslim conspiracy to subjugate the entire Subcontinent. This view was articulated by former RSS chief M. S. Golwalkar: "The creation of Pakistan is the first successful step of the Muslims in this 20th century to realize their twelve-hundred-year-old dream of complete subjugation of this country." By extension of the same logic he argued that the large Muslim population in India was a veritable fifth column to be employed towards attaining this end: "It would be suicidal to delude ourselves into believing that they have turned into patriots overnight after the creation of Pakistan. On the contrary, the Muslim menace has increased a hundredfold by the creation of Pakistan which has become a springboard for all their future designs on our country."[3]

Today, 43 years after partition, Hindus still think they are being wronged in many ways. The BJP's clamor for the abolition of article 370 of the constitution, which gives special rights to the state of Jammu and Kashmir, the only Muslim-majority state in India, can be seen in that perspective. Article 370 prohibits people from other parts of the country from buying land, starting a business, settling down, or even taking up a government job in Jammu and Kashmir. The BJP asks: Why this special status? Is it only because the state has a Muslim majority? Then will the same privilege one day be extended to several districts of West Bengal, which now have Muslim majorities through unbridled immigration from Bangladesh? Or to Assam, where Muslims could indeed become a majority in the foreseeable future through immigration from Bangladesh? In the BJP's scheme of things, Indian security is seriously compromised by giving such special status to a Muslim-majority state bordering a hostile Islamic republic. If they had had their way, they would have initiated a large-

---

[3] M. S. Golwalker, *Bunch of Thoughts* (Bangalore: Vikram Prakashan, 1966), pp. 167–168.

scale settlement of people from other states, mainly Hindus, to "rationalize" the population balance in Jammu and Kashmir.

Even on the Ramjanmabhoomi shrine issue, the Hindu anger has its origins in the belief that if the Muslim "invaders" of medieval times made it their business to raze Hindu temples and build mosques in their place, the modern-day Hindus, in a country where they enjoy political power and overwhelmingly majority status, should be able to restore what they consider to be one of their most hallowed shrines. A solution to the Ramjanmabhoomi problem often suggested by liberals entails declaring the controversial shrine as a national monument belonging to neither the Muslims nor the Hindus. The Hindu organizations' retort is: "Why don't the Jews and the Muslims declare all of Jerusalem a protected monument?" Even among relatively liberal thinkers a new school of thought is emerging; it holds that with the genie of Hindu revivalism now unleashed, it will be impossible to restrain it unless substantial symbolic concessions are made to the Hindus. One of these could be on Ramjanmabhoomi and perhaps even on one or two of the other disputed shrines, such as Mathura, where Hindus believe mosques were built on the debris of temples in the medieval period.

The Hindu assertion on the Ayodhya question might not have been so strident if it were not for the fact that the controversy was at least partly triggered by the Muslims themselves in an apparently unconnected act. In 1985 a faction of the Muslim leadership under Syed Shahabuddin began a nationwide agitation to "free" the mosques. Arguing that under the Islamic tradition each mausoleum was a place of worship, they demanded that the government turn over to the Muslims hundreds of mausoleums declared protected monuments throughout the country. These included even such popular tourist attractions as the tombs of Muslim rulers Humayun and Safdarjang in Delhi. Each Friday thousands of Muslims gathered in front of these mausoleums and offered mass prayers. The movement did not achieve anything. But two years later when the Hindu fundamentalist groups were busy whipping up a nationwide frenzy over the Ramjanmabhoomi question, it came in handy. If the Muslims could agitate to get historical mausoleums converted into mosques, couldn't the majority community seek the "freeing" of the birthplace of its most revered god?

There were other factors exacerbating the situation and giving some substance to the assertion by Hindu fundamentalists that while the minorities continued to extract purely religious, even irrational, concessions from the government, the majority was suffering by not demanding anything. Two recent instances deserve mention here. In early 1986 the government of India made a major concession to Muslim fundamentalists by acceding to their demands in what is known as the Shah Bano case. Shah Bano was a 78-year-old woman in the central Indian town of Indore. Her husband divorced her, and she sued for maintenance. The courts granted her a small sum of Rs. 500 per month. This led to immediate furor among Muslim fundamentalists, who objected to the Anglo-Saxon interpretation of a Muslim marriage and argued that it should be governed by the Quranic law, which does not allow for maintenance. A truly secular and liberal response to that should have been that the nation has enacted a set of laws that the courts enforce and follow and that should apply to all citizens. Instead, the government amended the law in such a way as to take the question of maintenance in Muslim marriage away from the purview of the courts. There was consternation among the Hindu fundamentalist groups: If India is a secular country and if all citizens are equal, why should there be special personal laws for one community, a minority at that? Hindu fundamentalists have obviously not forgotten the bitter battle they waged in the fifties when the progressive Hindu Code Bill was enacted modernizing the Hindu law on marriage and inheritance and making divorce easy. So blatant was this capitulation by the Rajiv Gandhi government that it even embarrassed several prominent Muslim liberals. One of them, Arif Mohammed Khan, a minister of state in the Rajiv ministry, left the party over this question. Later, along with V. P. Singh, he formed the core group of the National Front that defeated the Congress in 1989.

The second major concession was over Salman Rushdie's *Satanic Verses*. As Rushdie has pointed out time and again, so eager was the Indian government to please Muslim fundamentalists that it banned the book after reading nothing more than a few reviews. Later, official Indian spokesmen claimed credit for the fact that India was the first country in the world to have banned the book, even ahead of the Islamic world. Should the government of a truly secular nation have done this? ask Hindu fundamentalists.

For a community that has, for four decades, lived with the uneasy feeling that too much was being conceded to the minorities at its expense, these provocations proved to be the last straw. Since partition, many Hindus have harbored fears about a decrease in their share of the Indian population. There is a widespread belief among the Hindu organizations that while the Hindus have come forward willingly to accept family planning, the Muslims have steadfastly refused to do so as part of a well-thought-out conspiracy to Islamize India. There is also fear of proselytization by Christians, which is occurring on a large scale, particularly in the tribal belts.

Finally, again in relation to Islam, there is a phobia of pan-Islamic expansionism. Hindu fundamentalist spokesmen have often argued that all that stands in the way of militant Islam spreading eastward from the Middle East to the rest of Asia are the Hindus of the Indian Subcontinent. The *jihad* of the *mujahedin* in Afghanistan, the continuing Islamic revolution in Iran, increasing fundamentalist fervor in Pakistan (despite the presence of a democratically elected government), the growing Islamic resurgence in the Soviet Central Asian Republics, and now the predominantly Islamic popular upsurge in Kashmir have strengthened this fear and helped the Hindu religio-political groups win more support.

What lies ahead is suggested by the way the BJP has reversed its fortunes after nearly two decades in the wilderness. The party, in its original avatar as the Bharatiya Jana Sangh, registered substantial gains in the 1967 general election when the Congress, under a raw Indira Gandhi, was in confusion, the national economy in tatters, and insecurities high in the aftermath of two difficult wars (with China in 1962 and Pakistan in 1965). Further, the cadres of the RSS, from which the BJP originates, had earned credibility by being visibly involved in the national defense effort in the 1965 war—manning traffic intersections, supplying food to troops, running civil defense drills—all in the organization's khaki uniforms and caps. But the subsequent period saw a rapid decline in the party's fortunes as Indira Gandhi made effective use of a combination of socialist sloganeering and jingoism.

The RSS and the Jana Sangh returned to the limelight only in the mid-seventies when they ran an underground campaign against the internal Emergency imposed by Indira Gandhi in 1975. They were jailed in the thousands. But with the lifting of the Emergency, the Jan Sangh merged with the new Janata Party, which was elected to power. The merger, however, was artificial and the parties mismatched, as subsequent developments showed. The Janata Party broke up because of the continuing ideological differences between the socialist stream and the right-wing Jan Sangh elements. It was during this stage that the top leadership of the party decided that its destiny lay in going it alone.

The Jana Sangh reemerged as the Bharatiya Janata Party. But after its resounding defeat in the 1980 mid-term elections, the party vacillated between an extreme Hindu line advocated by Rajmata Vijayraje Scindia, the widow of the former ruler of Gwalior state and one of the party's most important leaders, and the more moderate but somewhat confused philosophy of Gandhian socialism. A further blow came in the 1984 general elections when the party was wiped out and its top leaders, including president Atal Behari Vajpayee, were defeated. It was at this stage that a process of serious rethinking began among the party ideologues and the leadership of the RSS.

Through five years of introspection the party gravitated towards its roots and the original RSS thinking. The new slogan was *Hindutva*, or "genuine Hindu nationalism." The concept is based on a significant book by that name written by Vinayak Damodar [Veer] Savarkar in the early part of this century. Savarkar, who was later incarcerated by the British in the notorious jail in the Andamans, argued that Hindus were a nation and as the indigenous people of the Subcontinent formed a well-defined single nationality despite the difference in ethnicities, lifestyles, and even methods of worship followed by various sects and subcommunities. This introspection was accompanied by several tactical changes. The party campaign was now led not by Vajpayee, widely acknowledged to be the finest orator on the Indian political scene, but by the relatively prosaic Lal Krishan Advani. The other vital difference between the two is that while Vajpayee is known to be a relative moderate, Advani is considered to be much closer to the orthodox RSS line of thinking. In another major political decision, the BJP made electoral agreements with other centrist non-Congress opposition parties without making any compromises in its ideological line.

Quite providentially, other political factors combined in such a way as to give the BJP a winning platform in 1989. The controversy over the Ramjanmabhoomi–Babri Masjid shrine that emerged in 1986 combined with the religiously oriented problems of Kashmir and Punjab to provide sustenance to the BJP's new call for *Hindutva* and a resurgent Hindu society in the vanguard of an India that could continue to be "secular" as long as the Hindu majority had a leading say in its affairs and the minorities fell in line and thought of themselves as Hindustanis rather than as Muslims, Sikhs, or Christians.

Politics and Religion in the Eighties

Three issues with religious overtones have influenced the politics of the 1980s and helped bring communalism to the center stage of national politics: Punjab, Ayodhya, and Kashmir. It began with Punjab. In the sixties the clamor of Sikh separatism had been subdued by the trifurcation of Punjab, where the majority of Sikhs live, on a linguistic basis. The Indian government carved out three states: Punjabi-speaking, Sikh-majority Punjab; Hindi-speaking, Hindu-majority Haryana; and Himachal Pradesh, consisting of hill districts where Hindi and a variety of local dialects are spoken. Hindu fundamentalist organizations protested bitterly. The beginning of the eighties brought them face-to-face with a stridently separatist Sikh movement run from the Golden Temple in Amritsar, the Sikhs' holiest shrine and the supreme seat of Sikh religious and temporal power. This confused the Hindu fundamentalists, who have traditionally regarded Sikhs as Hindus. They could not see why the Sikhs, among the most prosperous and prominent communities in India, wanted to leave the union. As Sikh extremists repeatedly attacked Hindus, tensions began to build. Punjab saw the growth of splinter Hindu organizations including at least three Shiv Senas (Shiva's Army), unconnected with the better-known Hindu organization by the same name in Bombay but following an equally extremist philosophy.

Yet the mainline militant Hindu parties have exercised restraint. While there is considerable anger among the Hindu population in Punjab and the rest of the north against Sikh fundamentalists, the RSS and the BJP have actually exerted a sobering influence. This is despite the fact that the Sikh fundamentalists have made a special target of RSS-BJP leaders and workers. On at least three occasions they have fired at the RSS *shakhas* (morning drills) in Punjab, killing people.

Predictably, their sober attitude has not made them popular with the Hindus of Punjab, many of whom complain of having been let down by the BJP and RSS. The consequence is the rise of a plethora of 'iiv Senas in Punjab. Some of the leaders of these groups have been in the vanguard of the Ramjanmabhoomi shrine movement. So far, despite selective killings of Hindus by Sikh terrorists in Punjab, there have been few incidents of retaliation by Hindu mobs against Sikhs in major towns like Ludhiana and Amritsar, which have a Hindu majority. But whenever clashes have taken place, the new Shiv Senas have been involved.

On a deeper level however the Punjab crisis has contributed to communal disharmony in a different manner. It is widely acknowledged that the Sikhs are a very prosperous, successful, and influential community in India, enjoying a slice of the national cake far larger than justified merely by their share of the population. If they came to believe that they were discriminated against and, despite being less than 2 percent of the population, they challenged the might of the Indian state, the Hindu fundamentalists would have something to worry about. Since many Hindu fundamentalists feel that the problem in Punjab is a creation of Pakistan and indeed part of a larger pan-Islamic move to destroy India, it is connected in their minds with fears of agitation by India's Muslims.

The Punjab is one area where the V. P. Singh government will be put to a severe test. Initially it took a soft line on Punjab. The suspected terrorists elected in the Lok Sabha poll, including such prominent figures as Simranjit Singh Mann and Attinderpal Singh, were released in the hope that they would bring Sikh politics back within the national democratic mainstream. Governor Sidhartha Shankar Ray, a tough governor, was replaced with a pacifist, Nirmal Kumar Mukherjee. But as the newly elected Sikh leaders dithered between extreme and moderate stands and killings increased, the government was forced to fall back on the tough option, giving the police *carte blanche* to hit back. Belying initial expectations, there were indications of increased trouble in Punjab, or at least a continuation of the violent impasse there.

The Struggle over Ayodhya

Nearly 600 miles away from Punjab, a phenomenon that began in its current manifestation with small demonstrations in 1985 had, by the end of 1989, emerged as India's most serious communal problem.[4] The Ramjanmabhoomi–Babri Masjid shrine is centered in the ancient twin cities of Ayodhya and Faizabad, barely five hours by car from Lucknow, the capital of Uttar Pradesh. The legend of Ramayana has it that Lord Rama, revered by the Hindus as Maryada Purushottam, the righteous and perfect being, was born here to King Dasrath as the heir to the kingdom of Ayodhya. But in the congested area along the banks of river Sarayu, dotted with temples associated with the legend of Ramayana, now also stands a curious building that looks more like a mosque than a temple, but architecturally like both when viewed from up close. This is the structure that Muslims claim the first Mughal emperor, Babur, built in the 16th century. The Hindus claim the mosque was built by demolishing the temple at the birthplace of Lord Rama.

A perusal of history shows that in nearly 350 years the Hindus have launched 76 attempts to "free" the shrine; 4 during the reign of Babur, 10 during Humayun's reign, 20 during Akbar's rule, 5 during the period of Nasiruddin Hyder, 3 while Nawab Wajid Ali Shah was in the saddle in Awadh, and 2 during the British period. There have been 4 attempts since independence including the one currently under way.

The story of how Babur first constructed the mosque in 1528 A.D. is narrated in his book *Tuzak-e-Babri*, which says that when Babur was going to Ayodhya after his battle with Rana Sanga of Mewar he was approached by two Muslim fakirs who pleaded with him to turn the temple in Ayodhya into a Khurd Mecca (a small Mecca). Babur agreed

---

[4] The account that follows draws on the United News of India, *UNI Backgrounder*, Vol. 12, no. 11 (March 12, 1987) and Vol. 14, no. 40 (October 5, 1989).

but apparently also tried to assuage Hindu feelings while building the shrine by using a composite Hindu-Muslim design. He decreed that while Hindus could continue to pray in the shrine unhindered, Muslims could only offer prayers on Fridays. Further accounts of the Mughal period are available in Abul Fazal's *Ain-e-Akbari*, which chronicles Akbar's reign from 1542 to 1605. It recounts how Akbar's Hindu courtiers Birbal and Todarmal came to Ayodhya and agreed to have a platform built for the Hindus to pray inside the mosque. The platform is still there.

The modern phase of the Hindu agitation on the issue began a little over a century ago, when one Mahant Raghubir Das filed a suit with the subjudge Pandit Hari Kishan at Faizabad asking for permission to build a temple on this platform. The judge said a firm "no" and argued that "awarding permission to construct the temple at this juncture is to lay the foundation of riot and murder." Further appeals were similarly dismissed, and the controversy receded into the background when the trustee of the mosque was declared by the authorities to be an opium addict on September 16, 1938. The mosque fell into a state of disrepair. Ironically, the British records of that period routinely refer to the shrine as the "Janamsthan [Birthplace] Mosque of Ajoodhia."

After independence the controversy was revived when the civil judge of Faizabad, on March 3, 1951, allowed Hindus unhindered right of worship in the shrine. The Muslims were told to stay 200 yards away from it. It is no surprise that the judge's portrait now adorns a wall inside the sanctum sanctorum of the shrine. But as tensions arose the district administration decided to lock up the shrine again.

The controversy was revived again in the 1980s, as the Vishwa Hindu Parishad, the new, rapidly growing Hindu organization, adopted the "freeing" of Ramjanmabhoomi as its prime objective. On September 7, 1984, the VHP was able to collect nearly 100,000 devout Hindus on the bank of Sarayu river. The throng took a holy vow to "liberate the temple." The campaign gathered momentum in February 1986 as the sessions judge of Faizabad, Krishan Mohan Pandey, directed the district authorities to unlock the shrine for the Hindus. The Muslims challenged the verdict in Allahabad High Court, but even before the courts could do something Muslims all over the country were standing up in protest.

Between February 14 and 19, 1984, riots broke out in several parts of India. The Muslim case on the shrine was articulated by the Babri Masjid Action Committee. In the forefront of the Muslim campaign was a former diplomat, member of parliament, and articulate spokesman for the Muslims, Syed Shahabuddin. The efforts culminated in an unprecedentedly large Muslim rally in New Delhi on March 30, 1987. The rally adopted a resolution demanding that the controversy be solved judicially but by a court in southern India consisting of three judges, none of whom should be Hindu or Muslim. Shahabuddin called the rally an "act of piety" and wrote in his journal *Muslim India*: "The struggle for Babri Masjid has become a symbol of Muslim awakening; the battle for Babri Masjid is the training field for the bigger battles to come for the defence of democracy and secularism."[5]

But quite to the contrary, it became a breeding ground of communal strife and one of the greatest threats to Indian democracy and secularism since independence. Riots continued, peaking in 1987 with large-scale sectarian killings in the city of Meerut on the outskirts of Delhi. Then both communities planned long marches to Ayodhya, but the government was able somehow to prevent these. After the Babri Masjid Action Committee split in November 1988 the Rajiv Gandhi government was able to buy time. In February 1989 Rajiv Gandhi himself intervened but could not do much. The controversy was quickly building into a major issue for the general election scheduled towards the end of the year.

In May 1989 the controversy took an entirely new turn with the VHP announcing a program to build a Rs. 250 million temple at Ayodhya. This was immediately followed by a fund-raising drive. (According to Income Tax Department figures, nearly a third of the required amount has been raised so far.) More important, however, the fund-raising drive resulted in the involvement of devout Hindus all across the country in the campaign. This was followed by another communal masterstroke: the making of millions of bricks with Lord Rama's name engraved on them. These were then to be consecrated as *ramshilas* (Ram's rocks) at streetside religious ceremonies and taken to Ayodhya on November 9 by groups of devotees from each locality. This was an explosive plan as it was obvious that each consecration ceremony would be seen as provocation by the Muslims in that locality and each group of devotees driving to Ayodhya would leave communal disharmony in its wake. Besides, it ensured the presence of more than one million devout Hindus determined to lay the foundation of the temple at Ayodhya on November 9.

It was partly the fear of such a large mob getting out of hand and partly the confusion among the then-ruling party's ranks as to what approach to the issue would have the best effect on the elections, barely two weeks away, that led to police inaction and virtual surrender to Hindu activists. Until then, the government had tried to buy

---

[5] Syed Shahabuddin, *Muslim India*, Vol. 53 (May 1987), pp. 195–196.

time by having recourse to legal processes. The Allahabad High Court, the apex court in Uttar Pradesh, had ruled on August 14 that neither side could change the status quo at Ayodhya. The VHP, however, maintained that the issue was beyond judicial scrutiny. The government thought the way out was to persuade the Hindu activists to lay the foundation stone of a new temple building at a spot about 100 yards from the main entrance of the shrine, falling in a section of the area designated in the revenue records as plot 578. This piece of land was claimed by neither the Hindus nor the Muslims. It was owned by a local Hindu resident who had agreed to give it to the VHP for the foundation stone. But on November 9, as thousands of paramilitary soldiers stood by patrolling the two-tier barbed-wire-and-steel-pipe fence around the shrine, the Hindu mob pretended to go toward plot 578, then quickly turned to the adjoining plot 586, which was claimed by the Muslims as part of the mosque, and consecrated a spot there for the laying of the foundation stone. This spot lies just 64 yards from the main entrance of the shrine and in a straight line with it, conforming to the Hindu fundamentalists' decision to build the new temple exactly where the earlier one is supposed to have been, demolishing the mosque and even digging up the surrounding graveyard in the process. VHP President Ashok Singhal stated that position clearly in an interview with *India Today*: "If there is a graveyard it should be removed with the mosque."[6]

Sensing victory, the VHP announced that the next phase of the construction program would begin in February 1990, but it was prevailed upon by the V. P. Singh government, with help from the BJP, to postpone it by four months. The Singh government believes that its proximity to the BJP and the BJP's emergence as a strong third force in national politics could actually become a sobering influence on the VHP. But that supposition could be optimistic. The membership, leadership, and policies of the BJP and the VHP interlock substantially, and there is a huge gray area in which it is difficult to tell who is from the BJP and who is from the VHP. Understandably, as months pass the BJP will be under pressure from its orthodox cadres to give the signal to the VHP to go ahead with the construction.

At present it is difficult to foresee what solution the government could offer. V. P. Singh has often said that since the Hindus feel so strongly about the shrine and believe that it is the birthplace of their most revered god, it is fair that they should be allowed to construct the temple. The Muslims, he maintains, harbor fears that this could be the beginning of a series of similar demands vis-à-vis hundreds of

---

[6] Interview, November 9, 1989.

other mosques that were supposed to have been built by razing Hindu temples. In his view a solution could consist of allowing the Hindus to construct the temple in return for a commitment not to disturb any other mosque in the country. But in the current charged situation it is difficult to imagine either side accepting this.

The Revolt in Kashmir

Next on the list and perhaps as important as Ayodhya in terms of its long-term impact on communal relations in 1990 and beyond is the rising Islamic and secessionist revolt in the Kashmir Valley. Hindu fundamentalists have questioned the patriotism and nationalism of Indian Muslims since independence. The secessionist clamor among the 3 million or so Muslims of the Kashmir Valley buttresses that prejudice. In fact, it does more than that. Hindu fundamentalists view the Kashmiri revolt differently from secessionist moves elsewhere in the country ascribed to regional aspirations or tribal ambitions. Jammu and Kashmir is seen as the country's only Muslim-majority state, which has constantly threatened the integrity of the nation.

Hindu fundamentalists have always maintained that the best course in Kashmir is to abolish Article 370 of the constitution giving Kashmir special status and prohibiting other Indians from settling in the region and to bring in millions of Hindus from other parts of the country, thus changing the population balance in such a way as to make the borders secure. Further, the Kashmir situation lends weight to Hindu fundamentalists' favorite argument, that if Muslims elsewhere in the country claim to be nationalists it is because they are not a majority; once they grow in numbers they will talk the language of the Muslims in Kashmir.

In the past these arguments have not been accepted by a large number of Hindus, who ascribed the confused nationalism of the Kashmiris to the peculiar circumstances in which the state signed the instrument of accession with India. It was pointed out by Hindu liberals that the Jammu and Kashmir Liberation Front (JKLF), which led the secessionist movement, itself had a secular—even socialist—manifesto. In addition, Kashmiri society was known for its secularism, its practice of a rather benign form of Islam, and its Hindu-Muslim unity. Even now Kashmir hardly has any record of Hindu-Muslim riots.

But things changed a great deal during 1989 and in the first few months of 1990. The Kashmiri separatist movement has been taken over by Muslim fundamentalist groups, who have enforced the closure of all cinema halls, liquor stores, and beauty parlors and have decreed that women stay in purdah. Further, almost each time the authorities have lifted the curfew in Srinagar, the summer capital of Jammu and Kashmir state, mobs have come out in the streets following calls for *jihad* by *maulvis* (learned religious leaders) on the mosques' public address systems. In Pakistan-occupied Kashmir, *jihad* funds are being collected in hundreds of villages. The leadership of the movement is slowly but inexorably passing out of the hands of the JKLF into those of fundamentalist groups including Jamaat-e-Islami, Allah Tigers, Dukhtaran-e-Millat, and so on. Many of these groups openly claim to be affiliated with the Gulbuddin Hekmatyar faction of the Afghan *mujahideen*. The movement has received support not only from Pakistani Muslim fundamentalist organizations but even from the Iranian government. Fortunately so far the non-Kashmiri Muslims in India have not shown any concern or sympathy for the agitators in Kashmir. In fact Muslim leaders including Abdullah Bukhari and Syed Shahabuddin have publicly criticized the secessionist demands.

However, the situation is unlikely to remain static, and it is fraught with danger. The most ominous trend has been the attempts of frenzied, religiously charged mobs from the Pakistani side to storm across the line of control into the Indian-held area. On a number of occasions Indian border patrolmen were able to stop the mobs after resorting to firing. But if some day a mob is able to overwhelm a small Indian picket, the reaction in India outside Kashmir will be tremendous and will inevitably take a communal color. Already some Hindu fundamentalist groups have talked in terms of taking *jathas* (groups of devotees) to Kashmir to protect the national borders from "Muslim invaders." The worst-case scenario is an Islamic-oriented breaking away of Kashmir. This would not only leave the Indian Muslims suspect forever, but they would become targets of vicious Hindu fundamentalism that would be impossible to control or contain.

The Shadow of Communalism over the Elections

It was a striking but insufficiently stressed facet of the 1989 general election and the 1990 state-assembly elections that no national party, with the exception of parties on the left, fought either on a truly secular platform or without attempting to exploit religious, communal, or sectarian feelings. The BJP and the other self-avowedly religious-oriented groups did only what would be expected of them in any election. But an entirely new dimension was added to the scenario by the Congress's blatant use of religion in the campaign.

When Rajiv Gandhi kicked off his campaign in November 1989 by announcing that he would hold his first public meeting at Ayodhya, there was widespread hope that he would begin on a note of secularism, asking Hindus and Muslims to bury their differences and vote for his party. In a move that shocked many among his key supporters he began, instead, by promising to bring *Ram Rajya* (Lord Rama's Rule) back to India. This was accompanied by what can be described at best as his government's active acquiescence in allowing Hindu fundamentalists to truck hundreds of thousands of consecrated bricks to Ayodhya and to lay the foundation stone of the new temple at the disputed site. The apparent calculation was that since the *shilanyas* (the foundation-laying ceremony) took place on November 9, barely two weeks before the election day, there would be a dramatic turnaround in the Hindu vote. That didn't happen, as the BJP, VHP, and other Hindu groups launched an effective campaign to convince the Hindus that the *shilanyas* had been achieved through their efforts and not merely because the government had turned a blind eye to it. However, the Congress strategy put off the Muslims, the party's traditional vote bank. Thus the Congress lost the votes of both communities.

The disastrously communal course adopted by the Congress(I) Party during the campaign was no panicky last-minute switch. Even before the campaign got under way newspapers had carried accounts, and even a picture, of Home Minister Buta Singh's visit to Devraha Baba, a *sadhu* with supposedly mystical powers who lives in a tree on the bank of the Yamuna River near Mathura. The picture showed the virtually naked *sadhu* stretching his leg down from his perch and blessing Buta Singh by touching him on the forehead with his bare foot. Later even Rajiv Gandhi paid a visit to the *sadhu*. It was obvious that Rajiv Gandhi and his campaign managers had concluded that their political salvation lay in somehow winning back the estranged Hindu vote. So as the polling day drew closer and the writing on the wall became clearer, their campaign speeches changed hue. Three days before the first round of polling, Gandhi addressed a series of meetings in Delhi. In each one he exhorted the workers and supporters of the BJP and RSS—whom he called "patriotic even if believing in a wrong ideology"—to desert the Janata Dal, which, he charged, was going to barter India's interests away in dealing with Pakistan. As his appeals to the BJP supporters grew louder his rhetoric against Pakistan became more strident.

At the other end of the political spectrum, even the Janata Dal's campaign, though much cleaner, was not above board. Indirectly its greatest contribution to communalizing the election was the legitimacy it granted to the BJP by having an electoral agreement to share seats nationwide with the party. V. P. Singh himself maintained a relatively clean record throughout the campaign but blotted his book on November 9, the day of the *shilanyas*. For several days before, he had been announcing at his campaign meetings that he would visit Ayodhya on the day of the *shilanyas* to counsel peace and amity among the communities. The motive was seemingly noble, but the possibility of exploiting the situation for political ends, or at least ensuring that the Congress was not allowed to derive any advantage from it, must have occurred to him. But what he did on that day showed him in a particularly poor light. Afraid that he might be booed by the devout Hindu crowds gathered at the shrine, he stopped a few miles short of it, held a press conference, and returned without making a public appearance. If making the very epicenter of communal disharmony in India the pulpit for a message of tolerance and religious amity was his purpose, he clearly failed to gather sufficient courage to fulfill it.

Some of the more blatantly direct uses of religious symbols for electioneering came from the Janata Dal's election partners, notably Andhra Pradesh's Telugu Desam Party led by Nandamuri Taraka Rama Rao. At one stage the election commission had to intervene and ask Rama Rao to remove from street corners massive cutouts of him dressed as various Hindu gods. But in 1989 the generally vigilant Election Commission was fighting a losing battle, finally proving incapable of stopping the communalizing of the election process. Throughout the country the BJP and other Hindu groups freely used portraits and idols of Lord Rama in chains.

The Minorities' Crisis of Leadership

While 1989 saw an unprecedented rise in the power of the Hindu revivalist groups, the decline in minority leadership continued unabated. In previous years Syed Shahabuddin, an articulate diplomat-turned-politician, had shown indications of emerging as a spokesman of the Muslim community, particularly on questions like Ayodhya. He was popular with the media and led a stream of modern Indian Muslims who dreamed of an India where Muslims had a greater share of the national cake in terms of power and resources. But sometime in 1989, in the midst of tumultuous political developments, Shahabuddin lost his way. Estranged from the centrist Janata Party after major elements left it to join the Janata Dal, he set up a new party of Muslims, the Insaf Party. But the party got a resounding drubbing in the Lok Sabha election, and Shahabuddin himself lost badly in Bangalore South constituency.

Yet even before this reverse Shahabuddin had not been very influential, and it is a commentary on the state of Muslim leadership that it is difficult to name even a few prominent claimants to the spokesmanship of the community. The Congress(I) Party has itself failed to produce any Muslim leader of consequence after Maulana Azad, a liberal Muslim leader who emerged in the course of the independence movement. Dr. Zakir Hussain and Fakhruddin Ali Ahmed, both of whom rose to India's presidency, were too far removed from the Muslim mainstream to make a mark. There are other prominent Muslims who emerged in post-independence secular India in fields ranging from politics to science and sports. Mohammad Currim Chagla and Humayun Kabir were key members of the union cabinet in the sixties. M. J. Akbar, formerly the editor of the Calcutta-based weekly *Sunday* and the daily *Telegraph*, emerged as a kind of role model for young, educated Muslims and is now a member of parliament from the Congress(I). There were others: painter M. F. Husain, musician Zakir Husain, and two captains of the Indian cricket team (a rather significant position in a society where a cricket defeat or victory often becomes cause for national celebration or mourning). But Muslim politics in India is also governed by a strange paradox. Any Muslim who rises to prominence in the society is quickly dismissed as a "liberal," or worse, a "non-practicing Muslim" by his coreligionists. At one point in the last decade, Jammu and Kashmir Chief Minister Farooq Abdullah seemed to be emerging as a moderate Muslim leader, but developments in his own state in 1989 led to his being discredited and forced to resign. Now even the Janata Dal does not have Muslim leaders of consequence, with the exception of Mufti Mohammed Sayeed, a Kashmiri who is now the home minister. What this means on the political level is that the leadership of the community remains with orthodox clergy at local levels.

The Sikh leadership too became even more ineffective and discredited in 1989. Of all the Indian communities, the Sikhs have had the most developed politico-religious leadership system in the Shiromani Akali Dal, a party that drew legitimacy from the Sikh church and power from the support of the devout Sikh peasantry. The 1989 election saw at least six factions of the Akali Dal stand, often against one another. People overwhelmingly voted in favor of the faction led by Simranjit Singh Mann, but within the first few weeks after his election Mann lost ground when he failed to convey whether he was an extremist or a moderate. He claimed to be a nationalist but refused to take the oath of membership of parliament. He criticized killings of innocent people one day but talked in terms of a Punjab with its "own army and police" on another. These contradictions made him lose the support of both the moderates and the Hindus, who increasingly dismissed him as yet another hard-liner, and of the extremists, who thought he was too soft.

Is Indian Secularism on the Road to Extinction?

The Nepalese ruling elite employs a perennial, devastating dig at India, particularly in response to the Indian socialist liberals' support for a new referendum in the kingdom on multiparty democracy. Would India, the Nepalese royalists ask, gather the courage one day to hold a referendum to see if its people want a secular state? Indian liberals thought it would be possible to answer that taunt in the affirmative some day; in 1990 such a referendum looks like a hopeless dream.

In fact, given the overpowering background of religious revival among all sections of Indian society, it is reasonable to conclude that by the end of 1989 and in the subsequent months Indian secularism found itself under the greatest pressure since the Hindu-Muslim communal frenzy of partition in 1947–48. Even in the best years of communal peace, true secularism was a futuristic ideal, despite the fact that it is firmly enshrined in the constitution. In 1990, following one of India's worst years of communal violence and two elections fought on unabashedly communal lines, secularism looks more and more like an unattainable utopia.

The basic prerequisite for secularism in any society, more so in a multireligious one like India's, is a clear separation of church and state. In the past the dividing line had been blurred at best. In 1989 it often disappeared altogether. In Punjab, the Akali Dals of various shades used religious symbols, shrines, and slogans even more freely than in the past. The Congress(I) too had crossed a new threshold earlier in the year by adding a promise to further the glory of Christianity in its manifesto for the elections to the assembly of the tiny tribal state of Mizoram. With the BJP and other Hindu groups occupying the center stage and the Congress(I) ridding itself of its secular facade, the recipe for disaster in future elections was complete.

In fairness to the BJP and the other fringe Hindu groups, it should be said that they cannot be held primarily guilty for communalizing the electoral process; that dubious privilege belongs to the Congress(I). Although it now castigates the Janata Dal for aligning with the BJP, in the past the Congress(I) itself has entered into alliance with the Muslim League in Kerala. Also, in 1972 it bulldozed all opposition, mainly by projecting Indira Gandhi's image as the goddess Durga in the wake of the Bangladesh crisis. The December 1984 elections saw the Congress's systematic exploitation of the communal situation climax in a landslide for Rajiv Gandhi. The most overpowering message of Rajiv's campaign was that Hindus should vote for him if they wanted to prevent the Sikhs from breaking up the country. All over the country the party displayed cutouts of Indira Gandhi collapsing as her Sikh guards riddled her body with bullets. The cameo of Indira's funeral pyre—with a sobbing Rajiv standing in a corner while priests read out the mantras—was repeated several times every day on television. In Rajiv Gandhi's own Amethi constituency, where he was challenged by his widowed sister-in-law Maneka Gandhi, a Sikh, the Congress(I)'s election slogan was *Beti hai sardar kee, desh ke gaddar ki* ("The daughter of a Sikh, traitor to the nation"). In 1984 Rajiv Gandhi stirred the wind by beating Hindu communal groups at their own game. In the next round the tables were turned, and India was left to reap the whirlwind of communal disharmony.

Conclusion

It is safe to conclude that just as drought and the state of the economy dominated 1987 and corruption in high places was the theme of the following two years, 1990 will see the arrival of communalism as India's number-one problem. The three issues dominating the communal canvas will, in the order of importance, be Ramjanmabhoomi–Babri Masjid, Kashmir, and Punjab. In addition, the increasing strength of the Bahujan Samaj Party (BSP), the party of the Harijans (Scheduled Castes), will contribute to tensions within Hindu society. On each of these issues, the National Front government led by V. P. Singh will face major disadvantages stemming from its very composition and support base.

On Kashmir it will be torn between the extreme postures taken by its two allies, who do not participate in the government but are always keen to ensure that their views prevail in the ultimate decision-making. The BJP is committed to the abolition of article 370 and, if necessary, to a hard line on Kashmir. The left disagrees and wants a softer line. Further, the government will be constantly pressured by Rajiv Gandhi, who has taunted it as incapable of standing up to Pakistan. The government's biggest problem will be to prevent the continuing crisis in Kashmir from threatening the ever-so-fragile Hindu-Muslim relations in the country.

On Ramjanmabhoomi–Babri Masjid too, the same syndrome continues. While the Janata Dal has yet to make its policy clear, its two allies have already gone too far in committing to extreme positions. The government's only hope now lies in persuading the BJP to keep the VHP under restraint and to bear in mind the larger national interest—particularly in view of the crises in Kashmir and Punjab.

But so complicated is the interlinkage between these problems that a worsening situation in Kashmir or Punjab could easily toughen the VHP posture while pushing the BJP closer to its position. That could lead to communal strife, or a threat to the survival of the National Front government, or both.

On Punjab, as time passes and killings continue, the government could find itself increasingly removed from the alternative of restoring the political process through an election. Yet a recourse to that alternative is inevitable, and there are many in the government who think that the sooner it is done the less will be the attrition. Much will depend on what kind of group a new election brings into power. Over the past two years the trend of killings in Punjab has undergone a major change as terrorists concentrate more on killing rivals within their own organizations, suspected informers, and policemen. Since these were predominantly Sikhs, the killings did not bring the Hindu-Sikh relationship under new strains. But the option of changing that approach lies with the terrorists, and if the victims in Punjab are once again mainly Hindus there will be new tensions elsewhere that the government could find extremely difficult to handle.

The question of affirmative action for the Scheduled Castes and Tribes and the rise of the BSP will continue to pose different kinds of problems within Hindu society. Lately the BJP as well as the VHP has tried at least to talk in terms of equality among all Hindus. But these organizations continue to be dominated by upper castes, and there is no doubt that in the coming months they could come into confrontation with the BSP. This could force them into adopting more extreme communal postures.

Thus communalism has emerged as secular India's greatest challenge at a time when the nation has shown the political courage to sacrifice the security of a party tried and tested through four decades and to support instead a coalition government.

3
India's Foreign Relations: Reassessing Basic Policies

Leo E. Rose

As we enter the 1990s, the international system is undergoing a process of change so broad in scope and fundamental in structure that its impact is bound to be universal. The South Asian states, and India in particular, have responded to recent developments in Eastern Europe and East Asia with an admixture of awe, elation, and concern, combined with a strong sense of uncertainty about their long-term effects. As the major power in South Asia and the one with the broadest involvement in extraregional politics, India may well face greater difficulty than its neighbors in making the necessary foreign-policy adjustments.

There has been and continues to be a broad consensus across the political spectrum in India on the principles and objectives of the nation's foreign policy. These were first defined by Prime Minister Jawaharlal Nehru during the 1947–1960 period and incorporated such novel concepts (in 1950) as nonalignment, peaceful coexistence, and the "neutralization" of Asia in the East-West cold war. By 1950 virtually all of the Indian political public except the pro-Soviet leftist factions had accepted these basic policy principles as appropriate for newly independent India. And when in the mid-1950s Moscow began to wax enthusiastic about India's independent foreign policy, most of the leftists in India and elsewhere fell into line.

There have been occasions when New Delhi "tilted" India's nonalignment policy toward what might be termed a covert and limited alignment with one or the other superpower—in 1956 and 1971 toward the Soviet Union and in 1963 toward the United States—for a limited period of time. These alignments did not, however, elicit significant voices of dissent from within the political party system or from intellectuals or the press. New Delhi's cooperation in the 1960s and 1970s with the American and Soviet policies to contain China, for instance, elicited only pro forma criticism even from the pro-China wing of the communist movement and was strongly supported by most of those who advocated nonalignment and the regional policy of excluding external powers from decisive roles in Asia.[1] The Janata Party government that came to power in 1977 had called for a return to genuine nonalignment in its electoral manifesto, but once in office it maintained the "tilted" alignment with the Soviet Union that the Indira Gandhi government had carefully concocted.

But while the conceptual framework underlying India's foreign policy has been clearly defined for four decades, there is evidence of confusion in the implementation of policy: India's rhetorical statements about global issues and its regional policies do not always mesh. The Government of India (GOI), for instance, strongly endorses nuclear-free zones of peace virtually everywhere in the world except in areas of its own concern—South Asia and the Indian Ocean. Disarmament is a hallowed concept in New Delhi, but since the mid-1960s India has generally taken the initiative in the militarization of the region by the development of its own nuclear-weapons capacity, the massive acquisition of highly sophisticated military equipment from outside, and the development of defense industries. There were sound and even compelling reasons for the policy decisions in each of these cases in the context of India's own security requirements, but then there usually are in countries with huge defense budgets.

India's policies toward its neighbors in the region do not always reflect the general principles of its foreign policy either. New Delhi strongly supports the concept of full sovereignty of nations (that is, of nonintervention by external powers) and the reordering of the international economic system in favor of less-developed states. But India generally insists upon the acceptance of its preeminent position in the region, both by the other South Asian states and by the major external powers. Preeminence is not precisely defined, and India's objective is not classic client-state relationships, but this stance is seen by India's neighbors as a limitation on their sovereign powers. Also integral to India's definition of preeminence is its insistence on the exclusion of external powers from a major role anywhere in South Asia. Psychologically this may be a reaction to 1,000 years of colonial intrusions in South Asia, first by Islamic and then by European powers, but again it is perceived by other regional states as designed to limit

---

[1] In 1963 and 1971, the Communist Party of India (Marxist) [CPI(M)], based in West Bengal, was usually identified as the pro-China, pro-Maoist wing of the Indian communist movement. But the CPI(M) usually has preferred to avoid too close an involvement in Sino-Soviet disputes and has claimed the status of a nationalist communist party.

their sovereignty in developing relations with external powers as well as in enhancing their status in the region.

The remarkable events of 1989 and early 1990 have set in motion a reexamination of the basic principles underlying India's foreign policy. What will it mean, for example, to define oneself as nonaligned if virtually every state, including the so-called superpowers, is nonaligned? Such questions will be debated in New Delhi in the 1990s.

Foreign Policy under Rajiv Gandhi

The propensity in New Delhi in 1989 was to project Rajiv Gandhi's role as a world statesman rather than to emphasize his more active and probably more important role in several critical developments in South Asia. Rajiv's participation in international conferences and his visits abroad—to China in December 1988, Paris in July 1989, and Belgrade in September 1989—were highly publicized by the government media, as were the visits of numerous foreign leaders to India. In February 1989, for instance, the presidents of France and Turkey, the prime minister of Australia, the UN Secretary-General, and several South Asian leaders visited New Delhi for meetings with Rajiv Gandhi and his associates.

Some of Rajiv's critics described his seemingly endless travels and meetings with foreign leaders as mostly show and little substance, but this characterization is unfair. Broader international developments in Asia and, in particular, in East-West relations, affected India's relations with several major powers in ways potentially important to Indian interests. While Rajiv and some of the foreign leaders did at times use effusive and rather meaningless rhetoric in their joint statements, they held several quiet dialogues on substantive issues as well.

The China Relationship

Rajiv Gandhi's highly publicized visit to Beijing in December 1988—shortly after Gorbachev's second visit to Delhi—raised speculation about the possibility of substantial improvements in Sino-Indian relations. The immediate results were not impressive. The PRC and India rededicated themselves to the Panchshila, or five principles of peaceful coexistence (first enunciated in the 1954 Sino-Indian Treaty), and signed agreements for cooperation in science and technology and in cultural relations. A joint working committee to consider, once again, the border dispute between the two powers was established, but there was no evident progress toward a resolution either in the Beijing meetings or in subsequent discussions in 1989.

Most of the attention in Sino-Indian relations continues to be focused on this border dispute. However, there were also improvements in the relationship in 1989 that received little public attention but may prove to be of some importance. Beijing was quietly appreciative of India's policy toward the Chinese government's violent suppression of dissident groups in Tibet and of pro-democracy forces in Tiananmen Square, both of which India called internal affairs of the People's Republic of China (PRC). This may help explain why China responded cautiously to the dispute between India and Nepal and refused to provide economic aid on favorable terms to Kathmandu. New Delhi, for its part, was quietly appreciative of PRC Premier Li Peng's comments during his November 1989 visit to Pakistan, Bangladesh, and Nepal, in which he urged all three to come to terms with India.

There also appeared to be a return by India and China in 1989 to a cautious policy regarding their disagreement over the line of control in sections of their long Himalayan border. From 1963 to 1986 both sides had abided by a policy of mutual restraint in assigning military units to these areas. Then, in 1986, according to unofficial but usually knowledgeable Indian sources, New Delhi decided to send a small military unit into one of these areas, the Sumdurong Chu Valley directly to the east of the India-China-Bhutan trijuncture.[2] The Chinese responded in far more flamboyant style in 1987 by the placement of a larger force, supported by helicopters; this led to a partial mobilization on both sides. There was fear, probably unrealistic, of another major Sino-Indian border conflict. But, in fact, by 1989 both sides had apparently returned to the old policy of mutual restraint in the disputed area. They still differ over where the line of control should lie, but they both keep their military forces out of the areas in contention. Sumdurong Chu is again just another complication among several in an overall border settlement between the two countries.

Neither Beijing nor New Delhi has been prepared to discuss realistically a compromise solution to the border dispute because such a solution could be politically embarrassing. The new V. P. Singh government may be more open than was its predecessor on this issue, but there is little evidence that the *ancien régime* in the PRC is capable of making novel decisions, even though there are obvious advantages

---

[2] While not a highly strategic area, the Sumdurong Chu Valley was the scene of the first major clash between Indian and Chinese forces in the 1962 war and is important to the Indian public, which still remembers the war as a major embarrassment.

for China in an overall settlement.[3] It is likely, therefore, that Sino-Indian relations in the early 1990s will continue to be reasonably normal and nonconfrontationist, but nothing like the *Chini-Hindi Bhai Bhai* (Chinese and Indians are Brothers) tacit alliance of the 1950s.

The Soviet Connection

There were no dramatic developments in India's relations with the Soviet Union in 1989 despite, or perhaps because of, the spectacular changes under way in the USSR's domestic and international politics. It is apparent, however, that both powers are in the process of reevaluating their security and economic relationship in ways that could, over time, reduce their importance to each other. Both New Delhi and Moscow prefer to maintain the public image of a close cooperative relationship on global issues, as most clearly expressed in their 1971 Treaty of Peace, Friendship, and Cooperation. And, indeed, the Indian media are filled with eulogies of Gorbachev's international policies, which are identified as closely conforming to those of India in the search for world peace. Usually ignored are the differences between the two governments on major substantive issues in international politics—for example, the evident Soviet preference for a U.S.-USSR–dominated international decision-making system is anathema to India.

Several changes in the overall Soviet perspective on key Asian policy issues have raised concern in New Delhi about the utility to India of the Soviet connection. Gorbachev has emphasized the primacy of China in the USSR's Asian policy in the late 1980s and 1990s, first in his highly publicized Vladivostok speech in July 1986 and then, in more direct terms with respect to India, during his visit to New Delhi that November and again in November 1988. This new emphasis raised a question about the reliability of Soviet support in the event of another Sino-Indian conflict. And indeed, one might conjecture that India revived its dispute with China over the Sumdurong Chu Valley on the Himalayan border—a comparatively safe place to arrange a "confrontation"—in the latter part of 1986 to test the *Soviet*, not the Chinese, response. Moscow kept very quiet, and Gorbachev told the Indians to settle their dispute with China peacefully. India had the USSR's response—though not the one it wanted—and the dispute faded away.

---

[3] Beijing has, on occasion, indicated an interest in a border agreement on the current line of control between India and Tibet, but at the same time has reasserted its claims to the entire hill area above Assam in the eastern section of the border. This raises doubts in New Delhi that China is seriously interested in a settlement.

The withdrawal of Soviet military forces from Afghanistan, completed in February 1989, and Moscow's clearly indicated interest in substantially improving relations with Pakistan have also raised doubts in New Delhi about what the Soviet role would be in another Indo-Pakistani conflict. Here also Gorbachev has indicated his reluctance to involve the Soviet Union and has strongly supported a peaceful resolution of disputes between India and Pakistan—not the policy adopted by Moscow during most of the period since 1955. This made it possible for Rajiv Gandhi in 1988 and 1989 to enter into serious and friendly negotiations with Prime Minister Benazir Bhutto and the democratic government in Pakistan without arousing intense criticism from pro-Soviet leftist elements in India, as would have happened in the pre-Gorbachev period.[4]

Throughout most of 1989, few Indians expected another conflict with either China or Pakistan, given the general trend of international relations in Asia and throughout the world. But such a conflict was not ruled out for the future, which raised the question of whether there was still something that could be identified as a limited security relationship between India and the Soviet Union. Some Indian commentators argue that while the Soviet connection was useful and necessary in the 1970s and 1980s, it would be more an encumbrance than a benefit in the 1990s. It is doubtful that either New Delhi or Moscow wants to do anything that would formally end their close cooperative relationship, but it is clear that both see the relationship as less significant to their national interests than at any other time in the last three decades.

Economic exchanges have been important in Indo-Soviet relations since the mid-1970s, but they too have come under closer scrutiny in the late 1980s. India has had a substantial surplus in the rather curious state-to-state trade system that has evolved with the USSR, averaging about 1 billion rubles (at the highly inflated international exchange rate for the ruble rather than the deflated rate that emerged in late 1989). But since this surplus can only be used for purchases from the Soviet Union and India finds little to import from the USSR except oil and arms, some Indians depict this trade system as a serious drain on India's limited resources. Oil and arms are important, but there are alternative sources for these items and, it is argued, alternative markets for at least some of the Indian products exported to the USSR. It is particularly irritating to some Indians that Moscow has

---

[4] Pro-Soviet New Delhi newspapers like the *Patriot* have been critical of Pakistani support of dissidents in Kashmir and Punjab, but the language used has generally been moderate, at least when compared to pre-1989 editorial commentaries.

been known to reexport certain Indian products (for example, coffee) for hard currency even though these goods were acquired under the special trade relationship.

There are reports that Moscow too is reexamining the utility of the trade system with India, but this is not yet evident in Soviet policy, which is still more concerned with finding products that the Indians are prepared to import. The USSR has even offered India assistance in its nuclear-energy program, but New Delhi has responded cautiously. The Indian concern about the quality and reliability of Soviet nuclear technology was clearly indicated in public announcements that the nuclear plant the USSR offered India is not a Chernobyl-model plant. Not mentioned publicly are reports that some of India's leading nuclear specialists have demonstrated little enthusiasm for Soviet nuclear facilities, particularly in comparison to alternative sources in the West and Japan or in India's own advanced nuclear-energy programs.

The Soviet Union continued in 1989 to transfer some of its most advanced weapon systems to India's ground, air, and naval forces. This was appreciated by most of the military leadership and by specialists on security issues, who still argue strongly for continuance of the large military modernization program introduced in the mid-1970s. But some Indians in 1989, like people virtually everywhere else in the world, were seriously questioning the wisdom of diverting such a quantity of resources to the defense sector. Remarkably, the previously sacrosanct Defence Ministry budget was debated in the 1989 budget session of parliament, something that had not occurred for decades. Supporters of the military modernization program argue that a high proportion of imported weapon systems and related technology is obtained from the USSR on very reasonable terms compared with world-market prices. Critics of the program note that India pays for the Soviet equipment by the export of Indian products that could be exported elsewhere for hard cash, and that Soviet spare parts are expensive and often unobtainable. Here again, the V. P. Singh government is unlikely to move quickly to change the existing arms procurement system, but it may well reevaluate this system.

Expanding Relations with the United States

As in most years since the mid-1950s, India and the United States had a stressful relationship in 1989. Much of the Indian criticism of the United States during the past decade has centered on the American multiyear arms and economic-aid program for Pakistan, which was concluded by the Reagan and Bush administrations and approved overwhelmingly by the U.S. Congress. The Indians termed this program another major incitement to an arms race in South Asia because it compelled India to import foreign arms in large quantities (in 1988 India imported more than five times the monetary value of the arms that Pakistan obtained from the United States, and even more in actual equipment) in order to maintain "parity" between Indian and Pakistani military capabilities.

Washington knew that Indian complaints about the U.S.-Pakistan security relationship had been used adroitly by the proponents of India's military modernization program, which was introduced in the mid-1970s at a time when there was no U.S. military-aid program for Pakistan. Since the U.S. government was interested in the long-range objectives of India's massive militarization program, it preferred to avoid expressing criticism except of those aspects of the program involving inputs into India's quite advanced nuclear and missile-system projects. There were the usual American expressions of concern about India's nonadherence to international nuclear nonproliferation principles and about the successful test-firing of the Indian *Agni* IRBM (intermediate-range ballistic missile), which can carry a one-ton payload up to 1,500 miles, as well as of the short-range *Prithvi*, *Akash*, and *Nag* missiles. The Indians gave their usual response, complaining about the discriminatory character of the nuclear nonproliferation treaty and expressing India's determination not to be caught with a military equipped with weapon systems that were two or three generations out of date. The nuclear issue remains an irritant in Indo-U.S. relations, but it was not allowed to interfere with the steady expansion of ties between the two powers during the Reagan administration and in the first year of the Bush administration.

The economic relationship became increasingly important in the last half of the 1980s as the United States replaced the Soviet Union as India's largest trading partner, with a relatively balanced exchange relationship. But there were irritants in 1989, in particular the U.S. government's "Super 301" regulations, adopted under strong protectionist-minded congressional pressure, under which India was bracketed with Japan and Brazil as the major violators of fair trade practices. The Indians objected, calling this a discriminatory policy against a developing country with a democratic political system. The GOI also took umbrage at the unsuccessful effort of a small group within a U.S. congressional committee that sought to cancel the U.S. aid allocation to India (about $15 million) because of alleged human rights violations. Most Indians acknowledge that human rights violations occur, but they also note that India has a democratic system in which such violations can be addressed by the public, as was dramatically demonstrated in the November 1989 elections.

Despite the negative aspects of Indo-U.S. relations in 1989, there continued to be substantive improvements in the interactions between the two powers. As noted above, trade continued to expand, rather slowly but in ways Indians consider important; for example, there was substantial growth in Indian software exports to the highly competitive U.S. market. High-technology transfers from the United States to India continue despite concerns in Washington about India's nuclear and missile-development programs. The figures for 1989 are not yet available, but it is probable that U.S. military and military-related contracts with India, primarily through the Memorandum of Understanding on Technology Exchange signed in 1984 by the two powers, were at least twice U.S. military sales to Pakistan—as was also the case in 1987 and 1988. If the United States has a "tilt" in South Asia on military sales, an argument can be made that it is toward India rather than Pakistan. This may explain the upgrading of exchange visits between high-level Indian and U.S. military delegations in 1989, which were conducted on very friendly terms.

There is a curious contrast in GOI public statements on the Soviet Union and the United States, reflecting Indian perceptions developed since the 1950s that may now require review. Indians of virtually all political persuasions speak enthusiastically of their relationship with the USSR. In the 1990s, however, it may be that, despite the best intentions on both sides, there is no place for the Indo-Soviet relationship to go, either on political/security issues or in their economic exchanges. In contrast, Indians rarely make positive public statements about any aspect of the Indo-U.S. relationship or the American role in the international polity or economy. Nevertheless, the growing importance of the Indo-U.S. relationship to India is understood and even appreciated at various levels of government in both New Delhi and Washington.

India as a Regional Power

Although in 1989 New Delhi preferred to direct public attention toward Rajiv Gandhi's involvement in broader international politics, there can be little doubt that most of the attention inside the GOI was focused on its difficult relations with several South Asian neighbors. Indeed, the year served as a testing time for the basic principles that have long guided India's relations with its neighbors in the region. On occasion India's regional policy, in a comparison to the United States's Monroe Doctrine for the Americas, has been termed a Nehru Doctrine, an Indira Doctrine, or a Rajiv Doctrine. It is doubtful, however, that this policy has had guiding principles so precisely and clearly defined that they could be termed a doctrine. But several broad, loosely defined policy objectives have, over the years, strongly influenced India's relations with both its South Asian neighbors and the major external powers.

The relationship between India and Pakistan has continued to serve as the fulcrum of regional politics in the Subcontinent, but on comparatively less stressful terms in 1989, when Prime Minister Rajiv Gandhi and Prime Minister Benazir Bhutto developed a good, seemingly friendly working relationship, than in past years. In contrast, however, India's relations with Sri Lanka, Nepal, Bangladesh, the Maldives, and even Bhutan were more controversial during much of the year, raising questions throughout South Asia about India's perception of its role in the region. The GOI was frequently described by its neighbors as a bully, a power with hegemonic ambitions intent on dominating the region. There was nothing particularly new in these critical appraisals of India's role as a regional power, but the language used was more intemperate in 1989 than at any time in the past, reflecting a highly emotional response to some of the GOI's policies and actions.

Building Friendship with Pakistan

Nineteen eighty-nine was a comparatively quiet year in Indo-Pakistani relations. This was due in part to the friendly ties that had been established between Rajiv Gandhi and Benazir Bhutto, but also to a more general Indian concern with avoiding actions that might be seen as endangering the stability of the newly established democratic system in Pakistan. While most Indians do not accept the validity of Pakistani allegations that previous martial-law regimes had been legitimized by the threat to Pakistan from India, New Delhi still preferred to assume a low-key role on issues that might provoke the Pakistani officer corps to move against the democratic government in the name of protecting national security.

There were, of course, persistent problems that defied settlement. Public attention in both countries continued to be directed toward the dispute over Kashmir, with Indians alleging that some Pakistanis (but not necessarily the Benazir Bhutto government) were supporting "terrorist" forces on the Indian side of Kashmir and in Punjab. There appeared to be progress on this issue by the fall of 1989. The Pakistani government offered what it described as firm commitments to New Delhi to refrain from assisting Kashmiri "terrorists." By late November, however, the stage was set for another confrontation with Pakistan over the increasingly critical internal situation in the Indian state of Jammu and Kashmir. (The dispute became heated in early 1990, with both sides engaging in the rhetoric of war; we shall examine the situation in Kashmir in more detail in relation to the new Janata Dal government.)

In another long-standing dispute, both Pakistan and India charged the other with aggressive action in relation to the line of control along the 20,000-foot-high strategic Siachen Glacier in Kashmir. By the end of the year, however, there reportedly was progress toward agreement on a formula for mutual withdrawal. The long dialogue over the expansion of economic relations also continued. Once again, a joint subcommittee was established to negotiate on economic relations, but on this occasion with a somewhat more open attitude on both sides.

Pakistan adopted a critical stance toward India's policies in Sri Lanka and Nepal, but its support of these small states was mainly rhetorical rather than material, and it was evident that the Islamabad government preferred to see India's disputes with these states resolved on reasonable terms. India and Pakistan also responded differently to the Soviet withdrawal from Afghanistan in February 1989, with India continuing to work with the old Soviet puppet Najibullah regime in Kabul while Pakistan sided with the *mujahideen* (Afghan resistance) interim government that continues to operate out of Peshawar in Pakistan. By late 1989, however, both powers had publicly accepted the need for a broad-based government in Afghanistan. Where they still seemed to differ was in their views on the bargaining process that should be used to form such a government and, more specifically, on which of the numerous Afghan political factions should be involved in the process and on what terms.

The nuclear proliferation issue continues to be a difficult problem in Indo-Pakistani relations as well as in both countries' relations with the United States. While there are strong apprehensions in Pakistan and India on the nuclear issue, there appears to be a pragmatic approach on both sides under which it has been tacitly agreed that each would develop nuclear-weapons capacity but exercise restraint in the actual production of nuclear weapons. It was in this general context that India and Pakistan signed an agreement in early 1989 not to strike each other's nuclear facilities, an indication of their willingness to live with a dangerous but not easily rectified reality.

Sri Lanka and the IPKF

The July 1987 Indo-Sri Lankan Accord, signed by Rajiv Gandhi and President Jayawardene, had seemed to lay the foundation for future relations between these two powers on terms that were satisfactory to

New Delhi. In particular, the GOI had appreciated the letters that accompanied the accord under which Colombo, in effect, agreed to
avoid anything that might be interpreted as a security relationship
with a third power.

By early 1989, however, everything in Sri Lanka, including the accord, seemed to be falling apart, and the beneficent role of the Indian
Peace Keeping Force (IPKF) had been transformed (in the perception
of most Sri Lankans, whatever their ethnic or religious affiliation) into
a hostile occupying force. The election of Ranasinghe Premadasa as
president of Sri Lanka in December 1988 was another complication for
India, as Premadasa had opposed the accord when it was signed and,
in the late 1988 election campaign, had called for the quick withdrawal of the IPKF. There was virtual unanimity among the major
Sinhalese political factions in support of this demand (even while they
kept killing each other), and the principal Tamil dissident faction, the
Liberation Tigers of Tamil Eelam (LTTE), also demanded the withdrawal of the IPKF. Several smaller Tamil political groups, primarily
in the Eastern Province, supported retention of the IPKF, but they
were minor elements in the totality of Sri Lanka's bloody politics.

In September 1989, Rajiv Gandhi finally agreed to the "deinduc-
tion" of the IPKF by the end of the year, but with several conditions
that made it unlikely that the force would actually be withdrawn by
that date—if at all. The Indian military made no objection to the withdrawal of the IPKF from what it saw as a no-win situation. The interventionist policy adopted toward Sri Lanka under the terms of the
1987 accord can scarcely be called a success, but it may have been a
useful lesson for New Delhi on the difficulties of crisis management
through direct involvement in the politics of neighboring states.

The Indo-Nepali Confrontation

What had appeared to be a normal, if noisy, debate between India
and Nepal in early 1989 over trade and transit treaties was transformed into a major political and economic confrontation when the
GOI refused to renew the existing treaties or enter into serious negotiations on new ones. Similar dialogues have occurred about every ten
years when the treaties were due to expire, but since 1960 they have
been settled quickly after initial clamor on both sides and informal
forms of pressure (for example, India's closing of the border with Nepal on patently ludicrous grounds and reopening of it when Nepal
had "learned its lesson").

In March 1989, however, India terminated the existing treaties and
insisted that, henceforth, its economic relations with Nepal would be

based upon most-favored-nation (MFN) principles. This in effect ended the special economic relationship between the two powers under which Nepal had received numerous concessions that were vital to the well-being of its economy. Applying MFN principles has had a major impact not only on Indo-Nepali economic relations but also on Nepal's transit trade with third countries, even though New Delhi was slightly more generous than the MFN principles specify by allowing two transit entry points rather than one. In any case, 1989 was a very bad year for Nepal economically.

There has been a good deal of speculation as to why New Delhi adopted and maintained such a hard-line position. A factor that was undoubtedly persuasive was the growing irritation in New Delhi over Nepal's persistent efforts since the early 1960s to modify or even abolish the special security relationship based on the 1950 Treaty of Peace and Friendship while insisting upon more concessions in the special economic relationship the trade and transit treaties.

In 1988 Kathmandu also took several actions that New Delhi interpreted as violations of the special security relationship. The first was Nepal's decision to award the contract for a major project near the Indian border to a Chinese company, a move unacceptable to India on the grounds that some of the Chinese employees might be intelligence agents. This reasoning might have made sense in the period following the 1962 Sino-Indian war, but it appeared to be a form of paranoia in the late 1980s.

A second action by Kathmandu that aroused concern in New Delhi was its entering into an agreement with China under which China shipped about 500 truckloads of arms, including anti-aircraft weapons, to Nepal through Tibet in mid-1988. Nepal had not consulted with India on these arms acquisitions as New Delhi insisted it was required to under the terms of the 1950 treaty and a 1965 agreement on this very subject. Kathmandu argued that neither of the agreements applied when the arms did not transit Indian territory, but New Delhi strongly disagreed with this interpretation of the rather ambiguous language in the agreements.

No doubt New Delhi would have strongly protested both the above decisions of the Nepali government, but it is possible that the GOI would not have taken any drastic action in response if it had not learned of a secret agreement between Nepal and China, apparently concluded in the late fall of 1988, providing for the exchange of intelligence between the two governments. This was more than the GOI was prepared to accept, and it adopted its hard-line policy toward Nepal.

New Delhi insisted that if the special security relationship was in effect terminated by the Nepali government, then the special economic relationship would also have to go. This is exactly what happened. The Indian policies have been described as a blockade by Nepal, but, strictly speaking, this characterization is not accurate. As noted above, the GOI applies MFN principles on trade and transit with Nepal. Although much less liberal than the concessional terms granted to Nepal under the trade and transit treaties, this policy does conform to general international principles for landlocked countries like Nepal.

Much of the rhetoric on both sides has focused on two issues. The one given the most attention is the Nepali insistence on separate treaties of trade and transit, whereas India's preference is for a single treaty, as was the case before 1978. While both sides sound intransigent on this issue, it is probably more symbolic than substantive. What is important, after all, is the terms of trade and transit, not whether there are one or two treaties. This is tacitly recognized by both sides. A possibly more difficult issue concerns the status of migrant communities in each country. Both governments have legitimate complaints, but it seemed likely by late 1989 that both would accept the pre-1989 system for movement between the two countries, with minor changes.

The Other South Asian States

Although most of India's attention in South Asia was directed toward relations with Pakistan, Sri Lanka, and Nepal, developments in the Maldives, Bangladesh, and Bhutan were of potential importance. The Maldives emerged in late 1988 as a seemingly critical factor in New Delhi's Indian Ocean policy when Indian military forces intervened to save the government from a coup attempt by a rival leader supported by Sri Lankan Tamil mercenaries. The intervention was welcomed by the Maldivian government and most of the populace, and, in contrast to the situation in Sri Lanka, no anti-Indian sentiment was evident. The U.S. government lauded New Delhi for its timely action and even the governments of the PRC and Pakistan (though not the Pakistani media) avoided critical comments. It was noted with appreciation throughout South Asia that the Indian forces were withdrawn once the Maldivian government was back in effective control and that the government of the Maldives stated it had no intention of concluding a security pact with India.

India's relations with Bangladesh have been stressful since the mid-1970s, leading some Indians to question the wisdom of the decision in

1971 to intervene in support of the disintegration of Pakistan and the establishment of an independent Bangladesh. Both sides have usually been careful to avoid overtly confrontationist positions on issues in dispute, but at the price of postponing the resolution of their differences on some important questions: the control and use of the waters of the Ganges and Brahmaputra rivers; the illegal migration of Bangladeshis into surrounding areas of India; alleged support by each country of tribal dissident movements in the other; Bangladesh's restrictive policies on trade with India; and conflicting claims to several islands in the Bay of Bengal that lie within both Bangladesh and Indian territorial waters under the general principles of the Law of the Sea.

In 1989 there was no evident progress toward the resolution of any of these disputes, but both governments proceeded cautiously in the face of the potentially explosive situation in the region. Dhaka, for instance, was careful in the policies it adopted toward the Indo-Nepali confrontation. While vocally supportive of Nepal and critical of India's "bullying" policy, Dhaka in fact failed to provide substantive assistance to Nepal—for example, it never offered to serve as an alternative channel for Nepal's transit trade with the outside world. While Bangladesh Biman, the national airline of Bangladesh, has made a good profit by serving as a channel to Nepal for some badly needed supplies, Chittagong harbor has not replaced Calcutta as the primary channel for most of Nepal's transit trade, nor has it substantially expanded its role in this trade.

As to India's relationship with Bhutan, New Delhi has long perceived it as exemplary. In 1989, however, there were signs of potential tension even here. Under its newly introduced policies directed at protecting Bhutan's indigenous culture, the royal government in Thimphu has taken several actions that have aroused concern in India, including the expulsion of thousands of Indians who have been long-term, if not exactly legal, residents of Bhutan. Both governments have played down their differences on this and several other issues, and they continue to emphasize their close cooperative relationship.

A novel and unexpected development in South Asia in the 1980s was the establishment of a regional organization—the South Asian Association for Regional Cooperation (SAARC)—in 1985. New Delhi had generally viewed a regional organization as a channel through which the other South Asian states could gang up on India, while the other states had thought of it as another means by which Indian hegemony could be reinforced in the region. In 1989 the general decline in India's relations with several of its neighbors in the region raised doubts about the viability of SAARC in the management of regional disputes. The more positive views on SAARC expressed by some members of the V. P. Singh government have revived optimistic appraisals of SAARC's future.

Foreign Policy in the 1989 Election

The ninth national election was held in India in late November 1989 under potentially explosive conditions in some parts of the country. One might have expected the controversies with Pakistan, Sri Lanka, and Nepal to be major issues, but that did not prove to be the case. India's military intervention in Sri Lanka, for instance, had led to bitter divisions within the Sri Lankan Tamil community, but this subject was virtually ignored in electoral politics among the Tamils in India. The main contending parties in the state of Tamil Nadu—the Congress(I) Party and the two largest Tamil regional parties—generally preferred to ignore India's policy in Sri Lanka and were cautiously ambivalent in the few statements issued on this subject during the election. The Congress(I) Party, in a coalition with a Tamil party, won most of the parliamentary seats in Tamil Nadu despite the strong criticism by some Sri Lankan Tamils of Rajiv Gandhi's decision in September to withdraw Indian military forces from Sri Lanka.

Similarly, the noisy confrontation between New Delhi and Kathmandu over the GOI's refusal to extend or renegotiate the terms of the treaties of trade and transit between the two countries played no role in the Indian election, even in the districts bordering on Nepal in which many Indians have familial connections across the border. The several opposition parties and factions that are well based in this area—and that won most of the parliamentary seats, defeating Congress(I) Party incumbents—were very restrained in criticizing Rajiv's Nepal policies, presumably because there was no significant public to appeal to on this issue. Pro-government sources in Nepal were strongly anti-Rajiv in their comments on the election across the border and were delighted with the defeat of the Congress(I). But they received little encouragement from the foreign policy positions assumed by the opposition candidates, which were hardly distinguishable from those of the Congress(I).

Even the deteriorating India-Pakistan relationship was only a minor factor in the 1989 elections. On occasion, during meetings in the districts bordering on Pakistan, Rajiv Gandhi and the Congress candidates criticized Pakistan's activities in Punjab and Kashmir as interventionist, but usually in comparatively moderate language. Similarly, the opposition candidates in these constituencies on occasion spoke in disparaging terms of the friendly Rajiv-Benazir relationship, implying that Rajiv had failed to protect India's interests, but this theme was incidental to their principal criticism, which depicted serious mismanagement of domestic economic and social-development programs and massive corruption as integral to the Rajiv system.

Foreign policy issues assumed significance in the election only through the corruption issue—specifically, the alleged payoffs to various members of Rajiv Gandhi's in-house coterie (and in some versions of the story, to the prime minister as well) by Bofors, a Swedish armaments manufacturer. By November it was clear that under-the-table payments had been made by Bofors as part of the process of gaining contracts for one of its artillery systems. What was still unproved was whether or not Rajiv or any of his confidants had profited from this deal, but the general assumption was that they must have, or that, at the very least, the prime minister's office had been negligent in moving against the culprits—both Indian and Swedish. Although this issue was domestic in origin, it increasingly became tied to India's economic relations abroad.

The Janata Dal Government: International Relations

A minority National Front government, headed by V. P. Singh, was formed by the Janata Dal based upon assurances of support, though not direct participation, by the BJP and the Communist parties. The new foreign minister, Inder Kumar Gujral, had held cabinet posts under Indira Gandhi in the early 1970s and was India's ambassador to the USSR, but he broke with Indira and supported the Janata Party government (1977–79). On assuming office in early December 1989, he and Prime Minister V. P. Singh both spoke of the need to establish better relations with the countries in the region than had the Rajiv Gandhi regime. The prime minister, in an address to the National Front parliamentary party on December 19, stated that his government would move to improve relations with Sri Lanka and Nepal as well as continue the efforts to resolve the boundary question with China and "further strengthen the traditional friendship with the Soviet Union, build upon the new trend of constructive and cooperative relationship with the United States, and strengthen economic cooperation with Japan and the European Community."[5] Although the rhetoric was impressive, it soon became evident that the new government had not yet considered the various policy options. It was time for India to commence serious negotiations with a number of governments,

---

[5] FBIS-NES–89–243, December 20, 1989, pp. 46–49.

a process that Rajiv Gandhi had suspended in the months preceding the election.

India's relations with the major external powers did not require any immediate decisions, although New Delhi could not ignore the amazing and unexpected developments throughout the communist world and the response of democratic countries to those events. As the USSR had done in 1977 when the Janata Party government replaced the Indira Gandhi regime, Moscow moved quickly to establish a good working relationship with the National Front government.[6] Yuli Vorontsov, the first deputy foreign minister of the USSR, came to New Delhi shortly after the new government took office and assured Gujral, "We are with India." But when Gujral brought up India's stressful relationship with Pakistan over the increasingly difficult situation in Kashmir, Vorontsov merely stated, "We are absolutely sure that the India-Pakistan tensions will not grow into conflict."[7] This kind of ambivalent response was not what New Delhi had hoped for from Moscow, since the Indians were less confident that a conflict with Pakistan was inconceivable. Alfred Gonsalves, India's ambassador to Moscow, stated, "It's my judgment that if the Indo-Soviet relationship is subjected to a test, there will be no difference from the past." But given the USSR's neutral position in the 1962 Sino-Indian war and the 1965 India-Pakistan war, this was not very reassuring. Because of the major crisis in the Soviet Union's economy, serious dissident movements in the Islamic republics within the Soviet Union, and the virtual collapse of the Warsaw Pact alliance system in Eastern Europe, the old view of the USSR as a support base for India in its

---

[6] In an interview with the author in mid-1978, Indira Gandhi described, in an indignant and sarcastic tone, Moscow's response to her defeat in the 1977 general election. She noted that up to a week before the election, the Soviet press had continued to laud her as the great leader of the people. Then in the last week, when the election became uncertain and her defeat a possibility, her name disappeared from the Soviet media. Shortly after Indira's defeat and the establishment of the Janata Party government, the Soviet press became harshly critical of her authoritarian and repressive policies during the Emergency. By late 1978, Moscow had concluded that Indira's Congress(I) Party was likely to win the next election, and it was again praising her leadership qualities. On resuming the prime ministership in January 1980, Indira sought to reestablish a good working relationship with Moscow. One of her first actions immediately after taking office was to instruct the Indian mission at the United Nations to defend the Soviet military intervention in Afghanistan in late December 1979. She regretted this almost immediately and sought to assume a more balanced position, calling for the withdrawal of foreign (i.e., Soviet) troops from Afghanistan, but without harming New Delhi-Moscow relations. Her contempt for Soviet leaders, and particularly for Brezhnev, was clearly indicated, however, in her private meetings with them in which she lectured at considerable length about what Moscow should be doing.

[7] *India Today*, February 15, 1990, p.30.

disputes with neighboring states may become even less plausible in the 1990s. It is assumed that Moscow will be increasingly sensitive to Islamic sentiments both within the USSR and in West Asia, and in such circumstances the Soviet relationship with Pakistan may become more critical to the Soviet Union. The facts of the case are that India no longer has much to offer the USSR in political and geostrategic terms in the 1990s, while Pakistan has become, marginally at least, more important, particularly if the situations in Afghanistan and the regions bordering Soviet Central Asia are taken into consideration.

The economic ties between India and the Soviet Union, however, continue to be important to Moscow, and preliminary negotiations between the two governments on this subject began in early 1990. These talks did not focus on the trade relationship, which continues to grow slowly, but rather on joint projects, mostly in the USSR, between private Indian firms and various kinds of Soviet enterprises. This relationship could be called a form of Indian economic assistance (that is, furnishing of capital as well as entrepreneurial and management skills) to the Soviet Union.

For their part, the U.S., Japanese, and West European governments did not see the transition to a new government in India as posing serious problems or requiring novel policy responses. Initially, at least, the emergence of the V. P. Singh government was perceived as having enhanced prospects for a reasonably quick and mutually acceptable resolution of India's ongoing disputes with Sri Lanka, Nepal, and possibly even Pakistan. The western powers and Japan, as well as the USSR and China, saw this as a positive development that they should encourage.

The one subject on which American, Japanese, and West European business communities have expressed concern is the economic policy of the V. P. Singh government as it evolves in 1990. The prime minister and several of his key economic advisers have assured foreign investors that the liberalization policies introduced by Rajiv Gandhi would be not only retained but implemented more effectively. At the same time, however, some members of the V. P. Singh government, and in particular of the old Socialist Party faction that still wields considerable political clout within the Janata Dal, have expressed their determination to reestablish a self-reliant industrial system that restricts foreign involvement. The rather casual remark of a former Socialist Party member, Railways Minister George Fernandes, about throwing PepsiCo out of India revived bad memories of the ejection of Coca-Cola and IBM in the late 1970s under the Janata Party government.[8] On balance, the focus on economic liberalization would appear to be better based, both within Janata Dal and on the broader political scene, but there are still strong political and economic groups that are interested in exclusionist policies.

In these circumstances, GOI concerns about the continued flow of foreign capital into India are not surprising. Foreign investments approved by the Indian government rose impressively in the 1980s, from Rs. 110 million in 1981 to Rs. 3.2 billion in 1989 (the exchange rate runs about Rs. 17 to the U.S. dollar). It is disturbing to the economic ministries that both American and Japanese investment approvals declined substantially in 1989 over 1988. West German and British investment approvals, on the other hand, rose dramatically in 1989, with West Germany displacing the United States as the largest source of approved foreign investment. The expectation, however, is that a large proportion of West German and British capital available for investment abroad will go to East European countries in the 1990s and that India will have to become much more competitive in attracting foreign capital. The result could be an involuntary return to the old policy of self-reliance unless American and Japanese investors can be persuaded of the attractiveness of the Indian market.

The change of government in New Delhi did not have an immediate impact on Sino-Indian relations, but there are expectations that progress in the resolution of the border dispute is now more likely. Over the last decade, I. K. Gujral has, on occasion, voiced support for a settlement that would define the *de facto* line of control as the *de jure* boundary. While there would be criticism of such an agreement from some opposition leaders in India, this could probably be controlled even by a minority government as delicately placed politically as the Janata Dal. A more difficult problem may lie within the National Front coalition. George Fernandes and several of his former Socialist Party colleagues still adhere to their 1950 position opposing the imposition of Chinese rule in Tibet. The prime minister, in contrast, has stated clearly that his government will retain Rajiv Gandhi's position that Tibet is an autonomous region of China but that what goes on in Tibet is an internal affair of the PRC. V. P. Singh, it is clear, will not seek to revive disputes with China over Tibet, the border, or any other old issues.

---

[8] Fernandes was industry minister in 1978 and is usually given credit—or blame—for forcing Coca-Cola out of India.

Sri Lanka and Nepal

When the National Front government took office in early December 1989, the foreign policy issues that demanded immediate response were the ongoing disagreements with Sri Lanka and Nepal. During the election campaign and thereafter, V. P. Singh stated that he would assume a kinder and more open posture toward the other states in the region and move expeditiously to settle all disputes. Some progress has been made in relations with both Colombo and Kathmandu, but problems remain.

V. P. Singh reassured the Sri Lankan government that India would abide by the March 31, 1990, deadline for the withdrawal of the IPKF from Sri Lanka. Moreover, New Delhi no longer insisted on a resolution of the intra-Tamil conflicts in northeastern Sri Lanka prior to the withdrawal of the IPKF on terms that would provide some protection to the Tamil "militia" and local government units established by the Indians in the Eastern Province. There were innumerable problems in the implementation of this promise due to the incredibly complex politics of Sri Lanka, but the last Indian troops were withdrawn on March 24, 1990, seven days ahead of schedule, and there was no serious criticism of this action within the Indian political system.

The main subject for discussion between the governments of India and Sri Lanka in the first part of 1990 has become their post-withdrawal relationship. Both Colombo and New Delhi support the conclusion of a treaty of peace and friendship to replace the 1987 accord, but they have quite different views on the terms of such a treaty. The Premadasa government wants a treaty similar to the 1971 Indo-Soviet treaty, which merely obligates both governments to consult in the event of conflict in the region. New Delhi, however, has insisted upon a treaty that would incorporate all the limitations on Sri Lankan relations with third powers that appear in the letters of exchange agreed to in the 1987 accord. The Premadasa government is strongly disinclined to accept such a treaty. But as a high Indian official told the author in January 1990, if Sri Lanka does not sign a new treaty with India, the 1987 accord and its various accompaniments will continue to be in force. This may be so legally, but the 1987 accord is unlikely to be the determining factor in Sri Lanka's international policies in the 1990s.

The issues in dispute between India and Nepal still appeared to be unresolved in early 1990. In fact, however, according to some sources, New Delhi and Kathmandu had reached a broad agreement under which their special economic relationship and special security relationship would be revived on essentially pre-1988 terms. The major obstacle to full normalization of relations then became the serious internal political crisis in Nepal resulting from the anti-government movement launched by the Nepali Congress Party's establishment of a working arrangement with the seven-party Left Front in 1990. The fact that several Indian political leaders, including two from the Janata Dal, visited Kathmandu and gave their blessing to the movement complicated relations between the two governments, even though V. P. Singh and I. K. Gujral have been more circumspect in their comments on the situation.

Pakistan and the Kashmir Dispute

The first quarter of 1990 might well have led one to conclude that the old adage "the more things change, the more they stay the same" still applies, at least with respect to Indo-Pakistani relations. By February 1990, both governments were indulging in provocative language, exchanging charges and countercharges that, in retrospect, will probably prove to be only slightly related to reality, and in the process reviving concern in both countries and elsewhere that yet another war over Kashmir is a distinct possibility. There are important differences from past crises, however. First, the current crisis is almost exclusively the product of a political upheaval in Kashmir or, more specifically, in the Kashmir Valley of the Indian state of Jammu and Kashmir. New Delhi charges Pakistan with provoking and assisting "terrorist forces," but most Indians understand—from history—the limited capacity of Pakistan to organize and initiate a movement that would have the overwhelming support of the people of the valley. Second, despite the strong language used on occasion, it appears that the top leaders in both India and Pakistan want to avoid another war but have difficult domestic political environments that complicate their efforts to limit the current confrontations.

The issues in dispute in 1990, as repeated endlessly by both sides in their most simplistic form, have not changed much over the past four decades. Perhaps the most unrelated to reality is the debate over the accession of Kashmir to India in 1947. New Delhi insists that the accession conformed to the terms set by the British for the partition of their Indian empire and that the people of Kashmir have demonstrated their support of accession through broad popular participation in several parliamentary and state assembly elections since 1950. According to an Indian External Affairs Ministry spokesman, the only issue still unresolved is Pakistan's withdrawal from the territory it occupied in Kashmir, which it calls Azad (Free) Kashmir and the Indians call Pakistan-occupied Kashmir. The Pakistani response is that the

1947 accession did not reflect the will of the people in Kashmir, that India has not honored the UN resolutions calling for a plebiscite on this issue in Kashmir, and that the people of Kashmir have the right of self-determination—a popular notion among Pakistanis in 1990 but not a right they recognized for Bangladeshis in 1971. New Delhi asserts, in response, that India will never consider any change in the status of Kashmir and characterizes Pakistan's support of Kashmir's struggle for self-determination as a blatant violation of the 1972 Simla Agreement.

It is the Simla Agreement, concluded between Benazir's father and Rajiv's mother, that has been the subject of controversy between the two governments in early 1990. New Delhi prefers to emphasize the clauses of the agreement under which both sides pledge not to use force to resolve the Kashmir dispute and to settle the issue bilaterally. India responded negatively to Benazir Bhutto's comment, in an interview with Agence France-Presse, that Pakistan would welcome third-country mediation, calling this a violation of the bilateral principle. Islamabad, in turn, notes that under the Simla Agreement the Kashmir issue should be settled through bilateral talks, asserts that Pakistan is thus a party to the dispute, and regrets New Delhi's refusal to hold such negotiations.

The most acerbic exchanges between the two governments, however, concern the Indian allegations that Pakistan has been training, arming, and providing other forms of assistance to anti-Indian groups in the valley. New Delhi has prepared a collection of confessions, pictures of "Pakistani arms" seized in Kashmir, and a list of 46 training camps in Pakistan for Kashmiri "terrorists." This was considered conclusive evidence by the Indians, but was somewhat less impressive to the outside observers who know how successful the police are at extracting confessions everywhere in India; how available foreign arms—Chinese, U.S., and Soviet—are in Pakistan and northern India; and how frequently the Indian lists of training sites in Pakistan for both Sikh and Kashmiri "terrorists" change. Prime Minister Bhutto denied all these charges, noting, "We fought two wars with India over the Kashmir issue and do not want a third war" and stressing the need to work with "extreme responsibility and care to prevent war hysteria."[9]

Nevertheless, something close to war hysteria had become evident by February 1990. The most common theme in New Delhi was not that Pakistan would launch a military action in support of the Kashmiris but rather that India might eventually have to respond militarily to Pakistan's "intervention" in Kashmir through its assistance to the

---

[9] FBIS-NES–90–036, February 22, 1990, p. 57.

dissidents. The ability of both governments to tone down the abusive rhetoric was limited by immediate domestic political concerns. In India, state-assembly elections were held in several major states in the Hindi belt on February 27, and the contending parties, including the Janata Dal, the Congress(I), the BJP, and the CPI(M), competed in issuing anti-Pakistan statements. In Pakistan the opposition continued its intensive campaign to overthrow the Bhutto government, using ethnic conflicts in Karachi and in Sind province as the focus of their attack. In response, Benazir suggested that the disturbances in Karachi stemmed from external (i.e., Indian) sources, thereby making it difficult for the opposition to use these clashes against her government and at the same time letting New Delhi know that allegations of interference can run in both directions.

The confrontation over Kashmir continued into the spring of 1990, with both the V. P. Singh and the Benazir Bhutto governments subjected to intense internal criticism for their alleged weakness (read moderation) in dealing with the other. But the important state-assembly elections were held in India in late February 1990 with no indication that the Pakistan issue had any impact on the results, and the anti-Benazir campaign in Pakistan may well have been weakened rather than strengthened by the Kashmir issue. Both governments remain vulnerable, of course, and cannot ignore developments in Kashmir. Fortunately, in 1990 none of the major external powers involved in South Asia is interested in encouraging another Indo-Pakistani conflict, and thus broader international politics are not likely to be relevant to this dispute.

India's New Roles

In early 1990 public attention in India to international issues was almost exclusively focused, once again, on relations with Pakistan. But this is somewhat misleading, for the principal question for New Delhi continues to be India's broader role as the major regional power in South Asia and as an important participant in Asian, Indian Ocean, and global politics. Formulating policy that combines these various roles is not simple, particularly in the complex world that is emerging. The Soviet Union will probably be less of a factor in the attainment of India's regional and extraregional objectives than it has been in the past. But because China is no longer a challenge to India's preeminence in South Asia and adjacent areas, Soviet support is no longer seen as necessary. India's decision in the 1970s to develop a "blue water" navy was made, in part, because of concern over the prospect of a Chinese naval capacity in the Indian Ocean. But India retained this program in the 1990 defense budget as an integral part of its broader regional security policy, which now covers the area from the Arabian Sea to the Malay Peninsula.

The United States now defines its role in South Asia outside of the cold war framework, which has served to ease relations with New Delhi and open up prospects for cooperation between the two countries. With the withdrawal of Soviet forces from Afghanistan in 1989, the containment policy previously directed, on different occasions, at both the Soviet and the Chinese presence in southern Asia no longer has relevance to U.S. objectives. This removes a point of disagreement between India and the United States on security policies in southern Asia and opens up a range of new policy options for both governments.

The task of reassessing the basic principles and strategies of India's foreign policy is just getting under way, and it is bound to elicit a lively and contentious debate within the small community of specialists on international relations, both within and outside the political system. This group is strongly disinclined to change the rhetoric or substance of foreign policy principles that go back to the 1950s and are enshrined in the programs of all parties, from left to right. But the world that is emerging in and around South Asia cannot be ignored, and two such skillful practitioners of the art of economic and political exchange as V. P. Singh and I. K. Gujral can be expected to broaden the horizons and objectives of India's international relations as the 1990s move forward.

4

Breaking Away: India's Economy Vaults into the 1990s

John Adams

During the 1980s the Indian economy reached and sustained a pace of growth well above that of the first three decades of independence. At the end of the decade, as agriculture has recovered from the extremely severe drought of 1987, an unprecedented surge of output has catapulted the national economy into the 1990s. India has not only broken away from the slower rates of the past but has laid the foundations for continued rapid growth. Because nothing in India is ever simple, however, and the economy is certainly no exception, the citation of these positive developments must be balanced by notation of the persistence of chronic deficiencies. These include regional economic imbalances, growing governmental deficits, and continued failures to achieve what is expected in health, primary education, and the reduction of poverty. In addition, preliminary statistics suggest that in 1989 the economy mostly held onto rather than extended the broad achievements of 1988 in agriculture and industry, giving rise to concerns that the gains of the 1980s might be impossible to match in the 1990s.

The year 1989 not only marks the end of a decade of distinctive economic achievement but is also a milestone in two other ways. First, the Seventh Five-Year Plan, which began in 1985–86, was wound up in March 1990. Coming into effect in April 1990, the Eighth Plan sets a new framework for the country's economic development during the near-term future. Second, because the election of 1989 brought a non-Congress government and prime minister into power, there are new cabinet members in key positions of economic command and freshly named members of a reinvigorated and revamped Planning Commission.

As India enters the 1990s under this new leadership, pertinent questions to pose are what alterations are brewing in the realm of economic policy and what implications they hold for India's farmers, businesspeople, state bureaucrats, and consumers. Those outside India may wonder what stances the National Front government will ultimately adopt towards foreign investment and technological collaboration, multilateral and bilateral aid, debt-service arrangements, and trade policy. Before formulating answers to these questions, however, it is necessary to determine why India's economy leapt ahead in the 1980s, to examine salient features of India's economic performance in 1989, and to discuss the economic meaning of the 1989 election.

The Earlier Decades Versus the 1980s

What has been most remarkable about India's post-independence experience with economic growth is the constancy of the policy framework within which that growth has occurred. There is a broad and enduring national consensus about the function of the economy in India's diverse society and about the nature of the government's role in the economy. Put briefly, the strongest element in this consensus is the commitment to socialism. In India, the chief dimensions of socialism are economic planning, public ownership of the "commanding heights" of the economy, the pursuit of economic equity, and state direction of crucial economic flows: savings, investment, credit, and finance; exports and imports; and foreign capital and technology. The achievement of self-reliance is also important. On a practical basis, this means growing enough food to feed all Indians; trying to absorb cutting-edge technologies from abroad while keeping to a minimum the presence of multinational corporations in the economy; and holding down the burden of external debts to public and private lenders.

The linked commitments to socialism and self-reliance were not completely articulated at independence, but they have deepened and become more complex with the passage of time. In the 1950s directive planning was introduced as a way of pushing the economy out of the doldrums of the late colonial period. In the parlance of development economists, a "big push" was needed to create social overhead capital, establish basic industries to produce things such as steel, machine tools, and electrical equipment, and get agriculture moving.

Problems with foreign-exchange shortages and food supplies arose in the 1960s. India felt unduly pressured by the United States, among other foreign powers, and wars with China and Pakistan heightened strategic concerns. Growing sufficient food, maintaining adequate foreign-exchange reserves, further widening the industrial base, and building up core defense industries became the components of a coherent policy of self-reliance. Outside India this strategy has been described as inward-looking or import-substituting, not always with flattering connotations.

During the 1970s the dual policies of socialism and self-reliance continued to shape the national economic effort. To borrow again from the development economists' lexicon, the aim was to achieve "balanced growth" across all major sectors—agriculture, industry, infrastructure, and social services. After about 1972 India began to experience spurts in exports every two or three years. At best, the economic style of the third decade of planned development could be described as one of consolidation and continuity, and both inside and outside India there was concern among experts that growth was too slow and perhaps even slackening. Criticism centered on the role of the state in directing and controlling economic activity, and arguments were made in favor of relaxing controls, liberalizing the economy, and opening India to wider international trade and investment flows.

Then, just as patience with India's respectable but plodding progress was wearing thin, economic growth perceptibly jumped to a higher trajectory in the 1980s. To draw once again on the jargon of development economists, the 1980s were identified as the decade of India's "take-off" during which the country sustained savings and growth rates that crossed and remained above crucial thresholds. Estimates of total output growth in each of the four post-independence decades clearly demonstrate this transformation: in the 1950s, output was up by 37 percent; in the 1960s, up by another 37 percent; in the 1970s, up by 33 percent; and, in the 1980s, up by 60 percent. With population growth averaging about 2.2 percent a year after 1950, the rate of expansion of per capita income had been barely over 1.0 percent per year from 1950 to 1979. Then, with annual growth in national output averaging 5.1 percent through the 1980s, per capita income growth more than doubled the earlier pace, cutting in half the time it takes to add another Rs. 100 to the average Indian's material well-being.

India's impressive record of economic expansion in the 1980s was attained despite the limitations of a comparatively unfavorable global environment. Protectionist tendencies were strengthening around the world, retarding the growth of world trade; a new conservatism governed aid transfers and private credit flows; and, in general, the world economy slowed down. The rate of growth of the main industrial market economies declined from 3.6 percent per year between 1965 and 1980 to only 2.7 percent per year after 1980. In contrast, India's growth actually rose from 3.7 percent per year before 1980 to just over 5.0 percent per year afterward. India also stood out in the decade because its economic performance was much superior to that of other low-income countries: prior to 1980 the reverse had been true. Output in India's peer countries grew at only 1.7 percent in the 1980s (excluding China from the comparison because of the doubtful validity of its numbers). Thus, during the 1980s India grew almost twice as fast as the average rich industrial country and about three times as fast as the typical poor developing country.

Explaining the New Growth Trajectory

India's economic growth in the 1980s was felt across all of the economy's sectors, although not exactly evenly. Good agricultural years in 1988–89 and 1989–90 raised the decade's average growth of farm output to the neighborhood of 2.9 percent, in line with long-term trends. Industry was the star sector with an average growth rate of 8.0 percent per year. Among the industrial subsectors, manufacturing, electrical power, and capital goods had rates at or above this sectoral average. The output of consumer durables—appliances, scooters, cars—expanded at a high 14.7 percent annual rate. The relatively weakly performing sectors—intermediate goods, transportation, and consumer nondurables—still generated growth rates of about 6.0 percent per year. The large service sector expanded at 6.5 percent per year, led by banking and financial services and public administration. Export performance was uneven, but a surge in the last three years of the 1980s elevated the decennial average rate of growth to about 5.2 percent in dollar terms.

There are a number of possible causes of the acceleration of the Indian economy in the 1980s. These can be clustered into five categories, which overlap and interact. The explanation most commonly given in the expert establishment is that after about 1978 a liberalization of economic policy allegedly unlocked the government's long-binding shackles on the private entrepreneurial sector. The underlying notion is that by freeing up internal product and factor markets, importing more machinery and inputs, and borrowing larger doses of foreign capital, Indian policymakers positioned the economy for more rapid expansion.

A second possible reason for the changed growth trajectory is an improvement in the efficiency with which the nation's stock of capital has been used to produce national output. This is said to have resulted, in part, from the aforementioned liberalization measures, which to a limited degree fostered competition among domestic firms (manufacturers of scooters, automobiles, television receivers) and between domestic firms and foreign suppliers (of machinery and intermediate goods). Although there may be some validity in these closely related "policy regime" and "capital efficiency" arguments, even taken together they are certainly incomplete and unconvincing.

Three additional causal factors must be given significant weight in any satisfactory and comprehensive explanation of India's improved economic performance. The combined roles of technology and skilled human resources were obviously crucial to the speeding-up of growth in the 1980s. Also, a surge of the demand-side flows driving India's macroeconomy had a great deal to do with elevating its operating level. These expenditure flows included consumer spending, migrant remittances, and government disbursements. Finally, the 1980s may have benefited from the coming of age of long-term public-sector projects and the improved management of public-sector enterprises. For convenience, these last three potential causes of India's economic growth spurt can be named the technology, the aggregate demand, and the social capital factors.

The Policy Regime

It was and is surprisingly widely believed that Indian economic policy went through a major change in the late 1970s and early 1980s. Yet to those who have assiduously followed developments in the Indian economy for several decades, the promotion of liberalization policies has had throughout a mythical or illusory quality. Indira Gandhi is alleged to have begun reforms quietly during her last years, saying and doing things privately that she could not say or do publicly. Then, on assuming her mantle, her technocratic airline-pilot son is said to have pushed forward with her closet-liberal market policies, making them part of his electoral rhetoric and placing them high on his post-election agenda.

There are two difficulties in swallowing this interpretation. First, the depth of the purported reforms was never very great, even during the flood tide of official rhetoric. Second, the scant degree of reform that was achieved can hardly have been sufficient to have caused a doubling of the rate of per capita economic growth in an economy as large and diverse as India's. The register of liberalizing policies through the mid-1980s is well known. It includes the expansion of firms' installed factory capacities, the freeing from licensing requirements of several product groups, and the shortening of the list of items reserved for small-scale industry. Other policies were the reduction of corporate and personal taxes, the decontrolling of the cement market, and the opening up of industries such as telecommunications to greater private competition. Although this may seem an impressive roster, these gestures contained much less substance than met the eye; in effect, India's politicians and bureaucrats had engineered a vast *trompe l'oeil* canvas. Those who carefully probed the tangibility of the purported reforms recognized immediately that new controls and new interpretations of old rules significantly constrained the apparently generous concessions to the private sector. The relevant regulations and procedures were, in any event, so overlapping and redundant that peeling away one layer merely exposed another.

Above all, no one doubted that what little the government had given, the government could take away at whim. There was no fundamental change in the legal or customary division of authority between the state and private business enterprise. No one seriously thought that property or profits were any more secure from governmental decisions in 1985 or 1989 than they had been in 1980. It is this potential for reversibility, at the government's discretion, that so vitiates the force of India's tentative experiments with liberal policymaking.

This interpretation does not imply that the contours of India's economic policies are forever chiseled in marble. No sensible person would expect the Indian government not to make adjustments in economic policy from time to time, changing the boundaries between the public and private sectors, adjusting tax and tariff schedules, and formulating new investment and foreign-exchange guidelines. The Import-Export Policy for 1988–91, for example, reduced controls on exports, improved the access of exporting industries to imported inputs and machinery, and enhanced the export-profit tax exemption to 100 percent. Although such artificial export-prompting measures may be desirable, it is not evident either that they are fully consistent with a liberal, let-the-market-rule philosophy or that they mark a permanent reduction in the government's involvement in industry and foreign trade.

If there was any effect of the then prime minister Rajiv Gandhi's frequent endorsements of enhanced latitude for private business, it may have occurred because his remarks improved the climate within which business opinion was formed. His oft-voiced enthusiasm for things new and technological may have played a role in promoting private investment. The government also was more tolerant than previously of mergers and new stock flotations. India's securities markets boomed, particularly Bombay's Dalal Street, where the total value of listed stocks rose six- or sevenfold between 1980 and 1988. Businesspeople and their activities achieved an approval unparalleled in India's long cultural history. This newfound public esteem may have emboldened private economic agents, and they ebulliently undertook more aggressive investment decisions.

Capital Efficiency

From 1950 through the mid-1970s India had the low savings rate typical of a developing country. Then total savings rose steeply as a proportion of national income, largely because of increases in household savings. India's national savings rate roughly doubled, peaked at about 24 percent, and has since moved in a range 2 or 3 percentage points lower. According to the theory of economic growth, increased savings should lead to increased investment, or capital formation, which in turn provides a basis for a higher level of national output and income. Since India's output and income did not immediately rise proportionately with savings, a reason had to be found, and it was: India was using its capital stock inefficiently. Since the nation's capital stock was largely owned or managed by the government, blame thus attached to the planners and to inept, procrastinating bureaucrats and their heavy-handed steering of the private sector.

A well-known dictum of growth economics is that it takes 3 to 4 percentage points of savings and investment to generate 1 percentage point of national output growth. This relationship is determined by the aggregate capital-output ratio. Thus, according to this formula, with a savings rate of 24 percent, the Indian economy should have been growing at a rate of 6 to 8 percent a year, not at 3 to 4 percent. By growing at the lower rates, India was in fact exhibiting a capital-output ratio of about 6 (24 savings units divided by 4 growth units), instead of the standard 3 or possibly 4. This was widely taken to be a result of very poor utilization of installed capital stock, including private and public industrial investment and social overhead investment in infrastructure, power, irrigation, and housing. It was further asserted that the capital-output ratio rose into and through the 1970s, indicating ever-decreasing efficiency in the usage of India's scarce capital resources. The blame was assigned unambiguously to excessive government controls over the private sector, poor public-sector management practices, and a lack of bracing competition, through imports and exports, with foreign firms. The efficiency argument thus became entangled with the liberalization argument. When growth accelerated in the 1980s, the argument was reversed: because of liberalization, capital was being used more efficiently. The capital-output ratio declined in the Seventh and Eighth Plans, not to the magical figure of 3, but at least down from 6 toward 5 or 4—or so it was said.

There are many definitional and measurement problems in calculating capital-output ratios and in establishing their relationship to an economy's growth rate. There is also the usually unexplored question of how long it should take before an increase in the rate of savings and capital formation is embodied in an enlarged productive structure and yields output gains. One possibility is that the connection is not instantaneous, as is often assumed, and that capital sunk in one year may not bear fruit in the form of additions to output until projects such as dams or power stations are fully completed and brought on line. If in India this takes five years on average, then higher savings in 1975 and afterward would not have had a realizable impact on growth until about 1980 and subsequently—a not unappealing line of reasoning in view of what in fact happened.

There is certainly little in this convoluted debate to demonstrate an increasing tendency in the Indian economy to use its capital less efficiently over time. S. P. Gothoskar's sensible estimates of the capital-output ratios are as useful as any, though, to demonstrate that there was probably not a systematic rise in the capital-output ratio, and hence of inefficiency, through the 1970s. For the first six five-year plans, the last of which ended in 1983, the ratios are 3.06, 2.73, 5.36, 5.42, 4.65, and 4.85.[1] Furthermore, others have shown that India's capital-output ratios are not dissimilar from those of peer countries over the same period, leading one to wonder what the fuss is about.

The claim of a worsening capital-output ratio cannot be used to flog the public sector and scourge the planners and bureaucrats. This being so, then the principal prop of the argument that India should have and must now adopt liberalization and privatization tactics to realize efficiency gains falls away. Nor would it be appropriate to claim that enhanced efficiency, in this sense, was to a significant degree responsible for the acceleration of growth in the 1980s.

Technology

On September 30, 1989, Sonia Gandhi applied vermillion kum-kum powder to the bow of India's first indigenously built submarine, broke a coconut on the hull, then pushed the launch button, and sent the INS Shalki away from the Mazagon dock and into the waters off Bombay. Eight days earlier a test firing of the *Prithvi*, India's tactical surface-to-surface missile, had been successful. In the same month, M. R. Srinivasan, chairman of the Indian Atomic Energy Commission, announced that India would soon be able to export nuclear power plants designed to work under Third World conditions. In 1989, as in earlier years of the decade, India's use and manufacture of computers of all sizes continued to grow, as did software production. Exports of

---

[1] S. P. Gothoskar, "Factor Income Share Hypothesis and Income Growth," *Economic and Political Weekly*, Vol. 22 (October 3, 1987), p. 1695.

computer hardware and software of about US$200,000,000 were probably achieved in 1989, with the Soviet Union being a leading market. American firms farmed out an increasing amount of routine programming to Indian suppliers, often receiving the finished products by satellite transmission.

This anecdotal evidence of the rapid pace of India's technological advance can be multiplied many times. In the absence of any concrete way of measuring technological change in a society, impressionistic, qualitative judgments have to suffice. There is widespread appreciation that India now has an impressive scientific and technological establishment and the capacity to assimilate the newest technological advances occurring elsewhere in the world. Securing access to world-class technologies has been the most important element of India's foreign economic policy in recent years, though there is always the constraint that India does not welcome direct investment with majority foreign ownership, nor does the government want to appear to pay too much in monetary or political terms for access to foreign know-how.

How much India's increased application of technology contributed to growth in the 1980s is difficult to estimate. Nor is it possible to determine precisely the relative weights of the effects of borrowed and domestically created technologies on the growth process. Likewise, the human elements of technological change—skills, education, knowledge—are hard to disentangle from the physical elements—machines, circuitry, chemical compounds. Growth accountants have had difficulty estimating the precise contributions of skills and technology to growth, but their studies have generally found that such sources of growth dominate capital formation. It seems reasonable to infer that India's growth has been substantially based on technological changes and that future growth will continue to be heavily influenced by the country's success in borrowing and devising new technologies.

Aggregate Demand

Demand-side forces provided the catalytic stimulus to the acceleration of growth in the 1980s. India did not previously have a consumer-oriented economy, for two not entirely separable reasons. First, India's national plans have focused on mobilizing resources for social overhead capital projects and large-scale industrial development. The capacity to produce consumer goods in the private sector has been restricted by "permit raj": the network of official controls over capacity and access to capital markets. Consumer imports, especially of what are thought to be luxuries, have been stringently constrained. In addition, the small-scale sector has been given preference in the provision of such items as soaps, textiles, and automobile components, which may reduce product quality and raise prices, thus discouraging consumption.

A second restraint on consumerism in India has been an intrinsic conservatism in habits. Although there have always been exceptions, most notably the maharajas of old, as a general rule personal ostentation and displays of wealth have been frowned upon. Cooking and dietary customs have discouraged adoption of processed foods and certain tabooed classes of products. For most men and women, dress has been simple and relatively inexpensive. The hierarchy of caste and its enforcement have militated against unseemly exhibitions of family wealth inconsistent with social rank, and it has been unwise and unsafe for the wealthy to make public exhibitions of their affluence.

Official and cultural restraints on consumer spending and exhibitionism weakened appreciably in the 1980s. Perhaps the most notable of the results of the government's liberalization rhetoric was to create an environment in which the wealthier businesspeople and professionals could more easily spend money on home appliances, color television sets, and private means of transportation as production rose and waiting lists shrank. Younger couples holding less traditional values were not as hemmed in by age-old attitudinal and social restrictions as were members of their parents' generation. Advertising and continued exposure to international standards of consumption probably contributed to the erosion of conventional restraints.

National data affirm the transformation of India's patterns of consumption. From 1965 to 1980 consumption grew by only 2.7 percent a year. Investment rose by 5.0 percent and government spending by 6.3 percent annually; gross domestic product (GDP) grew at a modest 3.7 percent. After 1980 consumption grew by 4.9 percent a year, while investment rose at a rate of only 3.7 percent; GDP growth was 4.6 percent annually. The surge in consumption thus appears to have contributed to sustaining the nation's rapid economic growth after 1980. It is interesting, too, that Pakistan's consumption growth rate averaged 4.9 percent per year throughout the whole period, 1965 to 1987, while its GDP growth averaged 5.7 percent annually, well above India's. The lesson may be that economists have greatly undervalued consumption streams as intermediate-term sources of growth while overvaluing investment streams. Rising consumption levels, after all, are what growth is supposed to be about, and it is certainly the Indian consumers' turn for a little abundance if it is anybody's.

Lying behind the surge in consumption were causes other than changes in policy and attitudes. The more open import policies permitted firms, especially those producing vehicles and electrical consumer goods, to attain higher levels of output, at least so long as foreign-exchange supplies lasted. Remittances from overseas workers added discretionary income to the nation's spending streams. Government expenditures climbed rapidly, raising the incomes of public employees and the armed forces. High levels of government purchases had multiplier effects in the private sector. A new factor was that Indian consumers were given enhanced access to credit from the banking system. Money from the black economy may also have been more commonly unveiled and switched over into consumer purchases. The rapid rise in spending and incomes from these various sources fed back into new rounds of consumer spending.

For those who worry about the impact of such profligacy on the nation's economic future, it is worth noting that despite the newfound hedonism of the Indian consumer, the national savings rate was not reduced: to the contrary, the ratio of saving to income was 22 percent in 1987, much higher than the 16 percent savings rate that prevailed in 1965. Apparently Indians have discovered that they can have their *halwa* and eat it too.

Social Capital

A final and also underrated source of growth in the 1980s has been the satisfactory performance of public infrastructure. Both private and public manufacturing establishments and agriculture depend in critical ways on these social-capital sectors. During the 1980s, power production rose at an average rate of 9.5 percent per year. Railway services grew at about 4.7 percent annually, with little or no extension of trackage. Nonrail transport services expanded by 8.8 percent annually. On the financial side there was also healthy progress, as banking and insurance services averaged 10.1 percent yearly growth.

By lowering costs for industrialists and improving the reliability of power and transport services, these infrastructural services facilitate production and raise profits. Since most of these services are provided through the public sector, particularly the central government, some credit for this record must be given to the center. State-level electricity boards, in contrast, continue to do a very poor job of producing, distributing, and pricing power to agricultural, industrial, and domestic users. Often their revenues do not even cover their variable costs— fuel, labor—much less the replacement costs of their expensive, capital-intensive power stations. In railways and coal, the center can further improve its performance. Still, despite such difficult problems, the positive spillover effects of improved infrastructure appear to have contributed significantly to overall economic growth in the 1980s.

Economic Performance in 1989

In 1989 the economy turned in a mixed performance. The remarkable resurgence of 1988 was based on exceptional growth rates in almost every sector, and not all of these could be maintained. Gross domestic product rose by about 4.5 percent, compared to 1988's 9.4 percent. Agricultural output in 1989 was apparently at about the same high level as in 1988, but industrial growth slowed in the first half of the year. On the plus side, exports continued to expand strongly and infrastructure performance was again satisfactory, led by an increase in electricity output of about 11 percent. The most vexing concerns that the Congress government bequeathed to the National Front were financial: large governmental and balance-of-payments deficits, rising domestic and foreign debt, diminishing foreign-exchange hoards, and inflation. The chief fear was that attempting to cure these financial maladies by adopting policies of fiscal and monetary stringency would constrict the economy as it entered the 1990s and the nation embarked upon its ambitious Eighth Five-Year Plan.

The monsoon was again favorable in 1989, and food-grain output was expected to total 170 to 175 million metric tons, compared to the 172 million metric tons in 1988. These two bountiful years at the end of the decade salvaged what was otherwise a disappointing record. The previous high for food-grain output was 152 million tons in 1983, and the 1987 drought had reduced production to only 139 million tons. Stocks fell from 17 million tons at the beginning of the drought to 8 million tons in 1988 but rose to 10 million tons in 1989 and continued to accumulate into early 1990. The whole agricultural sector rebounded by 12.5 percent in 1988 following the 9.0 percent decline in 1987. In 1989 the static (although high) food-grain total probably limited the sector's expansion to no more than 2.0 percent.

Throughout the 1980s agriculture was sluggish. Growth of less than 3.0 percent per year was below both needs and expectations. Little progress was made in coping with repeated shortfalls in cotton, sugar, and oilseed production. Furthermore, food and nonfood crops alike showed disturbing instability. Forty years of improvement in irrigation facilities and 20 years of disseminating green-revolution technologies had not diminished the effects on output of the vagaries of the monsoon. Indeed, there was evidence that instability had, if anything, increased over time. For reasons that are not clear, fluctuations in the outputs of different regions and different crops appear to be moving ever closer together, thus increasing the amplitude of the total agricultural cycle. An additional concern about agriculture was the continued concentration of growth in the irrigated areas of the northwest and the failure of food production in many states to keep pace with population growth. Also, public investment in agriculture and irrigation shrank as a share of total investment in the 1980s. This did not augur well for the future vitality of the sector, which increasingly depends upon rising amounts of capital per hectare of land to raise productivity now that all the country's cultivable land is in use.

The biggest shock in 1989 was the near stalling of industrial growth in the first half of the year. Even in drought-stricken 1987 industrial output grew by 6.5 percent, and this was followed by 8.8 percent growth in 1988. It is thought that industrial output grew by only about 4.5 percent in 1989, a rate about half that of the decade's average. It is too early to say either what caused this slowdown or whether it is temporary, although some reacceleration appeared to be occurring at year's end. Since industrial growth of about 7.7 percent per year would be required to drive GDP ahead at the 6.0 percent a year targeted in the Eighth Plan and to enable the nation to reach its early targets, a failure to regain the higher growth trajectory in this key sector would doom the plan to failure.

Industrial growth through the 1980s was paced by consumer durables such as electronics, appliances, and motor vehicles, including scooters and motorcycles. Electronic goods and automobiles have a high content of imported parts, however, and the mounting numbers of motor vehicles increased the nation's demand for gasoline, which in turn added further to the import bill and foreign-exchange depletion. Still, since consumer durables have a weight of only 2.55 percent in the industrial index, neither the robust growth of the sector in the 1980s nor the slowdown of early 1989 could be attributed primarily to this component. Manufacturing growth in the decade was in fact very broadly based in the capital goods, chemical, leather product, processed food, and electrical machinery industries, among others. The leading failure was in textiles, where growth was a slow 3.3 percent per year. This, coupled with uneven food production, made it possible to say that India's growth had not contributed to meeting the basic needs of the poorest sections of the population, a perception that may have had some influence on the 1989 election campaign.

The unexpected industrial sluggishness of 1989 appeared to be due to a pervasive contraction of demand as consumers reined in their appetites and a government beset with budgetary and balance-of-payments lacunae cut back on its purchases in such areas as cement, road-building equipment, and mining machinery and curtailed imports of inputs and components. Steel production was actually lower in 1989 than in 1988. Despite the widespread weaknesses in manufacturing, there were considerable continuing strengths in other areas of industrial output in 1989. Mining output climbed by 11.0 percent; power production rose by 12.3 percent versus 6.6 percent in 1988; and crude oil output was up by 6.9 percent versus 4.5 percent in 1988.

The services sector continued to expand at about 6.0 percent in 1989, contributing a larger share to GDP growth than either agriculture or industry, and probably generated employment at about the same rate. Although growth in the services industries is sometimes disparaged, particularly when centered in the public sector, the service sector, which also includes finance, transport, and commerce among its components, is not unduly large for India's level of income and development.

Exports rose in rupee terms by 26.2 percent in 1987–88, 29.0 percent in 1988–89, and an estimated 37.2 percent in 1989–90; volume and dollar gains were very roughly 60 percent less because of the declining value of the rupee. The export promotion measures adopted in 1985–86 and the creeping devaluation of the rupee probably helped stimulate exports, but the slowly increasing interest and skill of Indian private businesses in entering overseas markets played a role too. In 1989–90 import growth slowed considerably, but petroleum imports remained large. Exports of several kinds, particularly of gemstones, were themselves import-intensive. Despite some improvement in the balance of exports and imports in 1989, the overall payments situation worsened.

India's foreign-exchange reserves fell from US$6.2 billion in 1987–88, to US$4.8 billion in 1988–89, to US$3.5 billion in 1989–90. Remittances from overseas workers were flat or even shrinking, although hard-currency deposits by nonresident Indians continued to grow. The chief cause of the deterioration of the balance-of-payments was mounting debt-service obligations. Until about 1987, Indians could claim that they had avoided the debt problems that now plague most Third World countries. Indeed, prudent and conservative external account management had always been a lauded characteristic of India's fiscal and banking leadership. By 1988–89, India's medium- and long-term foreign obligations (excluding nonresident deposits) totaled US$44 billion, up from US$22.5 billion in 1980–81. Debt-service payments rose sevenfold over the same period and equaled roughly one-third of export earnings. Although India's debt-to-GDP ratio was about 20 percent, compared to around 60 percent for highly indebted countries, there was a sense that India was moving quickly down a well-marked path that would lead to the hellish debt trap into which Brazil, Mexico, and Nigeria had fallen.

In 1989, as in previous years, the government resorted to deficit finance in order to meet its expenditures, even though revenue as a share of GDP had risen during the 1980s. Interest payments reached about 20 percent of the budget. Current expenditures on salaries, subsidies, and defense rose in total from 6.1 percent of GDP in 1980–81 to 8.0 percent in 1989–90. Borrowing was relied upon to finance current expenditures and thus could not be justified as mobilizing resources for public investment projects that would ultimately yield net income to the government.

One result of the fiscal deficit was rapid monetary expansion and inflation. The banking system was pressed hard to cover the government's revenue gap. Through November 1989, compared to the same month of the previous year, the basic money supply grew by about 12.5 percent and bank credit to the government climbed by 16.9 percent. For the calendar year, wholesale prices rose by about 7.3 percent, but this average disguises two competing trends: food prices actually fell by 3.0 percent, while nonfood prices rose by 12.8 percent and prices of manufactured goods by 11.2 percent. The prices of tea, sugar products, vegetables, textiles, and leather products were appreciably above those of the previous year. This particular bundle of goods is composed of products that bulk large in the budgets of poor and lower-income families. Food prices did not tail down until later in the fall than usual, following the harvest, and this whole set of price trends undoubtedly had an adverse effect on the Congress Party's reelection hopes.

There are several general observations to be made about India's economic profile in 1989. In 1988 and 1989 India experienced a prosperous period in which growth was broadly based across rebounding agriculture, buoyant industry, and expanding services. Exports were strong. Weaknesses in some industries showed up in early 1989, however, limiting growth in that sector to about 4.0 percent for the year, and agricultural output was probably up no more than 2.0 percent. The major troubles were in financial areas: a huge fiscal deficit, excessive monetary growth, rising inflation centered on key market-basket commodities, a large balance-of-payments deficit, and a rapid loss of international reserves. Because all of these monetary variables were subject to governmental management and discipline, there arose a pervasive public perception that things were out of control and that the economy was not being well handled. In addition, since the adverse financial trends were associated with the government's policy of liberalization, and by implication with the international agencies that had pushed India to adopt this policy, it was possible for critical intellectuals and opposition politicians to challenge the government for kowtowing to outside influences, always a telling charge in Indian politics.

Economic Factors in the 1989 Election

Although economic conditions are not the whole explanation, the results in India's ninth national election were strongly influenced by the state of the economy in late 1989. Ralph C. Meyer has discovered that the share of the vote going to the Congress Party has been highest when agricultural output and total national product has risen in the year prior to an election (such as in 1957, 1971, and 1984) and has softened when these indicators are weak (1962, 1967).[2] The incumbent parties suffered reverses in the elections of 1977 and 1979 that followed very bad crop years. The voters' sense of short-run economic well-being thus affects their willingness to reward incumbents with a renewed mandate.

The recovery of agriculture in 1988 and 1989 and the strong performance of industry over the two-year period created conditions that were apparently favorable for the electoral chances of Rajiv Gandhi and the Congress(I) Party. In fact, it is plausible that Rajiv stretched his term to its maximal five years in order to gain a tactical advantage, waiting for economic improvement and the dissipation of the shortages and price rises resulting from the 1987 drought. His luck was good: the availability of farm products was much better in 1989 than in the two previous years, and consumer-goods production was running at a fast pace in the industrial sector. In addition, the Gandhi government continued to release stocks of accumulated foodgrains onto the markets and facilitated imports of edible oils and other commodities where shortages were feared.

Despite these measures, bazaar prices for foods, sugar, and tea remained unusually high right through election day. A sense that prices were too high carried into November, and opposition party leaders played on the popular alarm at every opportunity. By December the expected stabilization and selective reduction of key consumer prices finally began, but by then the electoral die had been cast, and Congress was sitting on the opposition benches in parliament. There is irony, of course, in the defeat of India's most market-oriented prime minister by voters upset by marketplace prices.

Apart from their disquiet over inflation, voters may have been influenced by other elements in the economic scene. Unquestionably the liberalization issue held little appeal for the mass of voters, and Rajiv Gandhi and the Congress had distanced themselves from their earlier enthusiasm for it, reverting to a much more conventional platform promising attention to equity and employment. Perhaps sensing the way the wind was blowing, Rajiv pledged that agriculture would

---

[2] Ralph C. Meyer, "How Do Indians Vote?," *Asian Survey*, Vol. 29 (December 1989), pp. 1111–1122.

receive renewed attention. Tarred with the brush of corruption and suffering from an unfocused and vacillating image, Rajiv Gandhi's management of the economy was perceived as weak and uncertain. Finally, there was considerable discontent over what was felt to be continued neglect of the principal agrarian interests. This antipathy was most evident in the support of farmers for Devi Lal and the Janata Dal, within the framework of the opposition alliance.

An important issue was the quality of economic management, and on this score V. P. Singh appeared to offer more hope than Rajiv Gandhi. At local levels, the "outs" seemed to be superior alternatives to the "ins" of whatever party stripe. This could be seen as a condemnation of avarice and venality but probably expressed a collective wish for a higher quality of economic performance: for better prices, better goods, better education, better jobs, and better defense contracting.

The first test faced by V. P. Singh as the newly chosen prime minister was the appointment of a cabinet. Since a managed economy requires talented and effective managers, India's prime ministers have generally appointed outstanding administrators to head up key economic ministries. V. P. Singh's economic ministers meet this criterion of excellence. M. Dandavate, who was awarded the Finance portfolio, is a pragmatic veteran who brings honesty and wisdom to his post. Ajit Singh at Industry, Arun Nehru at Commerce and Tourism, and Arif Muhammad Khan at Energy and Aviation each has the requisite skills and political base to make a success of his position. Other portfolios with large economic responsibilities tended to go to representatives of regional or social groups. Overall, the cabinet can be styled as nonideological, experienced, and professional.

The appointment of Devi Lal as deputy prime minister was regarded as an unavoidable political expedient and a bit of an embarrassment. This is, however, not a completely fair judgment. The urban, industrial, and technological biases of the Gandhi group doubtless had rankled many rural Indians, and rural Indians still outnumber urban Indians by about two to one. The divergence of rural and urban incomes was probably more acute in the 1980s than in earlier decades, despite or perhaps because of the rapid growth of the economy. Even setting aside the effects of one of the worst monsoon failures of the 20th century, agricultural performance and the growth of agricultural incomes in the 1980s had been disappointing to many landowners. Some expression of rural disquiet was unavoidable, and Devi Lal and his associated agrarianists became its vehicle. If Devi Lal had not existed, farm voters would have invented him in one incarnation or another. Raw, rustic power demands national embodiment, and Devi Lal is its avatar.

In addition to choosing a cabinet, Singh also had the task of naming a new Planning Commission. The commission had fallen from its high estate of the 1950s and 1960s and was in some ways merely another emblem of the institutional decay affecting many components of India's structure of governance. Having no constitutional basis, its role was derived from a devolution of powers from the prime minister's office; and under the Gandhis those powers had been pulled back into that office, leaving the commission with its expertise but robbing it of potency. Singh expanded the membership to nine, named a veteran Karnataka politician, Ramakrishna Hegde, as head, and gave that position cabinet rank. This signaled that Singh wanted to restore the commission to a status approaching its former grandeur and might also indicate that he has some understanding of the institutional crisis that threatens India's governance. He appointed professional economists as well as politicians and grass-roots activists to the remaining chairs. With the Eighth Five-Year Plan scheduled to begin in April 1990 and already phrased in provisional form by the previous incumbents, Hegde and his team went immediately to work to put their own stamp on India's most important economic document.

Political Economy After the Elections

The interest-group structure of Indian politics is almost impossibly complicated. Still, since economic variables do matter in Indian elections and politicians do take stances that appeal to voters in terms of narrow material benefits, there is purpose in identifying economic interest groups and determining whether each is likely to gain or lose following the change in government.

The poor, mass groups in Indian society include marginal farmers, agricultural laborers, artisans and craftsmen, weavers and other household workers, petty traders, and urban porters and laborers. Because they are numerous and widespread, it is difficult to organize them for concerted action: their immediate and local concerns outweigh their long-term and collective concerns. Their lack of wealth in land or capital and their insufficient education make them dependent for income on their own labor and dexterity. Their economic disabilities are often compounded by the stigma of untouchability or low caste status.

Overall, the poor groups in Indian society have not clearly gained by the electoral outcome. Indeed, in rural areas they may have lost slightly in that the ascendancy of the dominant landed castes may mean a diversion of rural resources upwards in the structure of agrarian relations. Although it is too early to tell, elements in the BJP may also be less sympathetic to lower-caste Hindus and the system of reservations. Overall, however, the composition of the cabinet and the Planning Commission suggests that the interests of the poor are adequately represented, and early statements of Singh and his ministers have been promissory. Nor is it likely that the prime minister can afford to alienate these large constituencies in calculating how to consolidate power and strengthen himself and his party in future elections.

Those with the largest material stakes in the outcome of the election are the elite groups of Indian society. These groups control and own India's productive wealth: land, water, industrial capital, and professional human resources. They have relatively narrowly focused economic interests, and because of their comparatively small numbers they find it easier to engage in collective political action. They can be categorized by a double bifurcation: urban-rural and public-private. The urban elites include large-scale private industrialists and upper-level professionals. In the rural areas, the big and middle-sized farmers are the major players. On the public side, the senior bureaucrats, the military, and the upper managers of state corporations and banks constitute the chief interests.

India's middle groups are perhaps the hardest to identify and the most diverse, both economically and in terms of their social attributes. They are in between the rich and powerful and the poor and impotent. If they aspire to rise economically and socially, they also look with dread at the prospect of backsliding into poverty and social degradation. Since they depend primarily on their earned incomes for their well-being and to validate their status, they are socially insecure and extremely vulnerable to sudden price changes or adjustments in their pay scales and allowances. Thus their sensitivity to government policies and legislation that affect these topics is acute. Included in the middle classes are petty bureaucrats, small businessmen, and professionals.

Two largely urban groups that do not fit well into these rich, middle, and poor categories are students and urban labor, yet both groups are politically active and can be effectively mobilized. Both, too, are sensitive to material issues: employment possibilities, tuition and other fees, and wage and benefit packages. It is appropriate to treat them as lower-middle groups because of the precariousness of their economic positions, but also to recognize that they are much better organized to defend and advance their interests than other large nonpropertied groups.

The results of the 1989 elections will influence the manner in which these middle-range and elite groups are treated by the government. It was argued above that the hopes of the poor groups in India probably suffered a mild setback, and it follows that the nonpoor on balance made a small gain. Within the elite groups, the chief beneficiaries are the landed rural groups. Campaign promises were made to them, and cabinet and Planning Commission appointments have been indicative of attention to those pledges. The Eighth Plan and future agricultural price policies are likely to indicate a tilt in favor of farmers, with the largest benefiting most.

The rural bias means that urban groups may face a comparative loss. For the private industrial firms, this will take such forms as higher taxes, less abundant credit, limits on access to foreign exchange, and greater attention to the social and ethical probity of business conduct. The economic policy adjustments of the 1980s will not be completely rolled back, though they might be modified, and it is unlikely the new government will make many concessions to business. Within the industrial elite, however, those firms most closely identified with the Gandhis and their Congress Party will suffer in comparison to those that joined the camp of Singh and his allies prior to the election.

Professionals and the middle classes did well under Rajiv Gandhi, but envy and the Indian concern with equity and their antipathy to displays of affluence, particularly by those whose caste status is inconsistent with it, may constrain further gains by these groups. Still, Singh's support was drawn in part from these groups, and if India's economic growth continues at its current fast pace, they are likely to benefit. Continued and even enhanced attention to education may make students more valuable allies. Organized labor did not fare well under recent Congress rule and may now find it easier to press public- and private-sector employers for gains. Singh may find his government tested early on by militant segments of the labor movement, and it will be interesting to see how strong and unified a front his government can present if union demands are judged unrealistic.

The public-sector elites appear well placed under the new government. This is partly because the regular civil service and army are strengthened when parliament is in the hands of a coalition with possibly limited tenure. The current government's attempts to regain control of the economy and to establish better management practices betoken heavy reliance on the civil service. Like the civil service, the military fared well in the 1980s in terms of salaries and budget share. A civilian authority that has yet to prove its mettle is unlikely to reduce appropriations to the army. With troubles in Punjab, Kashmir, and the northeast and the omnipresent potential for serious communal strife, the military establishment's role in the early 1990s may be crucial to the preservation of national unity.

In addition to these shifts in relative power in the competition for political spoils, the election results had larger meaning. Indian economic policy was recommitted to its two dominant post-independence themes, socialism with equity and national self-reliance. In many ways the National Front is more attuned to the continuities of Indian economic policy than was Rajiv's Congress. The new government appears ready to enhance its managerial control and authority over economic affairs. This means, among other things, growing more food and restoring depleted stocks so that India can continue to avoid buying food abroad in times of need, which are also windows of vulnerability to outside influence. Foreign debt and foreign investment will be monitored and restrained: imports will be restricted, the balance of payments improved, and gold and foreign-exchange reserves rebuilt. Making the public sector enterprises work more efficiently is also likely to be a priority; this will affect power stations, communications, the railways, steel, oil, and natural gas. Public sector investment will thus go up as a share of total investment, while private investment's share drops. Exports will be further pushed because of the debt burdens inherited from the previous government.

On into the 1990s

On March 19, 1990, the finance minister presented the National Front's first budget. It contained strong signals of the new government's aims and style. The profile of taxes and incentives exhibits few surprises when examined in light of the configuration of electoral politics and economic forces that brought V. P. Singh and his alliance into power. The finance minister, M. Dandavate, remarked, "We have . . . begun a process to restrain the budgetary deficit and contain the inflationary pressure [and] tilted the balance of planning and investment towards the rural areas and in favor of employment." Several steps were taken to reduce the government's fiscal deficit by about 40 percent. The allowance for business investment was abolished, the import duty on crude oil was hiked, and excise taxes on tobacco, motor vehicles, and appliances and electronic goods were raised. At the same time, the personal income-tax threshold was moved up from Rs. 18,000 to Rs. 22,000, per year and low-income taxpayers got some relief. Postal and railway rates were to rise. The net overall effect of tax and rate increases and decreases was to mobilize about US$3 billion of new resources.

On the expenditure side, the military forces won a commitment to a 7.9 percent increase, which one might expect to rise during 1990 as problems with Kashmir and Pakistan continue to mount. Agriculture and related areas were pledged a 31 percent increase in plan outlay. A 23 percent rise was slated for poverty alleviation and 30 percent for employment programs, most of which would affect rural areas. Small-scale industries also appeared to benefit from new tax exemptions and adjustments. On April 3, 1990, a refashioned export-import policy edict adjusted tariffs and import restrictions, generally easing them on capital goods. Exports of services, including computer software, became eligible for a 20 percent foreign-exchange replenishment license.

Looking farther ahead and situating the economic events of 1989 and early 1990 in the context of long-term trends, one finds grounds for optimism and grounds for pessimism. The acceleration of growth in the 1980s has raised the limits of what Indians think is economically feasible, and both governmental and business performance will be judged by these new, higher standards. Rajiv Gandhi and V. P. Singh did not differ in promising to try to attain high targets during the Eighth Plan period and beyond. It is encouraging that the new government put together a good team of economic managers in the cabinet and Planning Commission and that its first budget responsibly addresses India's short-run fiscal, monetary, and balance-of-payments problems. The budget's tilt toward agricultural and related rural programs cannot be criticized on economic or political grounds.

From the viewpoint of the United States, the change in government in India signals a reversion to less easy relationships, certainly on the investment front. Within four months of taking office the Singh administration rejected a pending investment offer from Coca-Cola that had appeared to meet the previous government's requirements. There was discussion of repudiating a 1988 agreement that had enabled PepsiCo to sell its beverages and snacks in India in return for its undertaking broad agricultural schemes and pledging satisfactory export volumes.

A discordant note in international economic relations between India and the United States was sounded on May 25, 1989, when India (along with Japan and Brazil) was cited as an unfair trader by the United States. Acting in accord with the Omnibus Trade and Competitiveness Act of 1988, Carla Hills, the U.S. trade representative, said that India was insufficiently open to private foreign investment and also that firms should be granted access to India's internal insurance market. Indians were bemused if not shocked by the U.S. action: insurance is a state-dominated arena in India into which private firms do not venture. Allowing greater admittance into Indian industry for large-scale foreign firms such as America's multinationals was not something India could or would do, given its commitment to self-reliance and its post-independence antipathies. Very little was to be gained by either government in taking the U.S. injunctions seriously. On the Indian side, any concessions would be seen as yielding to cavalier American interference in domestic policymaking. On the American side, even significant Indian adjustments would have yielded tiny gains, given the small size of the Indian marketplace in the total world economy. The cost to the United States was great: heightened Indian suspicion at a time when trade and technical relations were on the whole robust and improving.

Hills's warning, issued under clause 301 of the Trade Act, was known as a "Super 301" action ("super" because that clause, originally incorporated in the 1974 act, had been fortified in the 1988 act). If India did not open negotiations and reach a compromise with the United States, trade sanctions could be invoked within 18 months in the form of selective tariffs of up to 100 percent on Indian goods. In the event, the Indian response was to do nothing, even though the Brazilians and Japanese succeeded in negotiating sufficiently adroitly to get themselves removed from the list. On May 29, 1990, Hills renamed India under Super 301 as an unfair trader, although she refused to add new countries to the list. Then on June 12 she reaffirmed that India's policies on foreign investment and restrictions on the insurance industry were unreasonable and had hurt American commercial interests but said that these concerns would be dealt with during the pending Uruguay Round of discussions being held within the framework of the General Agreement on Tariffs and Trade. This was a considerable softening of the U.S. position and was in line with how India thought matters should have been handled all along.

With the Super 301 flap apparently over, Indo-U.S. commercial relations will probably continue to improve in the early 1990s. The United States will remain India's chief trading partner and provider of a large balance-of-trade surplus. The United States will also continue to be the leading source of borrowed technologies, but large blocks of foreign investment from American multinationals do not appear to be in the cards. The ongoing reorientation of the Eastern Bloc economies will force a recasting of India's trade and other economic linkages with this group of countries and will probably compel India to look even more to the West despite official reticence.

Overall, India remains well poised to continue its rapid growth through the 1990s. The new leadership seems surprisingly confident and active in seeking to make an early and deep mark on internal and external economic policies. V. P. Singh and his associates are evidently eager and willing to provide that better quality of governance the Indian electorate sought in putting them into office. The government has reverted to nationalistic self-reliant policies in line with the wishes of most Indian voters. This move will undoubtedly alienate many external experts and is to some degree counter to world tendencies; but it does move India back into line with continental Asia's persistently revealed reluctance to integrate itself fully into the ranks of the market capitalist economies, as the examples of China, Vietnam, Burma, and Iran, among others, make plain.

5
Poverty in India: Some Recent Policies

Alan Heston

If you walk north from the food stalls and hotels on Juhu, the major suburban public beach of Bombay, you find that the number of middle-class strollers thins out about two-thirds of the way up the shore, giving way to a less affluent group of beach-using adults and children. From a distance you see large buildings and homes on the upper part of the beach, with one or two gray patches in the panorama. As you come closer, these gray patches materialize into hutments, and you realize that it is mainly their inhabitants who use the northern section of the beach. The huts are constructed of a mixture of makeshift materials, like other such tracts in Bombay, Rio de Janeiro, and many other Third World cities. Their occupants have no electricity, regular water source, or plumbing; the lack of the last amenity accounts, in part, for the willingness of the middle-class morning strollers to leave this section of the beach to the poor.

Locations like Juhu are scarce near Bombay, where members of the upper classes continue to build towering apartment buildings and spacious bungalows on private plots behind the beach. Some homes are palatial, with the capacity to seat 1,000 dinner guests, reminding one of traditional Indian dwellings except in style and, some might say, taste. No official surveys on the subject exist, but one suspects that as new bungalows and high-rise apartment houses spring up, other families are creating at least as much living space in new and remodeled huts, some of which run to two or even three stories. Many of the new hutment residents have recently been pavement dwellers; new urban immigrants, lured perhaps by glamorous images of Bombay in the movies, are beginning their own cycles on the streets of Bombay.

One cosmetic approach to eradicating the image of poverty that the homeless and the pavement and hutment dwellers present is to get them out of sight. This is done periodically in New Delhi by bulldozing temporary housing and relocating its inhabitants to allegedly healthier environs. In Bombay this approach has a political dimension: a major movement of Marathi speakers, the Shiv Sena, has arisen to campaign for the removal of all non-Maharashtrians from Bombay. Many of the pavement and hutment dwellers come from districts south of Bombay and are Kanara, Konkani, or Telugu speakers. The Shiv Sena-controlled municipal corporation has attempted to have their huts demolished and to move the inhabitants to another, allegedly improved location. Although the very rich may not object to such policies, it is clear that at least some of the slum clearance activity in Bombay is spurred by lower-middle-class support for an ethnic party.

The homeless, destitute, and very poor are not a vocal lobby anywhere in the world. In most democracies they are a small minority, often unable to lobby for their own cause either individually or as a group. They pull at the conscience of the majority, but politicians have little to gain by seeking their vote. In India those in poverty number more than 320 million (and about half of these are *very* poor), so the poor are a potential electoral force. Indira Gandhi appealed to this group with her slogan *garibi hatao* ("away with poverty"), but she was not able to deliver on this pledge. Further, under her administration no grass-roots organization emerged to speak for the very poor. Poverty continues to command the attention of social scientists, politicians, and the general public in India. But just as bulldozing tenements is one way to "remove" poverty, so academic and political discourse on poverty tends to substitute for real action.

The Meaning of Being Poor in India

There are superficial similarities between poverty in India and poverty in the United States, but there are important differences in level and scale. To get some sense of the level, consider three groups in the United States: the homeless, the elderly, and members of households headed by women. For all three groups, average income is at least $10.00 per person per day. The homeless spend this primarily on food and drink. For the elderly and for female-headed households, housing is an important cost; this expense is much smaller for the poor in India because of the generally warmer climate.

Suppose that the *very* poor in the United States have available $5.00 per day per person for food. How would we translate this amount into Indian terms in such a way as to take into account the fact that prices are lower in India than in the United States? While the exchange rate today is $1.00 = Rs. 17, an Indian does not need Rs. 85 to buy consumer essentials in India that would cost an American $5.00 in the United States. Detailed studies of the relative prices of identical goods in India and the United States suggest that a bundle of essential consumer goods that costs $10.00 in the United States can be purchased for about Rs. 60 in India, so that $1.00 = Rs. 6 represents the purchasing power of the rupee. Thus, $5.00 a day can be translated into Rs. 30 per day in India, or Rs. 900 per month.

But Rs. 900 a month is far above the poverty level in India, which today is about Rs. 90 a month per person. A skilled worker, like a mason, might make Rs. 1,500 to Rs. 2,500 a month, which might translate into Rs. 900 a month per family member if other members of the family were working. A casual or unskilled construction worker would be unlikely to make Rs. 900 a month, even in a large city like New Delhi. So the first lesson is that the income level of Americans in poverty, even allowing for lower prices in India, is equivalent to that of the middle classes in India.

In addition to the level, the scale of poverty is quite different, with over 30 percent of India's population in poverty by Indian standards and less than 0.5 percent in the United States at the level of $5.00 a day. The proportion of Indians in poverty by American standards would be well over 95 percent of the population.

How can millions of people live on less than a dollar a day? For the rural poor this means a diet heavy in rice, wheat, or millet, with milk, meat, vegetables, fruit, sugar, and tea being extras. Basic caloric intake can be achieved with a pound of cereal a day per person; Rs. 3 will buy one to three times this amount (depending on the grain, rice being the most expensive and millet the least; in the United States $.50 would buy about the same amount of rice as Rs. 3). But for these people, there is little change left after buying the essentials, and clothing and basic medicines are too often outside the budget. Life is precarious, and minor mishaps, like missing work, may mean that meals must be skipped or that otherwise small health problems develop into major, even life-threatening, events. In urban areas the very poorest of the poor probably fare somewhat better in such periodic crises, because they can hustle merchants and food shops for handouts or wait in line at a clinic more readily than can those in rural areas.

Many in India whom Americans might regard as in poverty do not in fact consider themselves poor. They compare themselves with the much worse-off groups that we have just described. More important, the cultural standard of affluence, partly molded through advertisements, movies, and television, is at a much lower level in India than in the United States. The ideal movie star in India in the 1980s, as was the case in Italy in the 1950s, is overweight by U.S. standards of pulchritude, which reflects the belief that plumpness means that you have plenty to eat and are not poor.

Average urban housing space in India is much less than in the United States, so that Americans visiting the apartment of a lower-middle-class family in Delhi might find the living space and physical condition of the building and furnishings suggestive of poverty. But once the Americans became aware of the dignity of the lives lived in such surroundings, they would understand that one needs a different set of glasses to view poverty in India. For a great part of the year, for example, much of life can be lived outdoors, and verandas and rooftops are the preferred places to sleep for rich and poor alike in the very hot weather. These outdoor spaces effectively augment the square footage of living area, that consideration so important to New Yorkers. Without their Indian glasses, Americans might be surprised to learn that families living in such humble surroundings can do many things that are beyond the reach of most middle-class Americans, like receiving house visits from a doctor or from a tailor who makes up clothes for the entire family. With our Indian poverty glasses in place, let us look at what Indians say about their poverty and their programs for alleviating it.

Trends in Poverty in India

Two basic problems plague the measurement of the distribution of income in all countries. First, the rich do not report their incomes accurately, often because of the illegality or sheer size of those incomes. Since one does not really know what the top groups earn, one must use approximations. Second, the incomes of the poor are not measured well either, because the poor are hard to find. In the recently completed U.S. census, a special survey of the homeless was initiated because postal addresses were not sufficient to canvass all Americans. There are similar difficulties in locating those in poverty in India.

The basis for measuring poverty in India is the National Sample Survey, one of the world's major surveys of household expenditures. However, the sample frame is not well designed to capture the urban pavement and hutment dwellers. The survey requires those interviewed to recall family expenditures during the past month for a detailed list of items. Although it captures major trends in India, like an increasing proportion of expenditures on consumer durables, the survey is not sufficiently accurate to describe the situation of the very poor. However, this is the basis for most estimates of India's poverty line.

One difficulty with surveys of expenditures is that they usually record expenditures directly but infer prices from independent information about quantities, or quantities from independent information about prices. If one wants to look at the situation of the poor over the years, one needs to express the expenditures in constant prices based on a particular year. Several alternative sources of constant price information exist in India, and the choice of source can affect the measurement of trends in poverty by 10 percent or more. The different sources explain the differences between the Planning Commission and World Bank estimates that are cited below. Even when poverty lines have been converted into constant prices, there remain a number of controversies among experts on the trends in poverty in India. There is not space here to discuss the many issues involved, but it is important to look at the poverty line because it is the main criterion for most programs.

The Poverty Line

As part of its Third Five-Year Plan (1961–66), India adopted for rural areas its famous poverty line of Rs. 20 per capita per month in 1960–61 prices. This expenditure level, which is about Rs. 90 today in rural areas, would provide an intake of 2,150 calories per day for males in rural areas and 2,100 calories per day for males in urban areas as a threshold above which all poor were to be raised. In 1983–84 the Planning Commission put the number of persons below the poverty line at 270 million (about 36 percent of the population), whereas the World Bank estimates given below suggest a higher figure of 318 million (about 40 percent of the population). This poverty line was intended to provide quantitative goals for income distribution, which had in most other countries been merely rhetorical and entirely qualitative in nature. By attaching numbers to poverty goals, the poverty line made it possible to measure achievements in poverty reduction.

The Indian poverty line represents the first explicit attempt of a democratically elected government in the Third World to make the reduction of poverty an operational planning goal. China, of course, had made revolutionary strides between 1949 and 1960 in redistributing land and other productive assets and in improving health and distributing amenities through the "iron rice bowl" and other communally provided services. These were truly remarkable achievements, but they were carried out in an environment in which the flow of information tended to be controlled by the center rather than arising from below. (As A. K. Sen has noted, this lack of information from the grass roots permitted the occurrence in China in 1959–60 of the largest number of famine deaths in any country in this century, even though the overall availability of food in China has in general been more than in India.)

Sen provided one of the early critiques of the poverty measures, arguing that the distribution of poor persons below any poverty cutoff line was also very important. Contrast two hypothetical cases: Case A, in which all those below the poverty line of Rs. 90 in 1989 had incomes of Rs. 85, and Case B, in which half the people had incomes of Rs. 85 and half, Rs. 40. Most people would regard Case B as much more alarming than Case A. Sen's index would systematically give more importance to persons farther below the poverty line. In Table 1 this distributional aspect of poverty is partially taken into account by also counting the "ultra-poor," those whose income is more than 25 percent below the poverty line. With the poverty line of Rs. 90 as the standard, those with less than Rs. 90 per month are in poverty and those below Rs. 67.5 (.75 X 90) are in ultra-poverty.

TABLE 1

Number and Percentage of Rural and Urban Indians in Poverty and Ultra-Poverty in 1970, 1983, and 1988

	1970	1983	1988
Rural India			
Number (in millions)			
In Poverty	236.8	252.1	252.3
In Ultra-Poverty	134.6	128.2	123.4
Percentage			
In Poverty	53.0	44.9	41.7
In Ultra-Poverty	30.1	22.8	20.4
Urban India			
Number (in millions)			
In Poverty	50.5	64.6	70.1
In Ultra-Poverty	28.4	31.5	32.9
Percentage			
In Poverty	45.5	36.4	33.6
In Ultra-Poverty	25.6	17.7	15.8
Total Population			
Percentage			
In Poverty	51.6	42.9	39.6
In Ultra-Poverty	29.2	21.6	19.2

Source: World Bank, *India: Poverty, Employment, and Social Services*, Washington, DC, 1989, pp. 175–176.

Three points should be made about these trends. First, the absolute numbers in poverty have been rising in both rural and urban areas. Second, because urban areas often receive migrants in poverty from rural areas, they have a more difficult problem than rural areas. This means that although the number in ultra-poverty in rural areas has decreased and in urban areas has increased, this may simply reflect migration of the poor to urban areas. Third, the percentage of persons in poverty has decreased in all periods, and the total number in ultra-poverty has also decreased. These can at best be called modest gains.

Nutrition and Health Status

Given the difficulties of using expenditure surveys, it is not surprising that some have tried to measure directly the caloric intake available to the poor. Such research leads to conclusions about the numbers of persons below a minimum caloric intake, say 2,000 calories per day, and thus is closely related to measurements using the poverty line. One of India's most respected agricultural economists, P. V. Sukhatme, who has made a number of contributions to this work, has questioned many of the findings of nutrition surveys.[1] Such surveys often leave out calorie sources like tapioca, an important source of nutrition in Kerala but not generally consumed in other states.

Sukhatme has raised the more general question of whether a norm like 2,000 calories per day has much value when the caloric requirements to maintain the same body weight for persons of the same age, sex, height, and daily physical activity vary among individuals. Sukhatme points out that if you use 2,000 calories a day as a norm, there will be some individuals who need more, and probably a significantly larger number who need less, calories to maintain normal activity.

The perceived relationship between the poverty line and health may be misleading because such inferences are based on two common measures of health status, height per age and weight per height. Low caloric intake in children may lead to low height per age level, whereas in general, malnutrition leads to low weight per height level. In the absence of detailed national surveys of health status, inferences are often drawn for larger populations on the basis of local surveys that use both types of criteria. The results often suggest that large proportions of populations are malnourished and functionally impaired—for example, 53.5 percent of the population of Nepal according to a study conducted in the 1980s. If over half of a population is malnourished, it becomes a problem of

---

[1] P. V. Sukhatme, "On Measurement of Poverty," *Economic and Political Weekly*, August 8, 1981, pp. 1318–1323.

such magnitude that one does not know where to begin. The percentage for Nepal would be reduced to 7.5 if the weight-per-height criterion alone were used. Herein lies a major controversy in which India has been deeply involved. Some argue that if small people—as classified by the height-per-age standard that happens to be based on the population of Cambridge, Massachusetts—are not functionally impaired (for example, many of the Gurkha soldiers of Nepal), they should not be classified as malnourished. Yet there are seriously malnourished persons by a weight-per-height standard who should be targeted. These issues cannot be resolved here, but the warning is given that the poverty line dividing the poor from the rest of the population does not necessarily separate the malnourished from the well nourished or the functionally impaired from the healthy.

One final point should be made about poverty in urban versus in rural areas. The urban poor are seen and often heard, and they have a higher poverty line (that is, they require higher incomes to meet basic needs) depending upon which Indian city they live in. The urban poor are dwarfed in numbers by the rural poor, who live in the 700,000 villages of India. Most of the programs touched on in this chapter deal with the rural poor because India's leaders regard this sector as the major poverty problem. There are a number of urban programs, often specific to a municipality, that are concerned with delivery of health services, provision of essential commodities at subsidized prices, creation of income-producing opportunities, and other services. These programs are often innovative, but they will be given less space here than rural programs. In general, Indian planners believe that urban poverty can be dealt with only when conditions are so improved in rural areas that the stream of poor migrants to the cities is reduced. It makes sense to attack poverty in rural areas so that when the pavement dwellers of Calcutta move up to better housing, there will not be another set of migrants to take their place.

Regional Incidence of Poverty

India's governmental structure consists of 14 major and 11 smaller states as well as several federal territories. The traditional unit below the state is the district, of which there are about 400, which are in turn divided into subdistricts. For other purposes, India is also divided into development blocks, or multivillage administrative units, and into "natural" regions based on climate, soil, and terrain. A recent study examined the incidence of poverty in 56 of the 62 agro-climatically homogeneous regions of rural India.[2] The proportion of the population in each region in poverty was calculated using Sen's index, which weights degree of poverty by the size of the gap between household income and the poverty line. The study looked at the relationship between average consumer expenditure in each region and poverty share, or the Sen index.

A mapping of poverty reveals a broad belt running east to west. The high-poverty regions include areas of West Bengal, Bihar, and eastern Uttar Pradesh in the east. The swath moves slightly south, taking in parts of Orissa and Madhya Pradesh, and then west and north, taking in parts of Maharashtra, Gujarat, and Rajasthan. Other pockets of poverty, albeit less severe, are in parts of Tamil Nadu and Andhra Pradesh. The proportion of persons in poverty in this main east-west belt reaches a high of 85 percent in the southern part of Orissa, 67 percent in southern Bihar, 72 percent in eastern Gujarat, and 82 percent in southern Rajasthan. By way of contrast, the two regions each of Punjab and Haryana state and two of the three regions in Jammu and Kashmir have ratios under 5 percent. Not surprisingly, these latter regions have higher than average per capita consumption.

Table 2 provides data on trends in poverty in rural and urban areas

TABLE 2

Regional Distribution of Poverty

Rural Areas

	Percentage in Poverty				Percentage in Ultra-Poverty		
	1970	1983	1988		1970	1983	1988
South	62.6	47.7	44.7	South	39.1	25.8	23.2
East	65.3	60.4	57.4	East	42.0	36.2	33.1
Central	47.7	41.3	38.3	Central	26.5	20.2	18.0
West	49.0	41.8	38.5	West	24.3	18.9	14.4
Northwest	11.0	8.5	7.1	Northwest	4.1	2.0	1.7

Urban Areas

	1970	1983	1988		1970	1983	1988
South	56.1	42.3	29.7	South	36.3	22.7	20.6
East	41.8	43.5	40.9	East	23.5	23.0	20.5
Central	42.7	36.2	33.2	Central	23.4	17.3	15.2
West	39.3	31.6	19.8	West	20.1	14.3	12.7
Northwest	15.9	13.9	12.1	Northwest	5.1	3.6	3.2

Source: World Bank, *India*, pp. 175–176.

[2] L. R. Jain, K. Sundaram, and S. D. Tendulkar, "Dimensions of Rural Poverty: An Inter-Regional Profile," *Economic and Political Weekly*, special number (November 1988).

for each of five major regions of India. The regional differences are easy to summarize. The states of the east, the richest area of India in natural resources, have low levels of income per capita, low growth, and the least satisfactory performance with respect to poverty reduction. The south, which a few years ago had levels of poverty similar to those in the east, has achieved reduction of the absolute numbers in poverty in rural and urban areas.

Table 2 indicates that progress in the central region has been somewhat better than in the east but significantly behind the remaining regions. In Table 3, these data are arranged in a slightly different way for 1973 and 1988. The number in poverty and ultra-poverty in each region is expressed as a percentage of the number for all of India. The total population for each region is given in column 1 so that uneven spread can be seen in another way. The east had 23.7 percent of the rural population of India but 38.3 percent of those in ultra-poverty in 1988, as indicated in columns 1 and 5 of Table 3. Information is also given for the Scheduled Castes and Scheduled Tribes (SC/ST) and for expenditures on social services and education in the regions in 1988–89.

The Scheduled Castes and Scheduled Tribes are the largest of a number of groups designated in the Indian constitution of 1950 for various types of affirmative action. Unfortunately, data are not available to provide trend figures for these "backward" groups. As Table 3, column 1 indicates, these groups are predominantly rural, and the percentage of their members in poverty is a large proportion of their population. As I shall discuss later, the so-called backward classes, representing almost one-fourth of rural India's population (150 million out of 635 million in 1989), are clearly one group to be targeted in programs aimed at reducing poverty in India.

Columns 6 and 7 of Table 3 include additional information on per capita social and educational expenditures in the regions. Social services include health services as well as publicly distributed supplies of basic commodities at subsidized prices targeted for the poor. On an all-India basis social expenditures per capita in 1980–81 prices increased from Rs. 68 to Rs. 114 per capita and from 30 percent to 33 percent of state budgets during the decade ending in 1986–87. For education, the comparable all-India averages are Rs. 39 per capita at the beginning of the decade and Rs. 61 per capita at the end, a decrease from 24 percent to 22 percent of state budgets. Social expenditures increased as a percentage of budgets in all regions except the east, and education expenditures decreased as a percentage in all regions except the east. (In the east education shows up as a larger percentage of government spending because social expenditures there grew less than the overall average.)

TABLE 3

Share of Indian Population in Poverty, 1973 and 1988, by Region and for Scheduled Castes and Tribes, and Social Expenditures

Region/ Group	Percent 1988 Population	1973		1988		Per Capita Expenditure in 1980–87 (in rupees)	
		Poverty	Ultra-Poverty	Poverty	Ultra-Poverty	Social Services	Educa-tion
	(1)	(2)	(3)	(4)	(5)	(6)	(7)
South							
Rural	22.8	27.9	30.6	24.4	25.9	155	70
Urban	27.3	35.5	41.0	32.3	35.6		
East							
Rural	23.7	29.4	33.1	32.6	38.3	96	50
Urban	16.4	15.5	15.5	20.0	21.4		
Central							
Rural	30.4	27.1	26.4	28.0	26.8	81	47
Urban	24.0	20.3	19.7	23.8	23.2		
West							
Rural	12.2	11.4	9.9	11.3	9.8	158	80
Urban	19.6	18.4	16.7	17.4	16.3		
Northwest							
Rural	5.0	1.1	0.7	0.9	0.4	155	81
Urban	4.9	1.7	1.0	1.8	1.0		
SC/ST							
Rural	24.2			33.0	36.8		
Urban	9.3			13.1	14.7		

Source: World Bank, *India*, pp. 175–176. Note that regional figures do not add up to 100 percent because certain centrally administered areas are not in any region. Columns 6 and 7 are in 1980–81 prices.

Anti-Poverty Policies and Programs

At independence, India inherited two principal types of programs from the British; they might be termed the colonial safety net for the poor. One was a system for distributing food grains mainly to the urban poor at subsidized prices, and the second was a system for providing rural employment in years when droughts or floods reduced incomes from agriculture. These programs were retained, and India soon initiated its own major efforts aimed at raising output, educational levels, and health status, beginning with the Community Development program in the 1950s. Community Development established an administrative framework for including all areas of India within a system of development blocks separate from and independent of national and state administrations. It retained the top-down structure and small scope for local initiative that was characteristic of British administration. Soon after it was established, Community Development was judged ineffective and overambitious. In the 1960s the development blocks were integrated with a new system of local government known as Panchayati Raj, which was based on an older form of village council (or *panchayat*) government. While not a great success in the economic or social spheres, Panchayati Raj has provided an important electoral arena where local politics are played out and state and national political careers are launched. In addition to many official programs, nongovernmental organizations have a long tradition in India and include missionary groups, educational societies, charitable hospitals, and other voluntary organizations. Mahatma Gandhi's ashrams represented a holistic version of these programs, and some government support for this tradition is still given in the form of subsidies for local handicraft production.

As in most countries, there has been and remains a broad difference between those who believe more can be achieved for the poor in India by policies that result in high overall growth of the economy and those who believe more can be achieved by specific programs aimed at raising the position of those in poverty. The 1980s have seen expansion and new directions in public policy toward the poor, and the new government in India is likely in the 1990s to further extend programs directly aimed at improving the position of the poor. In the remainder of this chapter many of these targeted programs will be discussed, along with programs aimed at general economic growth and job creation.

Regional Policies

In the study of regions cited earlier, one of the most interesting findings was the relation between the level of average consumption and the incidence of poverty.[3] The facts seem to point very strongly in the direction of a trickle-down effect. Consider the average consumption figures for southern Bihar and southern Orissa of Rs. 37 and Rs. 28 per month per family in comparison with Rs. 73 and Rs. 76 per month for regions in Punjab. This somewhat more than doubling of monthly expenditures is associated with the reduction of the percentage of persons in poverty from 70 percent to less than 10

---

[3] Jain *et al.*, "Dimensions of Rural Poverty."

percent. Then is the cure for rural poverty simply a matter of raising incomes in certain regions? And if this is the answer, would it be feasible in India?

India has been trying to raise incomes in poor regions for some time, and this has not proved easy. An examination of per capita incomes since independence suggests that the experience of the Indian states is not much different from that of the world in general: a few of the poorer states, for example Orissa, have lost ground between 1970 and the late 1980s, whereas several of the middle-income states like Tamil Nadu and Rajasthan have made rapid gains in income. The high-income states on average maintained their levels, with Punjab and Haryana having done very well and Maharashtra, less well. Although we do not have data on per capita income by Indian climatic zones, it would be a safe bet that climatic regions with low per capita expenditures have experienced very low growth since 1950.

Is this difference in regional performance something that can be cured by policies aimed at rapid overall growth? Will national growth carry the momentum forward to bring along the poorer regions? Or will the poorer regions require special programs similar to the Tennessee Valley Authority in the United States? Some would say that low incomes and a high incidence of poverty produce a leadership style, or void, in which the well-off maintain their position in part by keeping the incomes and status of the poor low and by thwarting initiatives for change and growth. In this view of lagging regions, often the best potential leaders choose to emigrate rather than speak out for reform in their homelands. This was certainly a pattern for many years in the southern United States, and it has also been a pattern in parts of eastern India. Low-income and slow-growth regions may need resources and stimulus from the outside and perhaps also major social changes through education and new leadership.

The Ninth Finance Commission

In contrast to China, where the provinces contribute tax revenues to the center, in India the central government collects certain revenues that are distributed to the states. These allocations are reviewed every five years by a Finance Commission, and the Ninth Finance Commission (NFC) is in the process of submitting its final report at the time of this writing. State income differences have never been as large in India as in some other large countries, like Brazil and China. Originally the Finance Commissions primarily distributed funds on a per capita basis, but recent commissions have been asked to consider state inequalities. One of the problems in this task is that incomes are not evenly distributed within states; for example, among the poorer climatic regions mentioned above was eastern Gujarat, which is part of a state that is above average in income. In addition, the activities of the central government, which not only distributes tax revenues but also spends on projects and lends money in each of the states, have to be considered.

The NFC was instructed to find a methodology for taking the taxable capacity of a state into account in making its distributions. The idea was that any redistribution to a state should be based not on what the state actually collects in taxes but on what it could collect if it made an effort equivalent to that of other states. In fact, the estimation of taxable capacity has turned out to be a controversial issue, and the first report of the NFC appeared to favor the better-off states, which in turn has delayed acceptance of the report.

Although the NFC report is not yet available, some sense of the magnitude of the contemplated resource transfers can be conveyed. On a per capita basis transfers to the four major high-income states would average Rs. 142, or 4.4 percent of their average state domestic product (SDP) of Rs. 3,200, while transfers to the five major low-income states would average Rs. 199, or about 12.4 percent of their average SDP of Rs. 1,600. These reallocations proposed by the NFC, like those proposed by its predecessors, are relatively small. The difference of Rs. 57 is only 3.6 percent of the difference in SDP between the two groups of states, which also happens to be 3.6 percent of the level of SDP of the poorer states. For purposes of comparison, one could consider the plan to develop southern Italy in the 1950s, which involved transfers from richer regions of Italy totaling over 15 percent of the income of southern Italy. These NFC transfers are much too small to offset lower state revenues and lower private savings in the poorer states. As a consequence, capital formation is usually much higher per capita in the more affluent states. Also, public sector investments by the center are not distributed in favor of the poorer states. One is left with the conclusion that in terms of resource transfers, public policy, despite much rhetoric to the contrary, has not tended to equalize state incomes. In comparison with other countries, however, Indian performance at the center has probably been better than average.

Individual states also have backward-area programs that have been similarly modest in the results they have obtained. Firms have often been willing to invest in these backward areas because they can borrow at low interest rates or receive other concessions. However, most of these concessions make it attractive for firms to choose capital-intensive investments, so that often few new jobs are created by new firms moving into backward regions.

Poverty Programs in Rural Areas

A. K. Sen has used the term *entitlement* to characterize the potential of individuals to buy the goods they want, or, in cases of extreme deprivation, the goods they need to survive. In rural areas, as Sen describes it, there are large numbers of people, perhaps 40 percent of the population in Bangladesh and India, who are landless and whose only entitlement is their own labor. When the monsoons fail, these groups are hit in two ways. First, they get fewer days of work because there are fewer crops to harvest and fewer agricultural tasks to perform. And second, there are upward pressures on grain prices because of the smaller harvests. These landless laborers find that they earn less income, which in real terms translates into even fewer subsistence goods. In extreme situations, like the Bengal famine of 1943, the entitlements of these groups are inadequate to maintain life. Because monsoon failures are often concentrated in fairly remote areas, large numbers of the rural landless have persistently low and variable levels of income and often only a precarious hold on adequate food and health.

Integrated Rural Development Programme (IRDP)

It follows from this picture of rural India that one target group includes those in the countryside whose entitlements are basically their own labor and who have few skills and little or no education. Other assets may include a homestead site, but typically they include little or no land or other capital. Programs for these groups include the National Rural Employment Programme (1978–79) and the Rural Landless Employment Guarantee Programme (1983), which in some states offer 50 or so days of employment per year. These programs do not provide long-term skill training, nor are their beneficiaries restricted to the rural poor, except to the extent that landlessness and poverty are highly correlated. The combined employment provided by these programs is about 700 million person workdays. There are 44.4 million poor rural households, and the goal of providing 100 workdays per year for one member of each household would call for 4,440 million workdays. Thus, for these programs to reach their target, they would have to be increased more than sixfold.

In contrast to these short-term income-generating programs, the Integrated Rural Development Programme (IRDP) as implemented in

the Sixth and Seventh Five-Year Plans (1980–90) was intended to provide the poor with assets that would allow them to develop long-term
increases in their potential income. A model activity would be the
provision of animals, which in principle could feed on the common
property of a village and which could generate income from milk,
transport, or other rural work. The IRDP was supposed to have
reached 27 million poor rural families between 1980 and 1988, on the
average providing Rs. 3,000 (approximately US$500) in assets.

However, the program frequently brings the poor into conflict with
better-off villagers, who have often tried to privatize common property like grazing land, thereby thwarting the efforts of the poor to develop animal husbandry as their source of income and employment.
The IRDP has been administered through the existing bureaucracy
and has been criticized for, among other things, helping the nonpoor
and making most of its loans to those living in the more prosperous
regions of a state. Its annual costs have been roughly the same as
those of the employment programs.

Those too poor or unable to work or to utilize productive assets are
clearly left out by these programs. Of those receiving assets under
IRDP, a significant number have sold them, often at a loss. The loss
occurred because IRDP itself increased local demand for animals, so
that prices were bid up and excessive values were put on animals
provided to the poor as capital, with larger farmers realizing a capital
gain. It is estimated that these programs enable less than 10 percent
of participating families to move out of poverty.

Advances Among Special Groups

One of the cruel ironies of social policies is that they most often
help those in targeted groups who need help least, which in turn often operates against the broader interests of those groups. As mentioned earlier, India has had affirmative action policies for Scheduled
Castes and Tribes and some other minorities since 1950. We have
seen that most of the "backward" castes live in rural areas. However,
most of the affirmative action policies that have provoked backlashes
in India are those that reserve government employment and admis-
sion slots in higher-education programs for persons from Scheduled
Castes and Tribes, and most of these programs are in urban areas.
The poorest of the Scheduled Castes and Tribes appear not to have
received their share of IRDP resources. And because of their low literacy levels, which are usually about 60 percent of the average for all
rural males and 40 percent of the average for rural females, the likeli-
hood of their being able to take advantage of the IRDP is reduced.

Many other programs from which the Scheduled Castes and Tribes in rural areas can benefit are not enforceable, often requiring initiation by the injured party. For example, consider the long-deplored institution of bonded labor, which was formally abolished nationwide in 1976. The bond is usually a loan by landowner to worker, and in principle repayment frees the worker and his family. Bonded laborers are usually from Scheduled Castes and Tribes, and often the son takes over the father's bond. The abolition of bonded labor by legislation, like the abolition of dowry in India, has simply not been successful. Similarly, rural minimum-wage legislation has been passed in the states of India, but in order for it to be enforced complaints must be filed and administrators must rule on those complaints. And even if it were effective, like most minimum-wage legislation it would probably reduce employment opportunities.

Employment Creation

Rural employment programs have provided a type of safety net that in the 1986–88 drought period was effective in maintaining the incomes of the vulnerable. There is also potential for expanding agricultural and nonagricultural employment in rural areas, primarily by expanding irrigation. While programs to increase agricultural output do not directly target the poor and often initially help the better-off farmers, it is quite clear from the regional data that states with high agricultural incomes have smaller numbers of people in poverty. There remains considerable scope for expanding irrigated areas in eastern India, for example, where poverty levels are high but where, unfortunately, initiative has been low.

There is also an association in both India and China between non-agricultural employment in rural areas and high agricultural incomes. This occurs because high agricultural incomes create demand for inputs, including tube wells and other agricultural implements, which in turn creates a need for small machine shops as well as a demand for consumer goods and better housing, leading to more retail shops, more tailors, and more construction workers. Therefore, programs that can successfully increase agricultural output are likely to expand employment and have a significant positive impact on the incidence of rural poverty.

Reducing Poverty in Urban Areas

The average health status of those in poverty in urban areas is thought to be about the same as that of persons in backward rural areas. Tuberculosis is more common among the poor in urban areas, where it is often caused by poor housing, bad drainage, and crowded conditions. In most states, "fair-price shops" exist where essential commodities are available, often on a rationed basis at subsidized prices, to the urban poor. Many more nongovernmental organizations operate in urban areas, meeting health and educational needs and sometimes supplying employment and, periodically, direct aid. In the past decades the percentage of social expenditures going to health and education has been smaller than that going to special programs for supplying essential commodities and creating housing and employment for the poor. The most ambitious distribution system was created in Andhra Pradesh, namely the Rs. 2-per-kilo rice scheme that has been politically popular but fiscally dubious. This program also illustrates the problem of public distribution. While it has provided rice to the poor, it also makes rice available to all segments of the population up to some ration limit. The monthly subsidy for poor families is thought to be Rs. 9, while other families who purchase more because they have higher incomes are subsidized by Rs. 27 per month. This kind of state outlay takes away from other projects that might do much more for those in poverty.

Creating Industrial Employment

India's urban areas have not grown as fast as those in many other Third World countries, but the scale of the problem is still immense, with 40 million people in India's six largest cities and another 170 million in the other cities and smaller towns. Because most urban growth is by immigration of persons seeking employment, most observers regard rapid creation of jobs as the most important deterrent to poverty. However, India has a number of industrial policies that lead employers to reduce rather than increase employment. This was never more evident than in the 1981–85 period, when the growth in industrial output in factory employment would have created 8.8 percent more jobs each year if the same ratio of labor to output had been maintained in each sector. In fact, factory employment declined 0.2 percent each year due to employers using less labor per unit of output.[4] The good news is that the productivity of those working increased, but the bad news is that this was mainly the result of government policies discouraging large units from expanding employment.

---

[4] World Bank, *India: Poverty, Employment and Social Services*, Washington, DC, 1989, pp. 106–108.

There is little to prevent many different unions from representing workers at one plant—not unions organized by craft, like machinists, but rival general unions, usually identified with particular political parties. This produces frequent work stoppages, often unrelated to the production problems of a factory. Large factories are also subject to compulsory bonus schemes, minimum wage, and pension and insurance requirements that raise the costs of hiring substantially above the real wages. In addition, there are laws against laying off workers, legislation that U.S. unions would dearly love to have but that makes employers unwilling to hire labor without certainty of long-term need. Most of this legislation applies to firms above a certain size and imposes, in effect, a tax on the growth of small firms, which often discourages their expansion to efficient size. Given that real wages have also risen during the 1980s, it is not surprising that large Indian firms are acting like large firms in most other countries, trying to add as few workers as possible, even when sales are rising. The big difference between India and many other countries is that there are large pools of urban unemployed and underemployed in Indian cities, persons whom under other conditions firms would like to hire.

This situation has put much of the job-growth burden on small-scale enterprises. Small-scale industry typically uses more labor-intensive production methods and has been the major creator of urban employment. However, India reserves production of some products for larger firms if it is thought that they would be more efficient and would generate more output and employment than small-scale firms. Here again, general industrial policies in India represent an obstacle to expanding employment and thereby reducing the numbers of persons in poverty in urban areas. Finally, the whole set of licensing, quota, and permit policies that India imposes on the expansion of industrial capacity and on imports and foreign collaboration has tended to limit overall industrial output and employment growth.

Women, Position, and Poverty

In all of India, the participation of women in the work force is limited, in part by custom, but also in part by factors subject to public policy. Over much of rural North India, Pakistan, China, and some other countries, marriage typically means that the bride moves from her home village to the village of her husband. This puts little premium on investing in daughters, whose contributions of output and progeny will accrue to another family in another village. The woman, once married, will tend to favor her sons, as will her in-laws, because a son will be her support in that family for the rest of her life. This generates a cycle of low investment of resources in women by their families because the returns will not accrue to them, a cycle that becomes reinforced by women themselves because that is their own best strategy. This system is thought to account for neglect of female children and infanticide, which result in India and Pakistan in very high ratios of males to females. The same phenomenon occurred in China before the communist revolution and after the one-child-per-family policy. It has been suggested that the more women contribute to nonhousehold income, the higher is their status. Throughout North India there is a high ratio of males to females (105 to 110 males per 100 females), which is not observed in South India, where marriage typically does not require the woman to move outside her home village.

The two approaches to breaking into this cycle are investment in education and creation of more money-making opportunities, such as the IRDP has attempted for poor rural families. In almost all regions of India, voluntary organizations have been trying to increase opportunities for poor women to earn income. One of the most well known of these, the Self-Employed Women's Association (SEWA) in Ahmedabad, has worked in both urban and rural areas. One of the characteristics of such groups in India is that middle- and upper-class university-educated women, often with husbands in high positions, are the temporary intermediaries between the poor women and the authorities and must be dealt with to establish, for example, a cooperative or a commercial bank.

Recently, the gentle, and sometimes less than gentle, prodding of these groups produced government action. A case in point is *Shramshakti* (Power of Labor), the report of a national commission on women in the informal sector and self-employed women, chaired by Ela R. Bhatt, the founder of SEWA. Its extensive recommendations include consciousness raising, protective legislation, and empowerment. Many of the last set of issues are particularly difficult for poor women. Seemingly simple matters like maintaining a bank account or more complicated matters like putting ownership of land in a woman's name are difficult social innovations among poor and less-educated families. How successful these efforts will be remains to be seen. It is certainly clear, however, that the government is taking gender questions seriously in the draft documents for the Eighth Five-Year Plan.

More general policies that militate against female employment are minimum-wage and equal-pay-and-benefits measures, which, given the existing attitudes of employers and male coworkers, operate to reduce job opportunities for women. Before equal-pay provisions in the Bombay cotton-textile industry, women constituted one-third of the work force. They now constitute less than 10 percent; this is not solely due to equal-pay provisions, but these have certainly been a major contributing factor. With existing male, and some female, attitudes, and with a large number of unemployed persons, it is unfortunately true that measures that equalize pay and benefits for women are likely to reduce female and total employment and probably to operate against poverty reduction. This is why the creation of female-run businesses is often thought to be an attractive alternative.

Education and Health

Educational achievements and shortfalls in India vary substantially by region. Overall literacy in India was reported to be 36 percent in 1981, with female literacy at 20 percent. Kerala, the model state in which high educational and health achievements have been attained despite modest levels of income, had a male literacy rate of 75 percent and a female rate of 66 percent, while Rajasthan, Bihar, and Uttar Pradesh all had literacy rates of under 40 percent for males and under 15 percent for females. Clearly mass education has not yet been achieved in India, but enrollment rates for school-age children are reported to be 80 percent or more. Regions with a low proportion of literate females to literate males will also have low overall rates of literacy, low per capita consumption expenditure, and a large share of the population in poverty.

Another correlate of the education of women appears to be the health status of the family, and particularly of children. Women are the monitors of health and nutrition practices in the household, and it is frequently observed that better feeding, sanitation, and precautionary medical practices are associated with the education of women. Local demands may also generate government delivery of health services to specific areas, or at least that may explain why most indicators of government health inputs are less correlated with incomes than with educational levels, particularly of females.

Finally, women are the carriers of culture and change to the next generation because they are the first teachers of children. On most measures of attitudes toward change, education and willingness to innovate are positively associated. The important benefits of widespread education of males and females in India have not yet completely overcome longstanding conditions in India on both the supply side (a colonial and indigenous heritage of elite education) and the demand side (the unwillingness of families in rural areas to invest in the education of female children). Whatever the reasons, the evidence seems very strong that many of the measured and unmeasured correlates of poverty are associated with low levels of education of women.

Another strong force operating to reduce school completion rates in rural areas is that often large landowners do not want education for the children of their illiterate laborers. There is usually a common village interest in enrolling children in school because education grants are based on enrollments, not completions. Thus, a village teacher may wish to encourage students from "backward" castes to remain in school but feel unwilling to try to convince their parents, if the latter are in turn subject to pressures by landlords who employ children of school-going age. One may hope that these factors will change quickly with the spread of television and other media to remote areas.

Political Change

Rajiv Gandhi's defeat in the November 1989 Lok Sabha election has been attributed to corruption, failures in foreign policy, incompetence, and a general distancing of himself from the issues of the day. Inflation was an issue, but the economy as a whole had achieved a real growth rate of 5 percent to 6 percent per annum during much of the 1980s, which was considerably above the average for the previous decades. Reforms had been introduced into the control apparatus for industry, and permits for increases in manufacturing capacity and import licenses were issued with fewer delays. Foreign collaborations were encouraged, especially in industries whose technology was changing rapidly.

Although Rajiv Gandhi's administration was associated with some liberalization of controls, these reforms have been on the agenda of most other administrations for the past 25 years. However, Rajiv's administration appeared to condone two gaps that were increasing, one between those in poverty and those in the expanding middle class and another between the middle class and the very rich. While one could not say that poverty was an issue in the campaign, the increasing gaps in income between classes, especially when gains in income were associated with corruption in the administration, may have significantly contributed to the defeat of the Congress(I) Party.

Paradoxically, the reforms that Rajiv introduced eliminated the need for only some permits; others had to be obtained via new routes, namely having one's own industry exempted or one's clearance expedited. Often these routes bypassed the old bureaucracy and lowered its take of the bribes while allowing a new set of politicians to get a slice of the action. At the same time that Rajiv appeared to be liberalizing the economy, new avenues were actually being opened for businesses to obtain monopoly profits by means of lobbying and bribes, sometimes directed at the old bureaucracy and sometimes at persons associated with Rajiv's administration.

Despite claims that Rajiv's government was corrupt, there was general economic liberalization accompanied by broad-based growth. The expansion of India's middle class is evident to anyone who has visited Indian cities in both the 1970s and the late 1980s. But the greatly increased coverage by the Indian media in the 1980s of the lifestyles of Rajiv's wealthy contemporaries, in particular of their weddings and homes, certainly made middle-class viewers and readers aware that there was a new and very affluent Indian upper class that was also expanding.

The Janata Dal Party of V. P. Singh and the associated National Front campaigned on proposals to invest more in agriculture, in contrast to the Congress(I) Party's emphasis on industrial growth. The business community has expressed satisfaction with the ministers chosen by the new government, particularly with Madhu Dandavate in Finance and Ajit Singh in Industry. The new government considers growth in agriculture complementary to industrial growth, and this view has wide support among economists and many business leaders. Clearly investment in agricultural growth is likely to be more conducive to the reduction of overall poverty levels than are Rajiv's policies. As for liberalization, this was never a campaign issue, and Ajit Singh has assured industry that it will not be reversed. The new government has inherited a major balance-of-payments problem, continued budget deficits, and significant inflationary pressures, which, along with Kashmir and Punjab, will occupy its immediate attention.

What do the election results mean for India's war on poverty? In terms of new programs, probably little. However, two major issues raised in the campaign bear directly on the general economic situation of the poor. The first is the issue of corruption and the new rich, which helps bring the plight of their opposite, the continuing poor, into focus. As the disparity between the conspicuous displays of wealth of the very rich and the visible lack of amenities of the urban poor becomes more pronounced, there is likely to be a popular reaction. The National Front campaigned to bring honesty to government and to eliminate opportunities for politicians and businesspeople to make fortunes from activities that are not directly productive. This would have no immediate impact on the income of the poor, but it is clearly a campaign plank that a wide variety of Indian voters found attractive.

This brings us to the second proposal of the National Front, which is an attempt to deal with a different dimension of poverty, having to do with the political participation and self-respect of the poor. One of the campaign issues developed in the manifesto of the National Front was a response to a proposal of Rajiv's Congress(I) Party to restructure Panchayati Raj, the village governing councils. The Congress(I) proposals, according to their supporters, would have decentralized decision making and promoted growth. Local village *panchayats* would have dealt with district-level administrators (India has about 400 districts, and the district magistrate would have been a key figure under the Congress[I] proposal), who would in turn have dealt directly with the ministries in New Delhi. Proponents claimed that this restructuring would allow local initiatives to bypass cumbersome state government bureaucracies and would unleash the development potential of rural areas. The Congress(I) proposal was reminiscent of the Basic Democracies framework in Pakistan established by Ayub Khan in the 1960s, which linked the center directly to local units. The critics of both proposals regard them as a way to bypass intermediate levels of government and to increase power at the center rather than devolve it. They argue that the goal of more local participation is good but that decentralization should proceed from the center to the states and from there to the local level.

The National Front has offered its own proposals, which according to V. P. Singh call for "real devolution of financial and administrative powers while retaining the federal system. Under the cover of the Panchayati Raj, they [Congress(I)] want to hit at the federal system. They are mixing poison in sweetmeats." In a related vein, he asks, "How do we control the bureaucracy? How can the gap between the ruler and the ruled be bridged? That's again a global problem of administration. . . . I'm very clear it cannot be bridged through elected representatives only. There has to be a counterbalance mechanism at the people's level—of joint committees of people and also decision-makers."[5]

Apparently, the National Front aspires to a more open system of administration that would at the national level try to move toward nondiscretionary controls and toward more transparency regarding how decisions are reached. How this is to be achieved has not been spelled out.

It is on the village level that the National Front calls for participation of citizen groups as intermediaries between the bureaucrats and those seeking redress through the system. Slogans like "government of the poor and for the poor" capture the flavor of this approach. Such slogans are reminiscent of grass-roots programs that emphasize "working with the poor" as opposed to "targeting the poor," which

---

[5] *India Today*, December 14, 1989, p. 36.

has a top-down connotation. These proposals of the National Front were developed in response to the widely held view that at the village level the cards are stacked in favor of the larger landowners who can exert influence on local government administrators. In the foregoing discussion of bonded labor and the IRDP program, it was pointed out that many programs are simply not implemented at the local level. These failures usually operate against the poor in the villages. In its proposals to modify the Panchayati Raj, the National Front is seeking a mechanism to protect the interests of the poor. It is not clear whether the new government will succeed in its efforts at decentralization, but a study by N. S. Jodha suggests that success might produce large payoffs in fighting poverty.[6]

Jodha looked at two dry villages in Rajasthan, first in 1963–66 and again in 1982–84. There had been a slight rise in per capita income (Rs. 162 to Rs. 175 in constant prices of 1964–65) over the period, but the percentage of families in poverty had increased from 17 percent to 23 percent in these villages. Of those families in poverty in 1982–84, 47 percent reported gains in per capita income of over 5 percent, 15 percent had essentially no change, and 38 percent (35 families) experienced declines in per capita income. Jodha asked members of 35 households whose per capita income had declined over the previous 20 years how they perceived their fortunes to have changed over that time.

Jodha reports that these families perceived their economic situation to have improved; this is in sharp contrast to the standard poverty measures that are used in India. He did not simply ask if the families thought they were better or worse off, but he followed up with questions about various aspects of village life. With respect to the dependence of these families on a large farmer or patron, Jodha found that they felt significantly less dependent than before on their patrons for credit, for work as attached laborers, for residential space, for off-season loans, and for the marketing of their produce. These same households were less dependent than before on low-paid tasks and they did not need to take children out of school as often to help earn money. In general their financial liquidity and fixed assets had improved, they experienced a reduced incidence of guinea worm, a subcutaneous parasite, and the diet of this poorest group had become more varied, now including greens and sugar.

In the villages Jodha studied, competition between large landholders for resources including the labor of poorer groups, educational

---

[6] N. S. Jodha, "Poverty Debate in India: A Minority View," *Economic and Political Weekly*, special number (November 1988).

and medical improvements, and a number of small and not easily measured changes in the economic environment appear to account for the fact that people who have suffered declines measured in real family income regard their lot as improved. This suggests that political-administrative changes that expand the opportunities of the very poor and/or reduce the hold of the rich on them in the villages may be valued as highly as the ability to increase household expenditures. If V. P. Singh's government is able to bring off such changes in rural India, the perceptions by those in poverty of their situation may be substantially improved.

Improvements for the Poor

Since 1947 India has made important contributions to the measurement of poverty by determining a level of real expenditures that will provide a minimum standard of living. However, reaching a consensus on the trends in poverty in India over the past decades has not been easy. While learned debates on the extent of this poverty continue, a number of observers have suggested that the focus on a poverty line has prevented the development of broader measures of economic change.

Education and health services provided by the government, for example, are not measured in household-expenditure surveys because they involve no outlays; consequently any improvements in the provision of these services do not get counted when the number of poor is estimated. The degree of dependency of the poor on the rich, especially in the small-group context of an Indian village, is a major element in the perception of their economic status by the poor. Improved transportation and communication are greatly enlarging the world of the rural poor; inexpensive public buses in rural areas and access to radio and television have been greatly expanded.

This is not to say that India is meeting the challenge of its poor or that the gaps between the very rich, the middle classes, and the poor have not been growing. Much is to be done. But the measurement of trends in poverty in India appears to provide too static a picture. From my visits to the University of Bombay over a number of years, several snapshots are stored away in the back of my mind. Some of these snapshots are of families that made their homes under the enormous veranda of the Esplanade Mansions, a Victorian building adjacent to the university. I can remember on my first trip to Bombay feeling overwhelmed by the enormity of the odds against the children of one of these Esplanade Mansion families ever getting ahead. Five years later I observed this same family with better clothes and more belongings. Two of the family's three children were apparently attending school, and none of them were begging. On my next trip that family had moved on, and the total number of pavement dwellers at the Esplanade Mansions appeared to be decreasing. More objective surveys for Calcutta suggest that most pavement dwellers there now are transients and that over half of them have incomes above the urban poverty line.

None of this adds up to the kind of change that role models like Hong Kong have experienced since 1960 nor the kind of change that Indian political leaders had hoped to bring about. However, it does suggest that there have been improvements for the poor in the past 30 years in India, many of which have not been well measured. High rates of economic growth provide more jobs for the poor and allow their real expenditures to rise, even if they do not gain relative to other groups in the population. Increased access to public services and enlarged opportunities are not captured by the usual poverty measures. Health, education, an expanded range of economic opportunities, and the reduction of dependence on local patrons are all important to the poor in their evaluations of their situation. The new government has a large agenda, but early indications are that it understands that to improve the position of those in poverty it is important both to promote overall economic growth and to achieve a better balance in local bureaucracies between defending the establishment and protecting the rights of the disadvantaged.

SELECTED REFERENCES

Bhagwati, Jagdish. *Protectionism* (Cambridge: M.I.T. Press, 1988).

Government of India. *First Report of the Ninth Finance Commission (for 1989–90)*, New Delhi, July 1988.

Jaggannathan, N. Vijay, and Animesh Halder. "A Case Study of Pavement Dwellers in Calcutta: Family Characteristics of the Urban Poor," *Economic and Political Weekly*, February 19, 1989.

Kabra, K. N., and N. S. Jagannnathan. *Black Money* (New Delhi: India International Centre Monograph Series, 1985), no. 8.

Kohli, Atul. *The State and Poverty in India; The Politics of Reform* (New York: Cambridge University Press, 1987).

Kurian, N. J. "Anti-Poverty Programme: A Reappraisal," *Economic and Political Weekly*, March 25, 1989.

Lewis, John P., *et al. Strengthening the Poor: What Have We Learned?* (New Brunswick, NJ: Transaction Books in association with Overseas Development Council, 1988).

Lucas, Robert E. B., and Gustav F. Papanek, eds. *The Indian Economy: Recent Development and Future Prospects* (Boulder, CO: Westview Press, 1988).

Mellor, John W., and Gunvant M. Desai. *Agricultural Change and Rural Poverty: Variations on a Theme by Dharm Narain* (Baltimore: Johns Hopkins University Press, 1985).

Srinivasan, T. N., and Pranab K. Bardhan, eds. *Rural Poverty in South Asia* (New York: Columbia University Press, 1988).

Summers, Robert, and A. Heston. "Changes in the World Income Distribution," *Journal of Policy Modeling*, May 1984.

U.S.S.R.

AFGHANISTAN

CHINA

KABUL

Peshawar
Taxila SRINAGAR Leh

Nagaur

PAKISTAN

Lahore
Harappa
CHANDIGARH SIMLA

TIBET

Lhasa (Lasa)

Tsangpo River

Gangotri
Rampur
DELHI
Mohenjodaro
Indus River

Ahichhatra

NEPAL

SIKKIM

Gyantse (Gyangze)
Shigatse (Xigaze)

BHUTAN
Thimphu

Jaisalmer

Agra
Fatehpur Sikri

LUCKNOW
Ayodhya
Kanpur
Sarnath
Ganges River

Brahmaputra River

KARACHI

Udaipur
Bundi

Kausambi
Allahabad
Varanasi
PATNA

BANGLADESH

Yamuna River

Khajuraho
Bodh Gaya

DACCA

AHMEDABAD

Chanderi

Manipur River

Sanchi
BHOPAL

CALCUTTA

Narmada River

INDIA

BHUBANESHWAR

Ajanta
BOMBAY Ellora
Elephanta

Konarak
Ekamra

Godavari River

HYDERABAD

Pattadakal
GOA Vijayanagara
Hampi

Krishna River

INDIA

□ State Capitals

• Cultural
  Heritage Sites

BANGALORE
MADRAS
Kanchipuram
Mahabalipuram

Cochin
Thanjavun

TRIVANDRUM

© The Asia Society

6
The Future of India's Past: Conservation of Cultural Heritage

Vidya Dehejia

> It shall be the fundamental duty of every citizen of India to value and preserve the rich heritage of our composite culture.
>
> Constitution of India

India is both endowed with great advantages and presented with overwhelming problems by her vast heritage of cultural material from a succession of civilizations prolific in the creation of monuments. These civilizations were no less creative in the production of what one might term movable art—sculptures in a variety of materials, paintings, textiles, manuscripts, and an entire range of functional artistic objects. In addition there developed over the centuries a rich range of dance forms, musical traditions, and dramatic performances that survive into the present as "living heritage." Every generation is the custodian of the past and has a responsibility to transmit its cultural products to future generations in as unspoiled a condition as possible. However, to attempt to preserve everything of cultural significance is unrealistic. Rather it is essential to select for conservation the best and most representative examples of our heritage, a choice that can be made only when its totality is known to us.

The wealth of India's cultural heritage is justly famous. It is characterized by an impressive diversity of expression, both religious and secular. There are numerous archaeological remains, from sites of the Indus civilization dating back to the third millennium B.C. to excavations of the historic period (fifth century B.C. onward), and a rich array of monuments stands testimony to a variety of faiths.

Monumental stupas, constructed between the first century B.C. and the fifth century A.D. and covered with narrative sculptures, speak eloquently of the vitality of the Buddhist faith, and similar testimony is provided by the many rock-cut monastic establishments, decorated with sculptures and paintings, that were excavated into the hills along the west coast of India. Freestanding monasteries, constructed all over India until the 12th century A.D., with numerous images of Buddhist deities, testify to the continuing importance of India as the homeland of Buddhism. The first Hindu temples in stone appear as late as the fourth century A.D.; within two centuries, almost as if to make up for lost time, temple-building picked up an unprecedented urgency and vitality, and vast numbers of Hindu shrines were constructed all over the country. Temple-building in northern India slowed down after the 13th century due to the increasing presence of Muslim rulers, but such activity continued in South India with undiminished vigor right into the 19th century. From the 12th century onwards, the increasing presence of Islam in northern India resulted in the construction of numerous mosques. For the first time, secular monuments in stone such as tombs and towers, forts and palaces, made an appearance. The skyline of the country took on a new look, with onion-shaped domes appearing amidst the tall temple towers.

India's cultural heritage includes much in addition to monuments dedicated to the Buddhist, Hindu, and Islamic faiths. The Jains, for instance, built extensive temple-cities atop hills in western India between the 12th and 17th centuries and produced portable metal shrines and richly illustrated manuscripts. From the 15th century onwards, the Sikhs built temples and *gurudwaras* topped with domes and minarets. The Christian presence in India, which dates back to the time of the apostle St. Thomas, resulted in the construction of churches in various parts of the country. Art connected with churches was particularly vibrant from the 15th century, when the Portuguese took possession of Goa in western India; the body of St. Francis Xavier remains to this day the most prized possession of the Church of Bom Jesus in Goa. Jewish synagogues and temples, the most famous dating from the 16th century, abound in the Konkan area and in Cochin, both along the west coast of India, while the Bombay region has several 18th-century monuments of the Zoroastrian faith including fire-temples and "towers of silence," in which the dead are exposed to release their souls. In addition to such specifically religious monuments, from the 13th century onwards Rajput rulers built citadels all over Rajasthan containing palaces and *havelis* (groups of houses, each with a courtyard), while their artists produced albums of exquisite miniatures. The British in India, using a style referred to as Indo-Saracenic, built impressive town halls and court houses, libraries and railway stations. And down the ages, monarchs of all faiths have built observatories and granaries, ornamental gardens and waterworks. India's cultural heritage can be described as an *embarras de richesses*.

The Protection of Heritage Sites

At its 1972 Paris convention, the United Nations Educational, Scientific, and Cultural Organization (UNESCO) reiterated its position on the protection of world heritage, stating that it is the duty of each nation to ensure first the identification, then the protection and conservation, and finally the presentation and transmission to future generations of its heritage, both cultural and natural.[1] UNESCO has compiled a list of world heritage sites, and in India it recognizes 13 sites of cultural importance and 5 of natural importance. The 13 comprise (in the order in which they were recognized) the Ellora and Ajanta Caves, Agra Fort, Taj Mahal, Sun Temple at Konarak, Mahabalipuram monuments, churches and convents of Goa, Khajuraho temples, Hampi monuments, Fatehpur Sikri, Pattadakal temples, Elephanta caves, Tanjore temple and, just last year, the Sanchi stupa. (The Natural Parks are Kaziranga, Manas, Keoladeo, Sundarbans, and Nanda Devi.) UNESCO recognizes that the primary responsibility for conservation lies with the nation concerned, but, at the request of member-states, it will provide technical assistance for the protection of world heritage sites.

Conservation and Development

Is conservation a luxury that India can ill afford when she is hard pressed by the entire range of problems that face a developing nation? There is always a lobby that decries the importance of conservation when it appears to conflict with economic interests. For instance, when faced with the possible closure of the refineries and foundries that provided jobs to large numbers of local workers, with the goal of preventing discoloration of the marble of the famous Taj Mahal, the Agra Chamber of Commerce countered that conservationists were quite welcome to dismantle the Taj stone by stone and rebuild it elsewhere! Our answer must reaffirm the vital role of conservation; we cannot afford to take an irresponsible attitude toward our heritage in the interests of employment and productivity. It is essential to preserve cultural resources even though they cannot pay for themselves with direct monetary returns. Cultural resources are not wealth in the accepted sense of the term; but inasmuch as they lend the country its character, they are indeed its greatest wealth.

Unfortunately, such preservation is not always apparent. In the year 1913, the Archaeological Survey of India (ASI), the government

---

[1] United Nations Educational, Scientific, and Cultural Organization, *Convention for the Protection of the World Cultural and Natural Heritage*, Paris, 1972, Article 4.

body responsible for architectural preservation, listed 1,300 monuments of national importance in the greater city of Delhi; today only 960 remain. Silently, and without public or government awareness, 340 monuments have disappeared. In 1988 the pre-Moghul Chaumachi Tomb in Mehrauli on the outskirts of Delhi almost joined the ranks of vanished monuments. Enthusiasts of a citizens' group known as the Conservation Society of Delhi (CSD) were horrified to find a developer, armed with a written decree, about to demolish the tomb. The developer had apparently found a loophole in the uncoordinated zoning laws, but the CSD, with the support of an alert press, succeeded in getting a stay order from the Supreme Court.

Examples of this type could be multiplied. In Bombay, when the navy proposed demolition of the historic clock tower in its dockyard, various citizens' groups including the Bombay Environmental Action Group, the Save Bombay Committee, and the Indian Heritage Society intervened and saved the structure. In the Dalhousie Square area of Calcutta, yet another conflict has arisen, with the proposed demolition of historic buildings that once housed the offices of the British India government, in order to set up high-rise structures. As urban land values spiral, heritage structures tend to lose out. Developers rarely contravene the law; rather they take advantage of ambiguous clauses and seek new interpretations.

Much of India's historic heritage remains in active use today, complicating the problems of conservation. For instance, the 16th-century citadel of Udaipur is also today's town of Udaipur; the residents of Bhubanesvar crowd into the 11th-century Lingaraj temple for daily worship; the Maharani of Jaisalmer still occupies her medieval palace; and that spectacular monument of Indo-Saracenic architecture, Victoria Terminus, completed in 1887, is still Bombay's busy railway station. Clearly, the idea of protecting such monuments by isolating them is impractical as well as simplistic. A doctrine of integrated conservation is necessary to preserve a monument in regular use.

The very fact of India's cultural diversity, together with the inevitable reuse of monuments and sites, may pose an additional complication for conservationists, as exemplified by the recent controversy over Ayodhya, birthplace of the Hindu hero and deity Rama. It is believed that the mosque that now stands at that site replaced a Hindu temple in the 16th century. Today, some 400 years later, Hindus wish to see the mosque removed in order to rebuild a shrine to Rama. Comparable reuse of monuments does exist in other parts of the world. One can point, for instance, to the 15th-century conversion into a mosque of the Christian church of Hagia Sophia in Istanbul, or to the Gothic cathedral that stands to this day at the very center of the Great Mosque at Cordova in Spain. However, in India there are a number of instances of symbolic appropriation that precludes the possibility of scientific exploration of the earlier heritage.

Conservation need not be viewed as belonging to the opposite end of the spectrum from development. Frequently, the best way to preserve our heritage (we do not refer here to major spectacular monuments) is to keep it in use. The skillful rehabilitation of historic buildings can be economical, since this procedure is estimated by the Indian Public Works Department to cost about two-thirds as much as putting up a new building. We shall see later, when examining the Chanderi project, that the selective and adaptive reuse of certain categories of historic monuments can serve the goals of both conservation and development. The past is retained by being adapted, and the future is assured.

Conservation and Tourism

Another problem facing conservationists is the rapid increase in tourism, both domestic and foreign, and the fear among the professional guardians of heritage that an influx of visitors is likely to have an adverse effect on the nurturing of that heritage. All tourism in India can be called cultural tourism, because it involves contact with India's art and architecture through her museums and monuments, with her religious heritage through her sacred sites, with her arts and crafts through "cultural shopping," or with her traditions of music and dance through performances. Do conservation and tourism make incompatible bedfellows?

Domestic cultural tourism can foster a sense of national pride; occasionally it is responsible for actually generating an awareness of the country's rich heritage. The need for interpretive signs that explain the significance of sites cannot be overemphasized. Only if the present generation understands, appreciates, and cherishes its heritage will it be able to effectively transmit it to future generations. However, domestic tourism can also pose a variety of problems to heritage. Many of the visitors to Sarnath, the deer park where the Buddha preached his first sermon, are picnickers who care little about the historic aspect of the site. Apart from cooking in the area and playing amplified music, such tourists also use the site for active recreational sports, often causing unintentional damage and defacement. A National Park proposal, discussed later, suggests the creation of a visitor center with a park and a zoo to cater to such tourists. The main ruins compound may then be enclosed in a woodland setting to recreate the historic tranquillity of sacred Sarnath.

Foreign tourism is somewhat more complicated. UNESCO's concept of world heritage sites suggests that a country's monuments carry international and universal significance and that foreign tourists should have access to them. However, an entire camp of preservationists strongly opposes foreign tourism, complaining in particular of the clusters of five-star hotels that tend to rise in the vicinity of historic monuments, altering their historic ambience. This view is tellingly represented in a cartoon by Osbert Lancaster in which the chairman of Mammoth Hotels insists: "Let us get our priorities right. Historic monuments must not be allowed to stand in the way of the new, luxurious accommodation for tourists who come to see the historic buildings." Complaints abound of congestion, increased traffic, and camera-bearing crowds, reminding one of the rueful and witty remark of the mayor of Jerusalem (applicable to any other tourist city): "Visitors to Jerusalem have ended up seeing visitors to Jerusalem seeing Jerusalem." However, tourism with enlightened management can provide a supportive relationship to heritage and serve the interests of both tourism and conservation. The 1979 Tourism and Heritage Conference organized by PATA (Pacific Asia Travel Association) reflects this new concern and the desire of the tourist industry for cooperation with preservationists.

For India's beleaguered economy, tourism from abroad can provide much-sought-after foreign exchange and make a vital contribution to her future. In 1988 tourism was India's second largest foreign-exchange earner, overtaking traditional exports like tea and textiles to bring in US$1.26 billion, and second only to the sales of gems and jewelry at US$1.5 billion. The Indian government has announced that it intends actively to encourage foreign tourism. An example is its effort to create an atmosphere conducive to tourism at Bodh Gaya and other sites along the sacred route sanctified by the Buddha, which were visited even in ancient times by the Chinese pilgrims Faxian (ca. 400 A.D.) and Xuanzang (ca. 630 A.D.). The modern-day pilgrim, usually Japanese, who visits the homeland of the Buddha finds facilities lacking, accommodation unsatisfactory, and the environment far from ideal for the contemplation of nirvana. A US$132 million project has been initiated to upgrade the sites, with a 40 percent contribution from the Overseas Economic Development Fund of Japan. The project will create hotel rooms and provide train service between sites. With the aim of successfully integrating the concerns of tourism and conservation, and mindful of the possible damage to historic sites in the process of their development, the National Parks Service of the United States and the Delhi School of Planning and Architecture have been called in to act as consultants. Apart from encouraging tourism, the successful implementation of this project, with its accompanying and necessary conservation of sites, could actually prove beneficial to heritage.

There is today a general awareness of the need to preserve relics of the past. However, the task of the preservation and conservation of India's cultural heritage is a daunting one because of the superabundance of her monuments (immovable heritage), her sculpted images and paintings (movable heritage), and her traditions of dance and music (living heritage). There are thousands of temples, tens of thousands of bronzes and paintings, and dozens of dance traditions, to mention only a few categories of heritage to which attention must be directed.

Immovable Heritage

The Archaeological Survey of India

The first step in the preservation of India's heritage was taken, as might be expected, by the British administrators of India in the middle of the 19th century. The Archaeological Survey of India was established in 1861, purely to make a record of the monuments of India; shortly thereafter it was invested with the authority "to prevent injury and preserve buildings remarkable for their antiquity, or for their historical or architectural value."[2] Ten years later Alexander Cunningham, a retired major-general of the British India Army, was placed in charge of the survey, and he explored extensive areas of the country and published his "tours" as a series of reports. In order to discourage treasure-seekers from random digging into archeological sites, the Treasure Trove Act was passed in 1878 authorizing the government to claim possession of any unearthed treasure that exceeded Rs. 10 in value. Cunningham did a remarkable job of charting the ancient remains of India; he was followed by James Burgess, an architect by training, who toured the country and published his findings in a series titled *Annual Reports of the Archaeological Survey* and a set of volumes devoted to inscriptions titled *Epigraphia Indica*. Burgess introduced legislation that would make illegal any excavation other than those conducted by the survey. He even attempted to introduce an amendment to the Treasure Trove Act that would make it unlawful to export antiquities without an official permit, but in this he failed, and such an act had to wait nearly 75 years for implementation.

---

[2] Act XX of 1863, Sections xxiii–xxiv.

It was only in 1902, when Lord Curzon was governor-general of India, that a clear policy of conservation was formulated. "I cannot conceive any obligation more strictly appertaining to supreme government," Curzon wrote, "than the conservation of the most beautiful and perfect collection of monuments in the world." The Ancient Monuments Preservation Act of 1904 contained provisions for the acquisition of archaeological monuments, for their protection, and for their preservation without disturbing their religious character. Finally, in 1906, the ASI was placed on a permanent footing as an independent government department, headed by a director-general, John Marshall. An archaeologist who had worked in Greece, Turkey, and Crete, Marshall rejected the idea of restoration, which he considered akin to tampering with heritage; instead he emphasized that monuments were historical and archaeological documents. He embarked on a series of excavations and was responsible for systematic digging at Mohenjodaro, the famous Indus Valley site that dates to the third millennium B.C. He also excavated at Taxila, a major center of the Indo-Hellenistic Buddhist art of Gandhara in the early centuries of the Christian era.

Sir Mortimer Wheeler's tenure as director-general from 1944 to 1948 led to the constitution of an excavations branch within the survey and the introduction of international standards for excavation. Wheeler remarked that "the excavation of a site, like the ordering of a battle, must be thought out and coordinated by a single present and directing mind." Excavation and conservation courses were introduced, and two periodicals, *Ancient India* and *Indian Archaeology: A Review*, which are still being published, were launched.

Today the ASI is still the prime government body for the protection and preservation of India's immovable heritage. Roughly 5,000 monuments have been declared of national importance, and blue signboards at the entrance to such protected monuments proclaim the survey's control of the site, while accompanying boards provide historical context. The official position on conservation is reflected in the Ancient Monuments and Archaeological Sites and Remains Act of 1958 passed by the central government, which focuses on the protection of monuments. Conservation is generally interpreted exclusively as preservation, and stress is laid entirely on the upkeep and maintenance of a monument and its safeguard from harm or injury. For the latter purpose, the ASI employs guards to watch the monument around the clock and to ensure that no damage occurs. While the act enables an extension of protection to the immediate surroundings, the ASI generally conceives of monuments in isolation, although occasionally, as at Khajuraho or Sarnath, formally planted gardens surround historic structures. Even at Khajuraho, however, little attempt has been made to visualize the 30 or so temples still standing as an interconnected group, although as early as 1972 a UNESCO report laid emphasis on viewing a monument in its context. "A monument . . . affects and is affected by its setting, and its relations with that setting are intrinsic to its artistic value. Even when standing alone, with no other constructions nearby, it always forms part of a larger composition, natural or man-made."[3]

It is heartening to note that the funds available to the ASI were considerably enlarged by the Indian government under its Seventh Five-Year Plan (1985–1990). An allocation of Rs. 2,900 lakhs (approximately US$17 million) was provided for maintenance and repairs, and of this amount roughly US$3.4 million a year was purely for the preservation of monuments, with a separate budget for the remuneration of staff, for excavation, and for the ASI's School of Archaeology.

In the area of excavation, the efforts of the ASI are unrivaled, and over the years it has explored a range of sites and helped build up a picture of pre- and proto-historic India. Apart from the excavations at Mohenjodaro and Harappa, today in Pakistan, sites of the famed Indus Civilization have been uncovered near Delhi and in Gujarat. In southern India, an extensive series of sites of the megalithic burial culture, dating throughout the first millennium b.c., have been excavated. While the ASI has undoubtedly concentrated on prehistoric sites, it has also worked on excavations of the historic period. Sites uncovered include major cities like Kausambi or Ahichhatra and also more mundane civic structures of a utilitarian nature. An example of the latter is an elaborate water-supply system at Shringaverapura in Uttar Pradesh, where a series of brick tanks, fed by water diverted through a canal from the river Ganges, testifies to the sophistication of hydraulic engineering in India in the first century a.d. The zeal apparent in locating new sites for excavation has not been applied in equal measure to enlarging the numbers of standing monuments that require conservation. And yet, considering the many constraints under which it operates, much commendable work has been done by the ASI.

Several obstacles arise in the implementation of the Ancient Monuments Act of 1958. For instance, the act makes no provision for emergency repairs, and the ASI may not repair a monument until it has been legally declared to be under its protection. Tragic consequences may result, as in the case of Lechan Palker palace at Leh in Ladakh, a

---

[3] United Nations Educational, Scientific, and Cultural Organization, *Preserving and Restoring Monuments and Historic Buildings*, Paris, 1972.

mud structure in 11 levels, 190 feet high, built in the 16th century. In 1982 the ASI declared this remote Himalayan palace, located near the border with Tibet, to be a monument of national importance that should come under ASI protection. Negotiations for its purchase dragged on, however, and in September 1988 a significant portion of the palace crashed to the ground, destroying four of its stories. The ASI was aware of the intensity of the problem, but it did not have the power to effect emergency repairs and had to wait until legal possession had been secured. Yet another example is the case of the fortified town of Jaisalmer, founded in 1156. Eight potential disaster areas have been identified, the prime one being the portions of the city wall that are about to collapse. There is universal agreement that Jaisalmer is a national treasure and that urgent measures are needed to prevent it from crumbling. Yet, as long as the Maharani of Jaisalmer refuses to sign the contract by which the monument is declared of national importance, the government may not step in and effect emergency measures.

A problem connected with the Ancient Monuments Act and relevant to Jaisalmer is the act's lack of provision for financial reimbursement to the owner of a monument that is designated of national importance. Each case has to be negotiated on its individual merits, and a long, drawn-out dialogue generally ensues. Ironically, owners generally do not wish their property declared of national importance; in addition to lack of reimbursement, their very rights to the property are likely to be curtailed. A second look at the act certainly seems indicated.

The Indian Income Tax Act does little to encourage the funding of conservation or the gifting of heritage to the nation's museums. While monetary contributions for scientific research are deductible in full from an individual's taxable income, the situation is quite different in the case of contributions for conservation, whether of natural or human-created heritage. If substantial donations are made (exceeding 10 percent of total income), only 10 percent of the contribution is deductible; if donations are of smaller proportions (less than 10 percent of total income), then 50 percent of it is deductible. In contrast to the situation prevailing in the United States, the Income Tax Act provides no incentives toward the donation of valuable art objects to museums. Not only is there no provision for deducting the value of such gifted objects from taxable income, but in addition, a donor is actually liable for gift tax.

Indian National Trust For Art And Cultural Heritage

Compiling an inventory of India's cultural heritage has to be one of the first moves in any comprehensive conservation program. Across the country, the government has under its protection today only about 8,000 monuments considered to be of national importance. Roughly 5,000 of these are under the control of the ASI, while 3,000 are administered by the departments of archaeology set up by individual states. In a country with a continuous and rich culture dating back to the third millennium B.C., these numbers are woefully inadequate. In Britain, which is roughly the size of the north Indian state of Uttar Pradesh alone, and whose historic time span in no way rivals that of India, no fewer than half a million buildings are listed as historic monuments. In the United States, the National Register has 52,000 historic places on its list. Until very recently, one of the major organizational shortcomings in the protection of the architectural heritage of India has been the absence of a national inventory. Today this is in the process of compilation by the Indian National Trust for Art and Cultural Heritage (INTACH), established six years ago. This voluntary, nongovernmental organization has 155 regional chapters.

INTACH's aim is a listing of all notable buildings constructed prior to 1939 that survive in anything like their original condition and have significance to Indian history, archaeology, architecture, or culture. INTACH has selected buildings in four major categories, based in principle on the criteria used by the U.S. National Register. The first category comprises buildings that are of special value for a variety of reasons. They may represent a distinctive architectural style or the work of a master, or may otherwise possess high artistic or aesthetic value. They may be illustrative of social or economic history (theaters, markets, waterworks) or of technological innovations (dams, granaries, observatories). It is this category alone that the ASI has deemed worthy of protection.

A second group consists of structures associated with events that are significant in the context of India's history; an example is the Satichaura Ghats at Kanpur, site of the infamous massacre of the Indian Mutiny and Rebellion of 1857. A third category comprises buildings associated with the lives of those who have left their mark on Indian history; an example of such a structure is the Sabarmati *ashram* at Ahmedabad, intimately associated with the life of Mahatma Gandhi. There are those who may indeed be inclined to query the inclusion of categories two and three on the basis of their general lack of aesthetic value. Does one preserve a monument of historic import even when it lacks artistic features? The answer must be in the affirmative. As the 1972 UNESCO report on conservation emphasizes, "Architectural monuments are not merely works of art; they belong to a sphere of

more complex values, and cannot be judged by aesthetic and historical criteria alone."[4]

The fourth and final INTACH category consists of buildings that
have group value as examples of town planning; the Rajput town of
Udaipur is a prime example. It should be noted that the listing of
monuments includes, on the one hand, imposing buildings used by
the rulers or the community as a whole, and on the other, the traditional and vernacular architecture.

Once identified, these notable buildings are subdivided into three
levels of importance, by a consideration of their date of construction,
state of preservation, and architectural and aesthetic value. Grade A
buildings are of exceptional interest with unique features; to be saved
at any cost, they merit protection and maintenance on a permanent
basis. For grade B and C buildings, it is recommended that the town
and country planning departments of the various state governments
take responsibility for their maintenance and for the occasional judi-
cious reuse of structures in a manner compatible with their original
design and function. In the first five years of INTACH's existence, the
listing of historic monuments in 60 cities was completed, yielding a
total of 10,000 monuments. The listing in another 56 towns and cities
is under way, and it has not yet been commenced in several other important towns, cities, and rural areas.

Heritage Zones

Although the protection of monuments on the ASI list has been carried out adequately, it is time to extend the connotation of conservation to embrace its true meaning of preserving not only the monument but also its surrounding areas, in order to present the
monument in its original setting. One of INTACH's most significant
innovations is its concept of heritage zones, which marks a departure
from the conservation of individual spectacular monuments undertaken by the ASI. A heritage zone is an area of special architectural,
historical, or cultural interest, the character and appearance of which
it is desirable to preserve and enhance. Such a zone can be an entire
town, with its groups of buildings, streets, open spaces, features of
archaeological interest, sections of waterways, and the like. The intention is not merely to preserve the visual qualities of the area but also
to enhance its traditional character and revitalize it in the process,
putting old buildings to new (or original) uses and reviving the vi-
brancy of the zone. The concept of heritage zones thus shifts the em-

---

[4] UNESCO, *Preserving and Restoring Monuments.*

phasis from a monument seen in isolation to monuments in use by the people. It is clear that more than an architectural survey is needed; an economic and social survey is vital to determine the special requirements of the area. Heritage zones are not meant to be emptied of people; rather the zones are to be restored in such a manner as to maximize their utilization by the local population. The conservation of cultural heritage becomes an essential component of such schemes, and its success clearly requires the wholehearted cooperation of that population.

The active participation of planners and urban designers is a necessary component of heritage zone schemes, and one finds that the framework for such conservation is available through the Town and Country Planning Acts of individual state governments. Such acts, which enable conservation of monuments, buildings, sites, and areas and their renovation and redevelopment, are available in most states, with the exception of Rajasthan, Punjab, and Haryana. The Eighth Five-Year Plan (1990–1995) proclaims its strategy in this field as "conservation in the context of planned development."

INTACH has identified heritage zones in more than 50 towns, including such vastly different sites as 16th-century Jew Town in Cochin, the mysterious monuments of 7th- and 8th-century Mahabalipuram near Madras, Himalayan Gangotri from where the river Ganges emerges, Leh Town in Ladakh adjoining Tibet, and the British Dalhousie Square area of Calcutta. In several instances extensive studies are ready for implementation, and in a few areas work is in progress. The expenses involved in the revitalization of a heritage zone are considerable. The costs of the report preparation, borne either by INTACH itself or by its client, usually a state government, range from US$18,000 to US$30,000. The implementation costs vary vastly depending on the complexity of the project. For Ekamra, discussed later, the expenses have been estimated to run in the region of US$17.3 million. Apart from the ASI, which is funded by the central government, each state has its own department of archaeology with branch offices in each district. Money for the implementation of heritage zone projects will have to be budgeted from state government funds. The Orissa state government has already agreed to fund the Ekamra heritage zone.

I shall discuss in detail three projects that emphasize different aspects of heritage. The Udaipur proposal takes into account natural, architectural, and craft heritage; the Ekamra zone emphasizes religious heritage and attempts to reintegrate the temples into daily life; and the Chanderi project is development-oriented. The concept of isolated historic buildings belongs to the past, and these examples will reveal clearly that conservation and development can march hand in hand.

Udaipur Heritage Zone: Natural, Architectural, Cultural Heritage

Founded in 1559 by the ruler Udai Singh as the capital of Mewar state, Udaipur, city of lakes and palaces, is perched picturesquely upon the Aravalli hills. Its many palaces and temples, lakes and tanks, its steep winding streets and *havelis* add to its charm, while its pleasant, bracing climate has helped make the former princely town into an important tourist center. Udaipur has served time and again as a backdrop for fashion spreads, and the town was used as the exotic site for the James Bond film "Octopussy." A process of decay is, however, quite evident at Udaipur; if not arrested, it will destroy the fabric of the city.

INTACH's proposal for the Udaipur heritage zone takes into consideration its natural environment, its architectural setting, and the cultural riches of the area. In the realm of natural heritage, a prime concern is the receding water level in the lakes, one of the principal features of the city, and in many ways its lifeline. Compounding the problem is the fact that gardens, orchards, and other open spaces are sharply decreasing, while lakefront property is being divided into plots and sold for construction. The proposal calls for a comprehensive, conservation-oriented development policy for the mountains, lakes, and lakefront areas, with particular emphasis on preserving the environs of the lake.

Inadequate maintenance has been responsible for a considerable amount of deterioration in Udaipur's architectural monuments. A variety of smaller structures like ornamental gateways have become traffic islands; the magnificent fort walls have been punctured and demolished at will; and buildings are freely torn down so that their *jalis* (trellis-work screens) and other prized decorative elements can be sold. Once described with pride as the "White City," Udaipur now displays a variety of colors owing to unsympathetic renovation, while shops and a range of new constructions have sprung up in the vicinity of important old buildings. Innumerable signboards and hoardings ruin the view of the city, interfering with the concept of architectural heritage; the city walls themselves are scarcely visible behind the enormous multicolored advertisements plastered on them. A considered policy of architectural conservation is an urgent need, and the rise of new buildings must be restricted to maintain the character of the city. Enlightened developers have realized the value of converting old *havelis* into three-star hotels instead of replacing them with modern constructions. Such *haveli* hotels retain an old-world charm; yet, with careful planning, they can be renovated to include most modern amenities. It is important to restrict the height of buildings throughout the town. The proposed height restriction ranges from 6 meters (just under 20 feet) when building within a distance of 50 feet from the lake, to a maximum height of 50 feet in any part of Udaipur that lies more than 650 feet from the lake.

The third part of the proposal relates to the cultural heritage of Udaipur. The inner city area consists of 150 *galis* (long, narrow streets) inhabited by a variety of caste groups specializing in crafts such as painted miniatures, metal work, wood carving, weaving, embroidery, and the like. The *galis* are, in fact, named after these craftsmen. A major goal in development is to enable tourism to benefit the city, and one way would be to bring visitors into direct contact with the traditional artists. The restored *Bagor ki haveli* today houses a craft workshop where visitors can view some of the craftsmen at work and purchase their wares.

The Udaipur project, with its multipronged approach, involves a comprehensive conservation program, the success of which depends upon several factors. It requires ample finances, the skills of specialists, and the support of the state government. Further vital ingredients are a positive attitude towards conservation and the cooperation and participation of a motivated population involved in the cause of restoring the grandeur of their city.

Ekamra Kshetra Heritage Zone: Religious Heritage

Ekamra Kshetra, the ancient name for the Bhubaneswar region of Orissa, has a history reaching back some 2,500 years. The vast numbers of distinctive temples, built by a successive series of dynasties between the 6th and 15th centuries A.D., are responsible for its fame. Temple festivals dominate the day-to-day activities of the townspeople, and the majority of the population of 34,000 is dependent on temple economy and tourism.

However, this major Shaivite center with more than 300 temples is today in a pathetic state of disrepair. Shrines stand in ruins in the midst of paddy fields, others are used as traffic islands, while the existence of yet others is attested to only by the tops of spires seen above today's risen ground level. Water in most temple tanks is polluted, and in several it is silted or dried up. New construction abuts against ancient shrines with total disregard for their antiquity. In addition, with the abandonment of overcrowded Cuttack, Bhubaneshwar has become the new capital of Orissa. In the absence of planned development, Bhubaneshwar neither retains the dignified grandeur of ancient times nor has acquired the advantages of modern development.

The theme of the Ekamra project is "religious heritage," and the aim of the development of the heritage zone is to strengthen the structure of the city, which is based on the disposition of its spaces, sacred, secular, and open. The starting point of the study was an investigation of the medieval concept of *astha ayatana* (eight sacred precincts). In the course of attempting to locate the eight clusters of temples, 165 monuments not under government protection were identified, all in an advanced state of decay. No fewer than 48 of these unprotected shrines were classified as Grade A, or of national importance. The famous Lingaraj temple emerged visually, geographically, and symbolically as the center of Ekamra, and the plan advocates a series of open spaces in order to maintain views of the Lingaraj from several directions. Such open spaces are not merely of aesthetic value; they take into account the drainage patterns of the area and include low-lying areas, the tanks, and natural drainage channels, all identified as areas not to be built upon. Areas around the tanks and the clusters of temples are to be landscaped as public places so as to reintegrate the temples into the daily life of the people.

The Ekamra heritage zone has been demarcated into an inner core, an intermediate area, and a peripheral region that offers a transition to the new capital town. The development takes into account popular domestic tourism, which brings 250,000 visitors to the town annually. It is proposed to keep the innermost core free of all vehicular traffic and to provide a special heritage zone bus route with high-frequency minibuses to enable both pilgrims and tourists to visit the entire range of temples. INTACH's Ekamra Kshetra project involves the state government, local voluntary organizations, and other local authorities, who have extended enthusiastic cooperation. The aim of the Ekamra plan is not just to preserve the temples and areas of historic ambience that give the town its image; it is also intended to focus city life around them, to upgrade amenities, and to facilitate heritage tourism.

Chanderi Heritage Zone: Craft and Development Heritage

Located along an important medieval trade route and surrounded by high fortified city walls is the 15th century citadel of Chanderi in Madhya Pradesh, with its central Rajmahal palace complex. There is a remarkable visual cohesiveness to this town with its various distinctive buildings, its courtyards and *chowks* (squares), and its cobbled streets, all built of the local buff-colored sandstone. Chanderi is dotted with *baodis* (man-made tanks) of significant architectural character, which, to this day, remain the main source of the town's water supply. The historic town is in complete ruins and houses a population of only 20,000 inhabitants, almost all weavers who produce cloth of gossamer lightness. Using handlooms to weave silk and cotton threads together with *zari* (gold thread), they produce the finest of fabrics. Chanderi saris are among India's best known, but the advent of textile mills caused the craft to decline. However, changes are in the making. The construction of a dam across the river Betwa, which will inundate several villages, is expected to drive the displaced to Chanderi, while the recent revival of the handloom tradition is bringing prosperity and change to the town. New buildings with no reference to the historical character of the town were already in evidence when INTACH commenced work on its Chanderi project.

Two broad principles guided the rationale of the plan—that conservation should be development-oriented and that it should depend, as far as possible, on local materials, skill, and technology. The old town, with four gates piercing its city walls, was declared a heritage zone, and the new town planned beyond the walls has been connected to it by extending the main market street, with a symbolic gate linking the old and new developments. Designs for a new bank building, a market complex, and municipal offices are in harmony with the buildings of the old town. In this way, the old and new will not be totally separate entities, and the benefits accruing to one will be shared by the other.

One monument singled out for total restoration is the badly ruined Rajmahal that lies at the symbolic center of Chanderi. Forming the nucleus of the old town, this complex with its elegant canopied pavilions consists of the king's palace, queen's palace, royal baths, tank, minister's palace, a temple to Hanuman, and various ancillary structures like stables and guardhouses. Local builders using traditional materials and traditional technology are at work on this monument, and the restoration will actually cost SADA (Special Areas Development Authority of the Madhya Pradesh State Government) half of what it would have cost it to build an entirely new structure. When restored, this building will once again be the nucleus of the town. The ground floor will be used as an exhibition and sales showroom for Chanderi saris; the first floor will be treated as a museum to house a display of local sculptures; and the second floor will become a citizens' center. Rather than treating monuments as buildings of spectator-interest alone, the approach is to revitalize monuments and put them into use. While coming to terms with its history and witnessing the resurrection of the Rajmahal, the town is also planning its future.

National Historical Parks: Agra and Sarnath

One of the most significant moves in the field of cultural conservation is the proposal for national historical parks at Agra and Sarnath, put forward by the National Parks Service of the United States in consultation with the Government of India's Ministry of Tourism. At the core of the Agra park will be the key historic structures of the Taj Mahal and Agra Fort, and linked to these will be a string of other monuments, including Akbar's tomb at Secundra, the Agra tomb of Itimad-ud-daula, and a series of neglected Mughal gardens and lesser tombs lining the banks of the Yamuna River. Between the various monuments will be a series of buffer zones composed of green spaces intended both to protect the views and hold urban growth at a distance. Particular emphasis is laid on the importance of retaining open spaces on both sides of the river near the Taj in order to maintain the visual integrity of the historic scene. The plan suggests that the national historical park be extended to reach out to Akbar's capital city of Fatehpur Sikri, some 25 miles west of Agra. The U.S. Parks Service team, which includes a landscape architect, a historical architect, and an engineer, as well as planners interested variously in interpretation, cultural resources, and preservation technology, will produce the detailed concept designs. The team's investigations are being carried out with the cooperation of local engineers, archaeologists, and forest officers; the actual implementation will rest in the hands of various local authorities including the Agra Development Authority, the Tourism Ministry, the ASI, and the state town and country planners.

The Parks Service has highlighted the need for a series of detailed studies before it puts together its final proposal. One major investigation concerns the effect of air pollution on the quality of the marble—a factor of great concern to all those interested in the preservation of the Taj Mahal. Ever since the local press dramatized the discoloration of the Taj marble due to sulphur fumes from the oil refinery located 18 miles away, this matter has been of deep concern. A report on the discoloration, presented to the General Assembly of the International Committee on Monuments and Sites in Washington, D.C., in 1987, emphasized the need for constant monitoring of the quality of the air. While the oil refinery remains at its location despite much agitation to have it moved, all foundries in and around the town have been shut down.

A second study of vital importance concerns the dangerous level of pollution of the waters of the Yamuna River, into which open waterways discharge the domestic, commercial, and industrial sewage of Agra. The river was one of the factors that induced the Mughal emperors to make Agra the center of their activities, and the rebirth of the Yamuna as a river and as a viable source of potable water is essential. Related to this is the necessity for studies on the feasibility of constructing dams to regulate or even impound water flow. The possibility of having a body of water directly in front of the Taj is being studied. Although the Taj was originally built to withstand a body of water and incorporates a series of wells in its foundations, studies are required to determine if it would be dangerous to reintroduce water after a long period of dry foundations.

The second national historical park is the Deer Park complex at Sarnath, site of the first sermon of the Buddha, with various stupas, temples, lakes, and wooded areas. A study of this project carried out by a team from the Department of Landscape Architecture at the University of Illinois at Urbana-Champaign is subtitled "A Master Plan for Tourism Development," thus highlighting one of its major concerns. However, as we have seen earlier, the interests of tourism and conservation need not be opposed. Despite the doubts on the subject expressed by the ASI and INTACH's reservations on the involvement of the United States Parks Service, the Sarnath plan, while emphasizing tourism, gives weight to local religious, social, and craft concerns.

The plan contains several landscaping proposals that would add greatly to the atmosphere and historical authenticity of the site, the most significant being the restoration of the park to recall the earlier pristine deer preserve. It is proposed that local vendors, seen today all over the site, be relocated to a series of specially marked vending zones. Lodges constructed to accommodate visitors will follow an open monastery plan or a village plan, and local "rammed-earth" construction will be utilized; such lodges will be equipped with locally produced cloth, pottery, and furniture, thus aiding a self-sustained local economic cycle. The final report of this well-conceived plan is due to be presented by the end of 1990.

The Memorandum of Understanding between the National Parks Service of the United States and the Government of India's Department of Tourism, signed in May 1989, referred to cooperation on four projects. Third on the agenda, after the national historical parks at Agra and Sarnath, is Bodh Gaya, site of the Buddha's Enlightenment, mentioned earlier. The final project involves helping the Indian Institute of Tourism and Travel Management to set up a new campus and designing a tourist-related curriculum for it.

Wall Paintings

Although Indian painting is best known through its miniatures, mural decorations cover the walls of temples and monasteries, palaces and *havelis* all over India. Perhaps the most famous murals are in the Buddhist monastic caves at Ajanta, which are under the protection of the ASI and also on UNESCO's list of world heritage sites. The paintings, executed in the fifth century, have been a conservator's headache. In the 1920s Italian experts made liberal use of shellac mixed with alcohol as a fixative for the pigments. Unfortunately, the methods used were not successful in arresting deterioration; in addition, the coats of shellac underwent oxidation and altered the tonal values of the paintings. Remedial action, which began in 1953, included removal of the shellac using a variety of solvents. For the past several years, one or another of the painted caves has remained closed to visitors as the ASI proceeded with conservation work. Finally, last year, all the caves have reopened to the public.

The condition of the paintings continues to remain a matter of serious concern. A convenient system of lighting has been installed in the four main painted caves, enabling the vast numbers of tourists who visit the site to view the murals. Yet the lighting itself is a source of anxiety. A proposal to air-condition the caves was examined and rejected as not merely ineffective and wasteful but possibly harmful to the murals. A study in the variations of temperature and humidity within the caves was undertaken in 1975 in response to a proposal to close them to visitors. The report on the water vapor and carbon dioxide content concluded that such a move was not yet necessary but would need to be reconsidered if the tourist influx increased. Fifteen years later, a reassessment is certainly necessary. B. B. Lal, ex-director-general of the ASI, calculated that there has been a 75 percent loss of the paintings in the 15 centuries since their creation; at the existing rate of destruction, he estimates that they will be totally lost in another 5 centuries.

A major project to survey, scientifically examine, and conserve the many other wall paintings of India was launched a year ago by INTACH's Conservation Center together with the government's National Research Laboratory for the Conservation of Cultural Properties (NRLC), in collaboration with various state governments. In a pilot project at the Shish Mahal (Mirrored Palace) in the 17th-century Nagaur fort, dirt and water stains were removed, bulging plaster was reattached, and areas where it had fallen off were refilled and tinted to match the surrounding areas; a protective coating was applied to prevent further flaking of paint, and cracks were filled. An effort was made to lighten the blackened faces and limbs of the figures, with only limited success. An analysis of the pigment revealed the presence of lead, and experiments are continuing to overcome this problem, which is also apparent at Ajanta. Conservation has now begun at the Bundi fort and in other buildings at Nagaur. However, the most modern techniques used to restore valuable murals are still unknown in India.

Movable Heritage

India has a vast and impressive range of objects classified as movable heritage. Temples across the country own valuable sculptures of bronze, wood, and stone, as well as jewels, ritual objects, and ivories and textiles. Museums, private collectors, and art dealers own a wider range of objects that includes architectural units and coins, paintings, and manuscripts. In addition, private individuals who are scarcely aware that they own "art" possess shawls and musical instruments, silver utensils and jewelry, and photographs and religious pictures. Movable heritage is controlled in large measure by the Antiquities and Art Treasures Act of 1972, designed largely to regulate the export trade in antiquities and to discourage smuggling. The act requires every individual who possesses an object over 100 years old to register it, together with three photographs, with the government registering officer. Apart from being extremely cumbersome, the act is almost impossible to enforce. If the aim behind such registration is to build up an inventory of India's movable antiquities, the act seems like overkill. More could be achieved in that realm by making a master list of all objects in the nation's museums whether large or small, government- or privately owned, and particularly of those objects in unclassified storage.

The act also prohibits the export of articles more than 100 years old. Just as it is utopian to suggest the preservation of every ancient building merely on the basis of its having come down from the past, so too is it unrealistic to retain every object merely because it is old. As the 21st century approaches, it is sobering to realize that objects produced at the start of the present century will soon belong to this category. Once again, a selection of the best is indicated, after which the market can be allowed to take its course. India does indeed have a superabundance of movable heritage, much of it of the highest quality. However, there is a profusion of objects of secondary and tertiary quality: museum godowns are packed with medieval temple doorjambs, fragments of lintels, architectural elements of wood and stone, broken sculptures, and the like. How many of these are worthy of preservation? A systematic deaccessioning of such objects, followed by open auctions conducted by established auctioneers, could earn the government much-needed foreign exchange.

The advisability of transporting overseas valuable items of movable cultural heritage to project an image of culture has generated heated argument. A series of Festivals of India held in half a dozen countries—including the United Kingdom, the United States, Japan, France, Norway, and the Soviet Union—have presented the foreign viewing public with irreplaceable objects of India's heritage. If the intention of such festivals is to promote tourism, they probably serve their purpose; however, the same end could be achieved without the enormous expense involved or the great risks to the individual works of art. Lending a Gupta sculpture to a specialized exhibition on the art of India's Golden Age may be a creditable decision; sending that same image overseas to a festival to promote India's culture seems unnecessary.

A particularly vexing and paradoxical problem for conservationists is the threat to heritage posed by thievery and smuggling. Conservationists aim to ensure that heritage is successfully preserved, that the meaning of the term "heritage" is expanded, and that there is an increasing appreciation of heritage among the populace. Yet, as their aim is fulfilled, the market in heritage items increases, as does the incentive to steal such objects. The village guardian deity becomes a valuable piece of art and represents a hidden source of income. While it is impossible to estimate the dimensions of the threat from this quarter, it is unfortunately one of the by-products of the increasing awareness of cultural heritage.

Chemical Conservation

For more than 50 years the ASI has had a chemical branch that specializes in the preservation and scientific restoration of a variety of objects. In recent years, this has merged with the conservation laboratory of the National Museum, which restores and treats a wide range of objects including miniatures, scroll paintings, manuscripts, bronzes, wood and stone sculptures, and textiles. The Indian Association for the Study of Conservation of Cultural Property attached to the National Museum publishes a journal that gives details of the techniques used in preservation, conservation, and restoration. More recently INTACH established a well-equipped Conservation Center at Lucknow, with several restorers on its staff. The help and advice of the center has been sought by a variety of institutions including the Government Museum at Chandigarh, the State Museum at Lucknow, the Sarabhai Foundation at Ahmedabad, and Raj Bhavan at Calcutta, as well as by a number of private collectors.

Books and Manuscripts

Until recently, the vast majority of India's extraordinary range of manuscripts on palm leaf and paper remained unstudied, unpublished, and uncataloged. Ten years ago, a visitor to the Manuscript Library of the Sanskrit University at Varanasi would have found manuscripts wrapped in lengths of red cloth and stacked haphazardly on shelves. Catalogs, compiled as manuscripts were acquired, consisted of extensive handwritten entries that gave little information beyond the title of the manuscript. The only way to find anything was through the help of a knowledgeable librarian. The storage system was basic, and in conditions of high heat and humidity it could be dangerous to the collections. Recent years, however, have seen an intense awareness of the richness and importance of this aspect of our heritage, and a dramatic change has occurred in attitudes toward manuscripts.

The Indira Gandhi National Centre for the Arts (IGNCA), established less than five years ago, has been the moving force in this field. Their *Kala Nidhi* (Treasury of Arts) division was planned to house a computerized National Information System and Data Bank. One important scheme, initiated jointly with INTACH, is a Union Catalog of catalogs both published and unpublished. Information from 1,000 catalogs in India and overseas has been scanned and computerized, so that data on particular disciplines, from both published and unpublished material, can now be retrieved. Future researchers will have access to material that might otherwise have taken a lifetime to collect.

A second long-range proposal is to establish a microfilm and microfiche library of unpublished manuscripts from both Indian and overseas collections. The *Kala Kosa* (Storehouse of Arts) division has an ambitious program to identify and systematically edit and publish annotated texts and translations of fundamental works, together with commentaries on them, in the field of Indian arts, from architecture, sculpture, and painting to music, dance, and theater. The plan visualizes 108 basic texts in critical editions, together with glossaries, translations, and illustrations. As a pilot project, 3,000 manuscripts of three selected texts were computerized; the information will provide the base for the handling of variant readings of the texts that comprise the series. The initial phase, which will handle 24 texts, has seen the recruitment of scholars from both India and overseas. The first five volumes to be published include three texts on music, one on sculpture, and a Vaisnava temple text.

Although IGNCA concentrates its efforts on India's rich ancient heritage, it does not ignore the more recent past; photography, for instance, is among its concerns. IGNCA has acquired the valuable collection of nearly 2,000 glass-plate negatives, as well as a number of original prints, of the extraordinarily successful 19th-century Indian photographer Raja Deen Dayal.

Steps toward the conservation of India's books and manuscripts are also being taken by a variety of governmental institutions and universities in the United States. One such project, with a U.S. federal grant of half a million dollars (from the National Endowment for the Humanities and the U.S. Department of Education) is being carried out jointly by the University of Chicago and Harvard University. The aim is to microfilm 7,500 printed books from a range of Indological series that specialized in publishing Sanskrit texts. The books themselves are in brittle condition, and even with the most careful handling, pages crack and books fall apart. The resulting microfilms will be available through interlibrary loans or may be purchased as prints on a cost-recovery basis. The series chosen include, to mention just a few, the Adyar Library Series, the Benares Sanskrit Series, the Bhandarkar Oriental Series, the Chowkhamba Sanskrit Series, Gaekwad's Oriental Series, and the Scindia Oriental Series.

A project initiated by the University of Chicago will utilize money from the U.S.–India Fund in order to preserve by microfilming ("reformatting" is the library terminology) early 20th-century books on India. Important books published between 1901 and 1953 will also be brought under bibliographic control when microfilming is initiated. The project envisages work over ten years, at the rate of 6,000 volumes per year. Expertise from both India and the United States will be drawn upon, with the microfilming being done in India at the sites of various major collections.

Living Heritage

The third segment of heritage to be preserved and passed on to future generations is India's rich tradition of dance and music, of folk tales and folk songs, of storytelling, and of ritual diagrams on floors. This aspect of our heritage has ancient roots but is still a living tradition; in many areas, however, it is in danger of being lost as modernization and urbanization impose a new scale of values. One striking example is the rich *alpana* tradition found all over India, in which ritual and symbolic diagrams are produced on the floor with rice powder. Known by a variety of names—*kolam* in Tamil Nadu, *rangoli* in western India, *mugulu* in Andhra, *alpana* in Bengal—the tradition is in danger of being lost. In 1989 I found that while it was still traditional to have one of these auspicious diagrams at one's front door, the fashion in Bangalore was to buy them in stores as peel-off sheets. The importance of the documentation of such heritage has been realized and is part of IGNCA's *Janapada Sampada* (People's Wealth) activities under their division of ethnographic studies. For instance, a whole series of transparencies of rice drawings from Tamil Nadu has been acquired for their archives.

INTACH is collaborating with IGNCA on the documentation of folklore and oral traditions in India, and its Tamil Nadu chapter has prepared a survey of the folklore of districts in the far south of the state. Other projects include the recording of the oral tradition and folk songs of Kumaon and Manipur, such as the songs sung during the harvest and the sowing festivals. Traditions such as these are in danger of disappearing all over India as fewer villagers participate in such celebrations. One major contributing factor is the pervasive influence of radio and television, which have recently swept the country, replacing traditional forms of entertainment.

Integrated Conservation

Despite a certain amount of publicity and a great deal of concerted effort, the doctrine of integrated conservation is just beginning to be applied to India. The reasons for this appear to be threefold. First, there is an overwhelming interest in antiquities to the detriment of more recent and often "living" monuments. For instance, attention needs to be lavished on Colonel Cowper's 1833 Bombay Town Hall; while the exterior of the building has received attention in recent years, the interior, which houses the Library of the Asiatic Society, is in a shocking state of disrepair. Another neglected building is Sir Gilbert Scott's Bombay University Library of 1874, with its celebrated spiral stairway, used today by large numbers of college students. Considered planning is necessary to ensure the functioning survival of these and several comparable structures for future generations. It is telling that the organization responsible for architectural heritage is called the Archaeological Survey of India rather than a council for historic or cultural heritage; its name reflects the priority accorded to the archaeological and ancient historical heritage of the country.

Second, there is a shortage of resources relative to the number of conservation projects that await implementation. The generous government allocation to the ASI during the Seventh Plan is cause for optimism. However, the recurring requirement of substantial funds for conservation will have to be faced and the economics of conservation reassessed.

Third, there is an unfortunate absence of cooperation between the two main participants in conservation work in India—the government and the voluntary bodies. Further compounding the problem in an area like Tamil Nadu are the temple authorities, who play a considerable part in the upkeep of religious monuments. The many historic temples of southern India are in the hands of the state government's Department for Hindu Religious Endowments, and conservation may only be effected by the order of its commissioner. The conservation ideas of such a body, interested almost exclusively in the religious function of temples, differ vastly from those upheld by professional bodies such as the ASI.

It is also necessary for conservationists to maintain a continuing dialogue with the Department of Tourism, defining the areas of common concern to both. One school of thought among the professional guardians of cultural heritage, who fear erosion of sites at the hands of visitors, wishes to keep the general public away from its treasures if possible. But the growth of tourism is inevitable and, as we have seen, need not be a negative phenomenon; considered planning and professional management can ensure the successful conservation of the cultural heritage that is the very cause of tourism.

Cultural resource management, a term used widely in the United States, needs to take its place among subjects of national importance. Such management is concerned with what things will be retained from the past and how they will be used in the present and future. Once INTACH's listing of heritage has been completed, it will be practicable to make effective decisions on this issue.

The need for an overall conservation strategy cannot be overemphasized. The ASI concerns itself with immovable heritage in the form of Class A buildings, while the state archaeology departments conserve buildings that fall in the Class B category; INTACH's major thrust is heritage zones in which entire townships are preserved; the IGNCA's specialty is movable heritage, especially books and manuscripts, but also living heritage in the form of fast-vanishing traditions of dance, music, folklore, and the like. In addition, a number of local citizens' bodies function as voluntary conservation groups. These various bodies, each with specialized interests, devote themselves to different aspects of heritage.

While recognizing the special concerns of each body and the particular talents that each can provide, the Indian government must take the lead in overall planning for cultural resource management. Without actually directing the activities of individual bodies, a centrally constituted agency should review their various activities and offer suggestions on the directions each might profitably take in view of work being done by the others. The managerial component in conservation policy is crucial. Such an agency, taking a pan-Indian view of conservation, might profitably suggest, for instance, that the ASI declare as Class A protected monuments the unique wood-carved *gopurams* (gateways) of the bat-infested 17th-century temples at Tirukurunkudi and Tirupuraimaradur in Tamil Nadu; or that IGNCA give priority to the rich collection of Mughal and post-Mughal paintings and manuscripts in the library of the Nawab of Rampur; or that INTACH turn its attention early to Kanchipuram, that tragically neglected town of Hindu temples (8th to 17th centuries) and silk saris. Certainly, the individual institutions will at some stage address these concerns (given here as examples and not necessarily as first priorities). But a central agency would be better able to review the relative urgency of projects and, most important, to coordinate the activities of the various conservation bodies. Planning and management are essential to ensuring a successful future for India's past.

Suggestions for Further Reading

Akbar, M. J. *India: The Siege Within* (New York: Penguin, 1985).

Allchin, B., F. R. Allchin, and B. K. Thapar, eds. *Conservation of the Indian Heritage* (New Delhi: Cosmo Publications, 1989).

Andersen, Walter K., and Sridhar D. Damle. *The Brotherhood in Saffron: The Rashtriya Swayamsevak Sangh and Hindu Revivalism* (Boulder, CO: Westview Press, 1987).

Bhambhri, C. P. *The Foreign Policy of India* (New Delhi: Sterling Publishers, 1987).

Brass, Paul. *The Politics of India Since Independence* (New York: Cambridge University Press, 1990).

Chakravarty, Sukhamoy. *Development Planning: The Indian Experience* (Oxford: Clarendon Press, 1987).

Cleere, Henry, ed. *Approaches to the Archaeological Heritage. A Comparative Study of World Cultural Resource Management Systems* (New York: Cambridge University Press, 1984).

Cohen, Stephen Philip, ed. *The Security of South Asia: American and Asian Perspectives* (Urbana: University of Illinois Press, 1987).

Das Gupta, Jyotirindra. "India: Democratic Becoming and Combined Development," in Larry Diamond *et al.*, eds. *Democracy in Developing Countries: Asia* (Boulder, CO: Lynne Rienner, 1989), pp. 53–104.

Frankel, Francine, and M. S. A. Rao, eds. *Dominance and State Power in Modern India: Decline of a Social Order.* 2 vols. (New Delhi: Oxford University Press, 1989).

Ganguly, Sumit. *The Origins of War in South Asia: Indo-Pakistani Conflicts since 1947* (Boulder, CO: Westview Press, 1988).

Ghosh, Parthan S. *Cooperation and Conflict in South Asia* (New Delhi: Manohar Publishers, 1989).

Government of India, Ministry of Finance. *Report of the Economic Advisory Council on the Current Economic Situation and Priority Areas for Action*, New Delhi, December 1989.

Haksar, P. N. *India's Foreign Policy and its Problems* (New Delhi: Manohar Publishers, 1989).

Kohli, Atul. "Politics of Economic Liberalization in India," *World Development*, Vol. 17 (March 1989), pp. 305–328.

Kohli, Atul. *India's Democracy: An Analysis of Changing State-Society Relations* (Princeton: Princeton University Press, 1988); see also the updated paperback edition to be published in September 1990.

Mansingh, Surjit. *India's Search for Power: Indira Gandhi's Foreign Policy, 1966–1982* (New Delhi: Sage, 1984).

Menon, A. G. Krishna, ed. "Conservation in India," *Architecture + Design*, Vol. 6, no. 1 (November-December 1989).

Rudolph, Lloyd I., and Susanne Hoeber Rudolph. *In Pursuit of Lakshmi: The Political Economy of the Indian State* (Chicago: University of Chicago Press, 1987).

Sisson, Richard, and Leo E. Rose. *War and Secession: Pakistan, India, and the Creation of Bangladesh* (Berkeley: University of California Press, 1990).

Thomas, Raju G. C. *Indian Security Policy* (Princeton: Princeton University Press, 1986).

Weiner, Myron. *The Indian Paradox: Essays in Indian Politics* (New Delhi: Sage, 1989).

1989: A Chronology

1   India announces that it will withdraw 2,000 Indian Peace Keeping Force troops from Sri Lanka and that further withdrawals will follow.

Safdar Hashmi, a popular street-theater director, is beaten to death after refusing a demand made by Congress(I) politician Mukesh Sharma that he discontinue a drama in support of an opposing CPI(M) candidate. Sharma and four others are arrested for the murder.

6   Satwant Singh and Kehar Singh, convicted for the assassination of Indira Gandhi in October 1984, are hanged. The executions are carried out after a long, drawn-out legal battle and the final dismissal of the defendants' petition by two separate Supreme Court benches. The Indian government takes heavy security measures in order to control the violence spurred by Sikh protests of the executions. Despite these measures, on January 12 Sikh terrorists in Punjab murder 36 people in retaliation for the executions.

11   Minister of State for External Affairs Natwar Singh and Chinese Foreign Minister Qian Qichen meet in Paris to discuss the joint working groups that will be formed to negotiate on the Sino-Indian border dispute. The agreement to establish the working groups was reached during Prime Minister Rajiv Gandhi's official visit to China in December.

21   **Assembly elections take place in Tamil Nadu, Mizoram, and Nagaland. The polling is accompanied by scattered violence in some areas.** On January 23 the DMK is declared the winner of the Tamil Nadu elections, defeating the Congress(I) and the AIADMK by winning 146 of the seats in the 232-member assembly. The five-party front led by the DMK wins 170 seats in total. The AIADMK (Jayalalitha) wins 27 seats, the Congress(I) wins 25 seats, and the AIADMK (Janaki) takes only one seat. **The Congress(I) wins control of the state assemblies in Nagaland and Mizoram.** As a result of the elections, on January 24 President's Rule is lifted in both Tamil Nadu and Mizoram.

22   Madhya Pradesh Chief Minister Arjun Singh is directed to step down from his post by the Congress central leadership. Critics of the government have alleged that Arjun Singh and his family used profits from the Churhat lottery for personal gain. A Central Bureau of Investigation inquiry into the matter has been ordered. The following day, a nine-member ministry headed by Motilal Vora is sworn in.

31   Janaki Ramachandran, leader of the AIADMK (Janaki) and wife of the late Tamil Nadu chief minister M.G. Ramachandran, retires from politics following her party's poor electoral performance in the Tamil Nadu assembly elections earlier this month.

FEBRUARY

3   Prime Minister Rajiv Gandhi, addressing a rally of Congress(I) youth in Bombay, warns that India will take all steps necessary to ensure its security in light of recent developments in the nuclear program in Pakistan. Gandhi alleges that intelligence reports confirm that Pakistan has obtained nuclear technology from West German sources.

5   Pakistan's army chief of staff, General Mizra Aslam Beg, announces his country's first successful testing and firing of a surface-to-surface long-range missile,

estimated to have a range of up to 300 km. On February 8 Rajiv Gandhi issues a public statement expressing concern over the fact that the missile is capable of carrying a nuclear weapon.

8   All 31 ministers of the Andhra Pradesh ministry resign as recognition of their responsibility for budget proposals that were leaked to the press. A week later, Chief Minister N. T. Rama Rao inducts 23 new ministers into his cabinet.

10   On the first day of a meeting of National Front chief ministers in Delhi, National Front leaders announce that they will contest the Lok Sabha elections in a joint manifesto that they intend to release on April 15.

13   In Kashmir, one individual is killed and 20 are injured when police fire upon protestors in the first of the Indian demonstrations against the publication of Salman Rushdie's novel *The Satanic Verses*. This incident, together with the Ayatollah Khomeini's February 14 announcement of a "death sentence" for Rushdie, sparks a four-day wave of violent protests in the state, which leave two dead and hundreds injured.

14   **The Indian Supreme Court orders the U.S. multinational Union Carbide to pay US$470 million as "full and final settlement of all claims, rights and liabilities arising out of the 1984 Bhopal gas tragedy." A deadline of March 31 is given for the payment, and the court dismisses all pending criminal charges against the company. In the following week, opposition members in both houses denounce the government-sponsored settlement as a "betrayal" and a "sellout." On March 31 the Supreme Court rules that the Bhopal settlement is to be stayed until the constitutionality and legitimacy of the settlement can be ruled upon.**

15   In Sri Lanka, where 63 percent of the electorate turns out to vote in the country's national parliamentary elections, 57 are killed in election-day vio-

lence. The elections return the ruling United National Party to power with an absolute majority in the 225-member parliament, and Tamil candidates win 23 seats.

18   Prime Minister Rajiv Gandhi appoints R. K. Dhawan to the post of officer on special duty in the prime minister's office. Dhawan had previously served as a special assistant to Prime Minister Indira Gandhi.

23   Congress Party members of the Karnataka state legislature boycott the assembly, demanding a Central Bureau of Investigation inquiry into the land scandals that allegedly occurred in the state during Ramakrishna Hegde's tenure as chief minister.

24   On the same day on which parliament votes to condemn the Ayatollah Khomeini's death threat against author Salman Rushdie, ten individuals are killed in the violence that ensues during a Bombay demonstration against *The Satanic Verses*. A near-total *bandh* (protest) is observed in the Muslim sections of the city the following day to mourn those killed.

28   **Opposition party members boycott the presentation of the budget for the 1989–90 parliament because of accusations made by Prime Minister Rajiv Gandhi in the previous day's session that the opposition parties had encouraged communal, casteist, regional, and linguistic forces in the country.** Finance Minister S. B. Chavan presents the attending members of parliament with a Rs. 7,337 crore deficit budget, which he describes as "anti-poverty and growth oriented." The budget provides minor tax relief for those in the 18,000–25,000 rupee income range and calls for increased taxes on airline tickets, cigarettes, televisions, and other luxury goods. On March 1, following an apology by Prime Minister Rajiv Gandhi, which the opposition describes as "without grace," the boycotting members return to the Lok Sabha.

MARCH

3   Claiming a process of normalization has begun in Punjab, Prime Minister Rajiv Gandhi announces a new package for the state that provides for the release of all "Jodhpur [Jail] detainees," accused of waging war against the state in the aftermath of Operation Bluestar in June 1984, and the relaxation of restrictions on travel by foreigners to the state. On March 6 and 7, 188 Jodhpur detainees are released. However, many are rearrested for other charges pending against them.

4   Bihar Chief Minister Bhagwat Jha Azad and seven ministers submit their letters of resignation to the prime minister. Dissident Congress legislators in the Bihar assembly have been protesting for the past two months in an effort to put pressure on the Congress leadership to remove Azad. A week later, a 13-member council of ministers headed by Satyendra Narain Sinha is sworn in to replace the Azad administration.

9   Lok Sabha members V. P. Singh, Arun Nehru, Arif Mohammad Khan, and V. C. Shukla write letters to Speaker Balram Jakhar stating that they are formally members of the Janata Dal, in an effort to gain recognition for their party in the Lok Sabha. However, Jakhar reserves his ruling on whether to accord formal recognition to the Janata Dal, stating that he will need to look into the matter further in order to satisfy himself that the party fulfills the conditions stipulated for recognition.

14   Portions of the Thakkar Commission Report on the assassination of the late prime minister Indira Gandhi are published in the *Indian Express*. Opposition parties demand that the full Thakkar Commission Report be placed before parliament.

23   The trade and transit agreements between India and Nepal lapse. The Nepali Foreign Minister and his delegation leave India on March 27, still not having reached a renegotiation of the agreement.

27 The Thakkar Commission Report, assembled in two volumes of 657 pages, is put before both houses of parliament. The report on the assassination of former prime minister Indira Gandhi names six individuals whom Justice Thakkar found derelict in their duties and explicitly states that strong evidence was found warranting suspicion of Special Officer R. K. Dhawan's complicity in the assassination. Congress officials stress that the special investigating team has cleared Dhawan, indicating that there is no evidence that he was involved in the conspiracy.

APRIL

7 Former Indian Police Service officer Simranjit Singh Mann and three others are arrested and charged with sedition, murder, attempt to murder, and conspiracy to kill Prime Minister Indira Gandhi in Nagpur in September 1984 and at her residence in October 1984.

11 Nepal imposes a new import-tariff regime on a large number of essential goods, stating that it will no longer benefit the Nepali economy to give preferential treatment to Indian goods.

14 Prime Minister Rajiv Gandhi sends Home Minister Buta Singh and Defence Minister K. C. Pant to personally review the situation of communal violence and terrorism in Jammu and Kashmir and to prepare a first-hand briefing on the problems for his review.

17 Army, navy, and paramilitary forces take control of essential operations at 11 of the country's major ports, as 125,000 dock workers affiliated with all four major trade-union federations (each associated with a different party) begin the first day of their strike for a new charter and higher wages. Despite the government determination on April 19 that the strike is illegal and that all workers should immedi-

ately return to their duties, the strike is not settled until April 21. The settlement of the strike includes a higher wage for the dock workers.

21   The Karnataka assembly is dissolved and President's Rule is imposed on the state. On April 22 V. P. Singh and ten other opposition leaders meet and decide to call a protest for April 27 to express outrage against the Congress government's "policy of destabilizing non-Congress state governments." The protest is carried out and is largely peaceful.

24   The Janata Dal launches its election campaign with the release of a six-point manifesto emphasizing the party's commitment to addressing the special problems and concerns of farmers, women, and *harijans*. V. P. Singh announces that if the Janata Dal is voted to power it will allocate 50 percent of the central and state budgets to rural development.

28   Prime Minister Rajiv Gandhi announces the initiation of the Jawahar Rozgar Yojna rural employment and wage scheme. The program is aimed at benefiting rural farmers and will be implemented by the village-level *panchayats*. Fifty percent of the program cost, approximately Rs. 2,100 crores, will be supplied by the central government for the current year.

Eighteen members of the Jammu and Kashmir ministry resign in order to allow Chief Minister Dr. Farooq Abdullah to conduct a reconstruction of the cabinet in the wake of increased terrorist and "anti-national" activity in the Kashmir Valley.

MAY

4   The Indian government announces that, according to diplomatic sources, Nepal has deployed newly acquired Chinese weaponry along its southern border with India. On May 10 the government of India notifies Nepal that stand-by loan systems will not be renewed because of the failure to renegotiate the trade and transit arrangements between the two countries.

11   Despite warnings from Chief Minister Dr. Farooq
      Abdullah, a near-total *bandh* for the release of inno-
      cent individuals held on charges of subversion is
      observed in many areas of Kashmir. The *bandh*,
      called by secessionist groups, is mostly peaceful.

15   Opposition members from both houses resign from
      all finance committees to protest the appointment
      of AIADMK member P. Kolandaivelu as chairman
      of the public accounts committee. This post is tradi-
      tionally held by a member of the opposition. Oppo-
      sition leaders claim that the AIADMK cannot legiti-
      mately be considered an opposition party because
      of the electoral alliance between that party and the
      Congress.

      **A new bill concerning the village government
      (*panchayats*) is introduced on the floor of the Lok
      Sabha amid opposition protest. If passed, the 64th
      amendment bill, which the opposition claims is an
      attempt by the Congress government to control
      state activities, would give uniform and increased
      independent power to the *panchayats* across the
      country. In addition, the bill provides that the
      panchayats are to receive their funding directly
      from the central government. Shortly after the in-
      troduction of this bill, the 65th amendment bill, a
      similar bill applying to municipal governments
      (*nagarpalikas*), is introduced in parliament.**

22   After two months of delays and cancellations, India
      succeeds in launching the *Agni*, its first intermediate-
      range ballistic missile. The following day the Bush ad-
      ministration expresses concern over the test firing but
      states that this event will not affect current U.S.-
      Indian discussions on the transfer of technology.

24   The Nepali government accuses India of "unneces-
      sary harassment and economic blockade" in a state-
      ment to international media delivered at the United
      Nations. The following day, the Nepali government
      invites the Indian foreign minister to Nepal for talks

on the renegotiation of the trade agreement between the two countries.

25   The U.S. administration announces that it has judged that India, Brazil, and Japan participate in "unfair trading practices" and will put these three countries on a priority watch list for the coming year. In addition, the United States calls upon India to reenter negotiations on trade with Nepal.

31   The government announces several new economic measures designed to alleviate the country's severe balance-of-payments problems, thus preventing the need to seek an IMF adjustment loan in the coming year.

JUNE

1   In a dramatic announcement, Sri Lankan President Ranasinghe Premadasa states that he will ask the Indian government to begin the withdrawal of the Indian Peace Keeping Force on July 29, the second anniversary of the Sri Lanka Accord. On June 14 Prime Minister Rajiv Gandhi announces that withdrawal of the Indian Peace Keeping Force from Sri Lanka will be contingent upon the full implementation of the Sri Lanka Accord. The Sri Lankan government maintains its position that the troops should be removed from the country at its request.

4   The Janata Dal and the BJP initiate negotiations on the formation of an electoral alliance in all northern states except Maharashtra, where the BJP is already involved in talks with the Shiv Sena, a militant nativist communal party.

7   While addressing a joint session of Congress during her visit to Washington, D.C., Pakistani Prime Minister Benazir Bhutto proposes a nuclear-free zone in South Asia and a test-ban agreement between India and Pakistan. The following day, an Indian embassy spokesperson responds to Bhutto's speech by describing her regional approach as "unrealistic"

and stating that India sees the need for a more global approach to the problem of nuclear weapons.

10   The BJP announces that it will participate in electoral alliances with the Shiv Sena in the upcoming Lok Sabha elections. As a result, V. P. Singh announces on June 14 that the Janata Dal will not ally itself with the BJP in Maharashtra.

17   **India and Pakistan reach a partial understanding on the Siachen Glacier issue, agreeing to work toward a comprehensive settlement to avoid the use of force in the area.** The following day, Pakistani Foreign Minister Dr. Humayan Khan announces that troops will be restored to the positions they held prior to 1972, when an agreement on the border was signed between the two countries. However, India denies having agreed to this, stating that discussions on redeployment of troops will be based on their pre-1972 positions.

25   In Punjab, terrorists fire upon a gathering of the Rashtriya Swayamsevak Sangh, killing 26 individuals. An indefinite curfew is imposed on the area of the Faridkot district in which the incident took place. Both the BJP and Shiv Sena parties call for a *bandh* to take place on June 26 to protest the killings. This *bandh* is widely observed throughout most of northern India.

26   V. P. Singh and several other opposition leaders from the CPI(M), CPI, Janata Dal, and Telugu Desam parties participate in protests against governmental control of the electronic media.

JULY

4   Rajiv Gandhi promotes five junior ministers in what is viewed as a move to accord greater representation to scheduled-caste and tribal members in the Council of Ministers. Of the five individuals promoted, four belonged to Scheduled Castes or Scheduled Tribes.

8   Representatives from the Shia Conference, the Muslim United Front, and the National Conference arrive in New Delhi for the commencement of the National Political Convention of Muslims. Members of the convention call for "the emergence of a national party based on the concept of solid support of all deprived social groups."

9   Addressing the press, Janata Dal President V. P. Singh rules out a Janata Dal alliance or sharing of power with the BJP in the new central government to be formed after the upcoming elections. Singh states, "We will prefer to sit in the opposition if we win rather than sharing power with the BJP." He claims that the issues on which the two parties disagree, such as the granting of special status to Jammu and Kashmir, are issues on which the Janata Dal cannot compromise.

16   **Rajiv Gandhi arrives in Pakistan, the first official visit of an Indian prime minister to that country in 30 years.** Rajiv's opening remarks emphasize the need for creating an atmosphere of cooperation between the two countries and for settling the Siachen Glacier dispute.

19   **The report of the comptroller and auditor general on allegations of improprieties by the government in its dealings with Bofors, a Swedish armaments firm, is released. It holds the government responsible for the gun purchases.** The next day, neither house of parliament is able to proceed with business as members of the opposition parties demand the resignation of Prime Minister Rajiv Gandhi.

23   The government calls out the army and imposes an indefinite curfew in the southern Kashmir town of Anantnag to control rioting triggered by the disappearance of a holy relic from a nearby shrine. Thirty individuals are injured in the disturbances.

24   **In an unprecedented move, 73 members of parliament from 12 opposition parties resign from the**

Lok Sabha in protest of the government's handling of the Bofors gun scandal.

28   After two months of troubled negotiation, Indian and Sri Lankan officials meeting in New Delhi reach an agreement on the withdrawal of the Indian Peace Keeping Force from Sri Lanka. The following day, the date of the original Sri Lankan deadline for withdrawal, a token 600 troops are removed.

31   Rao Birendra Singh, former Union agriculture minister, resigns from both the Congress Party and the Lok Sabha over the Bofors scandal. In addition, another opposition member resigns, raising the total number of resigned members to 97.

AUGUST

10   Rail and road traffic is held up and several thousand opposition workers are detained throughout the country as opposition supporters observe the "Save India Day" *bandh* called by opposition party leaders to protest the Bofors scandal and corruption in government.

With most opposition members no longer participating in the Lok Sabha, the *panchayat* and municipalities bills are unanimously passed.

Haryana Chief Minister Devi Lal announces that his government will withdraw its proposal to the state assembly for a resolution denying married daughters a share in the landed property of their parents. The proposal had drawn a great deal of criticism from the press and feminist groups.

13   Andhra Pradesh Chief Minister Rama Rao charges that Doordarshan and All India Radio have refused to air his Independence Day message, demanding major changes to the script. Rao asserts that it is the responsibility of the media to broadcast the ideas and views of those who head state governments.

15   Addressing a public rally at the Red Fort for Independence Day celebrations, Prime Minister Rajiv Gandhi praises the *panchayat* and municipalities bills, saying they would bring *swaraj* (self-government) to the people. He accuses secessionist, communal, and anti-nationalist forces of attempting to hinder this movement toward self-rule for the people.

20   **The Janata Dal and the BJP announce that they will participate in seat adjustments with one another for the upcoming elections in order to pursue their goal of unseating the current Congress government.** However, both parties are reluctant to speak about the possibility of sharing power with one another in the newly elected government.

SEPTEMBER

4   While attending a four-day summit of the Non-aligned Movement in Yugoslavia, Prime Minister Rajiv Gandhi and King Birendra of Nepal meet together for the first time in 14 months. Although the two leaders discuss the lapsed trade and transit treaties, no conclusive decision is reached on the matter.

6   In an interview with *India Today*, retired army chief of staff General K. Sundarji alleges that the Indian government has stalled efforts to obtain the names of people who had received illegal payments from the Bofors company.

17   India and Sri Lanka announce that the Indian Peace Keeping Force will suspend all offensive military actions beginning September 25 and that an effort will be made to withdraw all Indian troops from Sri Lanka by December 31.

30   In Madhya Pradesh and Punjab, communal violence breaks out during Ramshila processions, leaving 50 dead and hundreds injured. As the violence escalates over the next four days, three Madhya Pradesh towns are put under indefinite curfew.

U.S. President George Bush appoints career Foreign Service Officer William Clark as Ambassador to India.

OCTOBER

11   No business is conducted in the Rajya Sabha as opposition members continue to demand that Rajiv Gandhi be called upon to discuss the documents on the Bofors scandal published that day by the *Hindu*. The Bofors documents hint at Rajiv's involvement in the scandal. The following day the editor of the *Hindu* announces his decision to discontinue the exposé series on Bofors. The author of the story, N. Ram, and his coauthor, Chitra Subramaniam, allege that the government has put pressure on the paper to discontinue the story.

13   **Despite heavy campaigning, the government is unable to gain the two-thirds majority vote necessary to pass the 64th and 65th amendment bills on village and municipal government in the Rajya Sabha.**

15   Rajiv Gandhi approves a program to hold 450 public meetings throughout the country in the next two weeks to highlight how the opposition has prevented the Congress from handing power over to the people by defeating the *panchayat* and municipalities bills in the Rajya Sabha. Former Bihar chief minister Bhagwat Jha Azad will head the national monitoring committee that will oversee the meetings.

17   **Prime Minister Rajiv Gandhi announces that all states except Assam will go to the polls November 22 and 24 (later, November 26 is added) to elect the next Lok Sabha. Assembly elections will be held simultaneously in Andhra Pradesh, Karnataka, Goa, Sikkim, and Uttar Pradesh.**

19   V. P. Singh appeals to the VHP to delay the laying of the foundation of the Ram temple at Ayodhya, scheduled for November 9, in view of the recent election announcements.

20   The five-party National Front coalition releases its manifesto, which promises to track down those who received commissions from Bofors and to punish those guilty for the scandal. The coalition also vows to eliminate corruption and to break down the ties between elected officials and vested interests.

23   Rajiv Gandhi announces that he will again contest the elections from the constituency of Amethi, where he won 83.7 percent of the votes in 1984. The following day, the prime minister registers in Amethi.

26   **In the wake of increasing communal violence between Muslims and Hindus in Bhagalpur, Bihar, the prime minister orders the Bihar government to ban the Ramshila *puja* processions.** The following day, as the death toll from the communal clashes rises to 119, the Indian air force drops paramilitary troops in the area to control the rioting. In addition, 12 districts in Bihar are marked "politically sensitive."

      Janata Dal candidate Rajmohan Gandhi, the grandson of Mahatma Gandhi, announces that he will challenge the Lok Sabha elections from Amethi, Rajiv Gandhi's constituency.

27   The Supreme Court declines to ban the Ramshila processions and the controversial program of the Vishwa Hindu Parishad for the laying of the foundation of the Ram temple at Ayodhya. In addition, the Supreme Court announces it will not allow any general bans on Ramshila rallies or processions.

28   The communal violence that began in Bhagalpur, Bihar, begins to spread to the rural areas of the state. The death toll in Bihar rises to 135.

30   Janata Dal President V. P. Singh nearly misses the deadline for filing his papers challenging the Lok Sabha elections in his constituency in Fatehpur when his flight from Delhi is delayed because of a bomb scare and a technical difficulty. Singh alleges that the

delays were part of a Congress plot to prevent him from registering as a candidate in the elections.

NOVEMBER

1   Several newspapers publish reproductions of documents, said to be excerpted from the diary of the former Bofors managing director Martin Ardbo, that suggest Prime Minister Rajiv Gandhi's involvement in Bofors. A Congress spokesperson maintains that the documents were forged.

5   **Leaders of the major opposition parties announce that they will boycott the poll broadcasts from All India Radio and Doordarshan to protest the censorship of their scripts. Opposition members report that they were notified by election media authorities that they must avoid any references to Bofors and any use of Rajiv Gandhi's name in their scripts.**

6   On a tour of his parliamentary constituency, Amethi, Rajiv Gandhi releases his party's election manifesto and pledges to return the *panchayat* and municipalities bills to parliament, to overcome the problems of terrorism, and to bring about balanced growth of the economy. He also assures constituents that the Congress government will give special attention to the problems faced by women.

9   India's Election Commission announces that it will cancel plans to use electronic voting machines in the upcoming elections as the reliability of these machines has not yet been proven.

The Ramshila procession of the Vishwa Hindu Parishad and celebrations for the laying of the foundation of the Ram temple take place in Ayodhya. Despite communal flare-ups in many parts of the country, the procession and celebrations proceed peacefully.

11   Syed Abdullah Bukhari, the Shahi Imam of Delhi's Jama Masjid, announces his support of the Janata Dal

in the upcoming Lok Sabha elections. Bukhari holds the Congress government responsible for provoking communal tensions in many areas of the country.

14   The death toll resulting from the continuing communal violence in Bihar rises to 256. Of these deaths, 219 have occurred in Bhagalpur.

22   **Polling begins in the Indian states for the Lok Sabha and state-assembly elections. The voting continues on November 24 and 26. On all three days nearly 60 percent of the eligible electorate turns out to vote.**

Widespread violence accompanies the polling in many states, leaving more than 100 individuals dead. During the first day of polling, Janata Dal candidate Rajmohan Gandhi is severely beaten by police in the Amethi district while campaigning. The following day, near his house in Amethi, Janata Dal candidate Sanjay Singh is shot in the abdomen and seriously wounded. On November 24, unidentified gunmen shoot at V. P. Singh as he stops at a polling place near Fatehpur in Uttar Pradesh; Singh escapes unharmed.

23   Repolling is ordered at 600 booths in various districts throughout the country, including Amethi.

28   **Early results of the parliamentary elections point to severe Congress(I) losses in eastern, western, and northern India, and a very strong Congress(I) victory in the south. In the state elections also, the opposition National Front wins overwhelmingly in Uttar Pradesh, while component parties, the Telugu Desam in Andhra Pradesh and the Janata Dal in Karnataka, are badly beaten.**

29   **Rajiv Gandhi announces his resignation as Prime Minister of India, stating that he accepts the verdict of the people.**

30   Veerendra Patil is sworn in as Congress(I) chief minister of Karnataka. On December 3 Chenna

Reddy of the Congress(I) takes office as chief minister of Andhra Pradesh. In Congress-governed states where the Congress(I) lost in the parliamentary elections, new Congress chief ministers are installed: Hardeo Joshi in Rajasthan (December 5); Jagannath Mishra in Bihar (December 6); Hemnanda Biswal in Orissa (December 7); S. C. Shukla in Madhya Pradesh (December 9); and Madhavsinh Solanki in Gujarat (December 10).

DECEMBER

1   Punjab Governor S. S. Ray orders the immediate release of senior Akali Dal leaders, including the former chief minister Prakash Singh Badal, from prison. Some analysts see this announcement as tantamount to a general amnesty in Punjab.

President R. Venkataraman invites V. P. Singh to form a new government. Earlier in the day, V. P. Singh is unanimously elected leader of the National Front. At first, Devi Lal is nominated and elected as the leader, but he turns the nomination over to V. P. Singh, who accepts the unanimous vote in his favor. Hopeful candidate Chandrashekhar's name is never proposed.

2   **V. P. Singh is sworn in as prime minister and Devi Lal is sworn in as deputy prime minister.** The swearing in, performed by President Venkataraman, is attended by Rajiv Gandhi and all the senior leaders of the National Front except Chandrashekhar.

Akali Dal (Mann) President Simranjit Singh Mann and four of his associates are released from the prison in Bihar where they have been held on charges of attempting to assassinate late prime minister Indira Gandhi. Special Judge H. K. Verma withdraws all charges pending against the four in the interest of "public justice," as all four have been elected to the Lok Sabha.

O. P. Chautala, the son of Devi Lal, is sworn in as Janata Dal chief minister of Haryana. Mulayam

Singh Yadav of the Janata Dal becomes chief minister of Uttar Pradesh on December 5.

3   BJP President L. K. Advani announces that his party will not share power with the National Front government at the center or the Janata Dal Haryana state government, but that the party will lend support to both governments.

Prime Minister V. P. Singh asserts that the Bofors company will have to refund to the Indian government all money said to have been paid to middlemen in the gun deal.

5   Prime Minister V. P. Singh inducts 15 cabinet ministers and ministers of state, including Madhu Dandavate (Finance), Arun Nehru (Commerce), I. K. Gujral (External Affairs), Mufti Mohammad Sayeed (Home), Ajit Singh (Industry), George Fernandes (Railways), Arif Mohammad Khan (Energy), and Maneka Gandhi (Environment).

Former environment minister Z. R. Ansari is charged in a Delhi court for allegedly "molesting and outraging the modesty" of a female social worker in his office last October. Ansari had been arrested at his residence the previous week.

7   During a three-hour visit to Amritsar, during which he rode in an open jeep in a complete reversal of security precautions required by Rajiv Gandhi, Prime Minister V. P. Singh, along with Deputy Prime Minister Devi Lal, offers prayers at the Golden Temple.

8   Nirmal Kumar Mukherjee, a respected retired senior administrative officer, is sworn in as the new governor of Punjab.

9   **Rubaiya Sayeed, daughter of Home Minister Mufti Mohammad Sayeed, is kidnapped by members of the Jammu and Kashmir National Liberation Front. The kidnappers threaten to kill Sayeed unless five JKNLF members are released from prison. Sayeed**

is eventually released on December 13 in Srinigar, hours after the release of the five extremists.

17 An all-party meeting on Punjab takes place. The delegates arrive at a broad consensus on taking steps to repeal the 59th amendment. The controversial amendment, passed in March of 1988, gives the government the power to impose emergency regulations in Punjab in light of internal disturbances.

18 The Akali Dal (Mann) leaders announce their decision to support the National Front government at the center. In addition, the party demands immediate elections for Punjab.

21 The National Front government headed by V. P. Singh demonstrates that it has the confidence of the majority of the Lok Sabha in a voice vote in the house. The BJP, CPI(M), CPI, Forward Bloc, Revolutionary Socialist Party, Jharkhand Mukti Morcha, Akali Dal (Mann), and Shiv Sena party members all vote in support of the government. AIADMK and Congress members oppose the government during debate but do not vote against the National Front.

22 A five-judge constitutional bench of the Supreme Court upholds the constitutionality of the Bhopal Gas Leak Disaster Act.

28 The government announces that the pullout of the Indian Peace Keeping Force from Sri Lanka will be completed by March 31, 1990. The troops will have left six of the eight districts they occupy by December 31.

29 A five-member board composed of individuals active in the media, art, and cinema is established to oversee the operations of Doordarshan and All India Radio. In addition, Information and Broadcast Minister P. Upendra introduces a bill into the Lok Sabha that seeks to establish a new autonomous Broadcasting Corporation, of which All India Radio and Doordarshan would form two wings.

Glossary

Some Common Abbreviations:
AIADMK: All India Anna Dravida Munnetra Kazhagam
ASI: Archaeological Survey of India
BJP: Bharatiya Janata Party
BSP: Bahujan Samaj Party
CPI: Communist Party of India
CPI(M): Communist Party of India (Marxist)
DMK: Dravida Munnetra Kazhagam
GOI: Government of India
INTACH: Indian National Trust for Art and Heritage
IGNCA: Indira Gandi National Centre for the Arts
IPKF: Indian Peace Keeping Force
JKLF: Jammu and Kashmir Liberation Front
LTTE: Liberation Tigers of Tamil Eelam
RSS: Rashtriya Swayamsevak Sangh
SAARC: South Asian Association for Regional Cooperation
SC/ST: Scheduled Castes and Scheduled Tribes
VHP: Vishwa Hindu Parishad

Abdullah, Farooq. Son and political heir of the "Lion of Kashmir," Sheikh Abdullah; *chief minister* of Jammu and Kashmir state until his resignation in early 1990.

Advani, Lal Krishan. Leader of the *Bharatiya Janata Party* in the *Lok Sabha*.

Akali Dal. The major party of the *Sikhs* for 40 years, it governed the state of Punjab until May 1987 when *President's Rule* was imposed. Split into several factions, the most significant of which is now headed by *Simranjit Singh Mann*.

All India Anna Dravida Munnetra Kazhagam (AIADMK). Former ruling party in the state of Tamil Nadu, ousted by imposition of *President's Rule* in January 1988 following the death in December 1987 of its founder, M. G. Ramachandran. Split into two factions, both of which lost badly to the *DMK* in the election of January 1989.

Asom Gana Parishad (AGP). Ruling party in the northeastern state of Assam representing the interests of native Assamese. It was formed just before the December 1985 elections from members of the pro-Assamese All Assam Gana Sangram Parishad (AAGSP) and the All Assam Students Union (AASU). It is now part of the *National Front*.

Ayodhya. Small city in East-Central Uttar Pradesh; the city of Rama, hero of the *Ramayana*, and location of the *Ramjanmabhoomi–Babri Masjid* shrine.

"Backward" Classes. Classes recognized by the constitution as disadvantaged and allowed remedial treatment. In practice, "backward" classes have been defined in terms of caste membership.

Bahujan Samaj Party (BSP). Literally "party of society's majority," a newly formed party led by Kanshi Ram, it seeks to attract support not only from *scheduled-caste* voters, but also from other oppressed groups: Muslims, *"backward" classes*, and others.

Bandh. Protest through general strike or closure of shops and offices.

Bharatiya Janata Party (BJP). Party formed from the *Janata Party* by elements of the *Jana Sangh*, with support mainly in northern India. Led by L. K. *Advani*, it is seen to favor a Hindu nationalist ideology and pursues a hard line on the Kashmir question.

Bofors. Swedish armaments company alleged to have paid commissions to middlemen, in violation of its agreement with the government of India, to secure a Rs. 1.1 billion contract to supply 155 mm howitzer field guns.

Chandrashekhar. Starting as a "Young Turk" of the *Congress(I) Party* under Indira Gandhi before the *Emergency*, he has been an opposition leader since 1977 and now leads a faction of the *Janata Dal*.

Chief Minister. The equivalent of the prime minister in the government of Indian states.

Communal. Refers to ethnic communities, most commonly Hindu and Muslim communities; a "communalist" is what opponents call someone whose political identity is bound up with his or her ethnic identity and who allegedly puts his or her community "above" the nation.

Communist Party of India (CPI). The less influential of the two major communist parties; at present a part of the Left Front in parliament.

Communist Party of India (Marxist) [CPI(M)]. The stronger segment of the the Communist Party of India after the split of 1964. The CPI(M) has run the government of the state of West Bengal since 1977 and competes with the *Congress(I) Party* for power in Kerala. At present part of the Left Front in parliament.

Congress(I) Party. Party of former prime minister Rajiv Gandhi and the dominant Indian national party since independence and, even after its defeat in the 1989 elections, the largest party in the *Lok Sabha*. Congress is the principal inheritor of the mantle of the independence movement. The "I" stands for Indira Gandhi, who led this faction after a Congress Party split in 1977.

Congress(S) Party. Congress (Socialist) Party; formed from the split in the Congress in 1977, with the *Congress(I) Party* the other segment. Formerly used parenthetical letters that stood for the party president's name: Congress(R), Congress(S), Congress(U). At present, part of the *National Front*.

Crore. 10,000,000. Ten million.

Desai, Morarji. Senior *Congress Party* leader, formally opposed to Indira Gandhi after the 1969 party split. Prime minister of the *Janata Party* government, 1977–79.

Development Block. An administrative unit encompassing about 80–100 villages, with a specialized set of officials coordinating and staffing rural development efforts.

Devi Lal. Deputy prime minister in the *National Front* government led by *V. P. Singh*. Previously *chief minister* of Haryana, he is seen as the most powerful representative of rural landowning interests.

Dravida Munnetra Kazhagam (DMK). Tamil nationalist party, led by M. Karunanidhi, who became *chief minister* of Tamil Nadu after the party's January 1989 election victory. It is now part of the *National Front*.

Emergency. Declared by Indira Gandhi's government in June 1975, it lasted 21 months; opposition leaders were jailed, press censorship imposed, and the constitution amended to restrict the judiciary.

Five-Year Plans. Formulated by the *Planning Commission* and approved by parliament, these analyze the economic situation of the country and set out broad goals and specific guidelines for investment and other economic policy, for both public and private sectors. The First Plan covered the 1951–56 period. The Seventh Plan covers 1985–90.

Golden Temple. Holy seat of *Sikh* religion, located in Amritsar, Punjab. The Golden Temple has been a center of Sikh militant activity.

Gurudwara. *Sikh* temple.

Harijan. The name Mahatma Gandhi coined for the *Scheduled Castes*. Literally, "children of God."

Haveli. Large, traditional city house, with a courtyard in its center.

Hegde, Ramakrishna. *Chief minister* of Karnataka until his resignation in August 1988, and leader of the ruling *Janata Dal*; one of the major opposition leaders even after his defeat in the 1989 state elections, considered to be a potential prime minister. At present, head of the *Planning Commission*.

Hindi Heartland. The belt of states in which Hindi is the major language spoken: from west to east, Rajasthan, Haryana, Madhya Pradesh, Delhi, Uttar Pradesh, and Bihar.

Indian Peace Keeping Force (IPKF). Units, mainly of the Indian army, sent into the northern and eastern provinces of Sri Lanka under the *Sri Lanka Accord* of July 1987, initially to disarm the *Liberation Tigers of Tamil Eelam (LTTE)* and the other guerrilla groups. When that provision of the accord broke down, the IPKF fought the LTTE in pitched battles at Jaffna, and it has since attempted to maintain law and order. Withdrawn in March 1990.

Indo-Sri Lanka Accord. See *Sri Lanka Accord*.

Jainism. A religion dating from at least the sixth century B.C., in which adopting an ascetic life to achieve liberation is a central belief.

Jammu and Kashmir Liberation Front (JKLF). Militant group fighting for the independence of Kashmir.

Jan Morcha. "People's movement" founded in October 1987 by *V. P. Singh* and others expelled from the *Congress(I) Party* in April 1987 as a nonparty opposition group. Now part of the *Janata Dal*.

Jana Sangh. Hindu-chauvinist party formed in 1951 with strength mainly in North India. Much of its political cadre was drawn from the *Rashtriya Swayamsevak Sangh*. See *Bharatiya Janata Party*.

Janata Dal. Party that formed the government after the 1989 elections, with the support of the *Bharatiya Janata Party* and the Left Front. Formed from the *Jan Morcha*, the *Janata Party*, and factions of the *Lok Dal*.

Janata Party. One of the principal opposition parties, and ruling party in Karnataka until the formation of the *Janata Dal*. Janata formed a national government coalition in 1977–79, with *Morarji Desai* as prime minister.

Jati. Caste or subcaste unit that defines acceptable interactions in marriage, dining, and other caste-related practices.

Kashmir Valley. Also the "Vale of Kashmir." The valley of the river Jhelum, a part of the state of Jammu and Kashmir (the other major regions being Buddhist-dominated Ladakh and Hindu-dominated Jammu), which is populated almost entirely by Muslims. The political heartland of the state.

Lakh. 100,000. One hundred thousand.

Liberation Tigers of Tamil Eelam (LTTE). Leading Sri Lankan Tamil militant group, which seeks a separate state for Sri Lankan Tamils on the island of Sri Lanka. After the breakdown of the *Sri Lanka Accord*, it continued to fight the *Indian Peace Keeping Force* and conduct terrorist operations against Sinhalese in the Eastern Province of Sri Lanka.

Lok Dal. Break-away faction of the *Janata Party* formed in 1979 because of opposition to *Rashtriya Swayamsevak Sangh* involvement in the *Janata Party*. Leaders of its two major factions, *Devi Lal* and *Ajit Singh*, are now, as members of the *Janata Dal*, part of the *V. P. Singh* government.

Lok Sabha. Lower house of India's bicameral parliament.

Mann, Simranjit Singh. Militant leader of his faction of the *Akali Dal*, was elected to the *Lok Sabha* in 1989. Having resigned from the Indian Police Service in protest of *Operation Bluestar*, he was jailed from 1984–1989, charged, among other things, with conspiring to assassinate Indira Gandhi.

Narayan, Jayaprakash. A founder of the Congress Socialist Party in the 1930s, he renounced partisan politics to lead the Gandhian "land-gift" movement of the 1950s and the movement for a "total revolution" that triggered the *Emergency*, for which activities he was jailed. His role as non-office-seeking leader was crucial to the *Janata Party*'s victory in the 1977 elections.

National Front. An alliance opposed to the *Congress(I)* and composed of the *Janata Dal*, the *DMK*, *Telugu Desam*, *Asom Gana Parishad*, and the *Congress(S)*.

Nehru, Arun. Former minister of state for internal security and cousin of Rajiv Gandhi. After his expulsion from the *Congress(I)* in 1987, he became a leader, with *V. P. Singh* and others, of the *Jan Morcha*, and then the *Janata Dal*.

Operation Bluestar. Military assault on the *Golden Temple* in June 1984 to flush out *Sikh* extremists using the temple as a refuge. Operation Bluestar led to widespread Sikh alienation and protest.

Panchayat. Literally, a council of five. A village or *jati* council. *Panchayati raj* is the system of rural local government introduced in 1959 and changed significantly since, with variations from state to state. A constitutional amendment to standardize the system and give greater powers to both *panchayat* and central government (thus weakening the role of state governments) was introduced by the Rajiv Gandhi government but was defeated in the *Rajya Sabha*.

Planning Commission. Government body that prepares *Five-Year Plans*, which provide a broad framework for public and private economic goals.

President. In India, the equivalent of a constitutional monarch, who gives formal assent to bills, but whose powers are severely restricted. Elected by members of parliament and the state legislatures for a five-year term. The present incumbent is *R. Venkataraman*.

President's Rule. Suspension of a state's assembly and direct rule of the state by the central government through the centrally appointed governor, typically when the state government loses its majority or is deemed unable to govern due to a "disturbed" political situation. It has sometimes been used by the center to topple opposition-controlled state governments.

Punjab Accord. July 1985 agreement primarily between the central government and the states of Punjab and Haryana intended to resolve the crisis created by *Sikh* grievances over treatment of their community and the state of Punjab by the central government. The agreement remains largely unimplemented.

Ramayana. One of the two major epics of India, describing the adventures of Rama, a warrior-king and the incarnation of the god Vishnu.

Rajya Sabha. Upper house of India's bicameral parliament.

Ramjanmabhoomi–Babri Masjid. Literally: "Birthground of Rama—Mosque of Babur." Ram (or Rama), the hero of the *Ramayana*, is believed to have been born in *Ayodhya* on a particular spot of ground, now occupied by a mosque believed to have been built by the Mughal Emperor Babur. A shrine to Ram exists within the mosque.

Rama Rao, N. T. *Chief minister* of the state of Andhra Pradesh and leader of its *Telugu Desam* party, which was routed in the 1989 *Lok Sabha* and state elections.

Rashtriya Swayamsevak Sangh (RSS). Militant Hindu organization associated with the *Bharatiya Janata Party*. The RSS draws its membership mainly from urban and lower-middle classes and seeks the consolidation of a Hindu nation.

Reservation. The provision for quotas in legislative bodies, civil services, educational institutions, and other public institutions, typically in proportion to the percentage in the population, for qualified members of *Scheduled Castes and Scheduled Tribes*, and, in some places, for other *"backward" classes*.

Scheduled Castes and Scheduled Tribes (SC/ST). List of "untouchable," or *harijan*, castes and tribes drawn up under the 1935 Government of India Act and subsequently revised. Legislative seats as well as government posts and places in educational institutions are reserved for members of these castes and tribes.

Sharma, Shankar Dayal. Vice-president of India, succeeding *R. Venkataraman*; elected to a five-year term in August 1987.

Shekhar, Chandra. See *Chandrashekhar*.

Shilanyas. The ceremony of laying the foundation stone (at *Ayodhya*).

Shilapuja. (Also "Ramshila puja.") The worship and thus consecration of the "rocks" (in fact, bricks) destined for the Ram temple to be built at the *Ramjanmabhoomi–Babri Masjid*. *Shilapujas* were organized by the *Vishwa Hindu Parishad* all over India, with the consecrated bricks then taken in processions to *Ayodhya*, ending on November 9, 1989.

Shiv Sena. Militant nativist communal organization based largely in the towns of northern India. It was founded in Bombay in 1966 to agitate against South Indian immigrants to the state of Maharashtra. In the 1989 parliamentary and 1990 state elections, it formed an electoral alliance with the *Bharatiya Janata Party*.

Sikh, Sikhism. The religion of Sikhism was founded in the 16th century by the first guru, Nanak, drawing on Hindu devotionalism and Islam. Persecuted by the later Mughal emperors, Sikhs developed into a martial community, led by the tenth and last guru, Gobind Singh; a Sikh kingdom in central Punjab was conquered by the British in the mid-19th century.

Simla Agreement. Peace pact signed in 1972 by India and Pakistan, formally ending their 1971 war over Bangladesh and affirming the line of control between India and Pakistan in Kashmir.

Singh, Ajit. Industries minister in the *National Front* government. The son of *Charan Singh*, he returned from a career as an executive in the United States to don his late father's political mantle.

Singh, Charan. Leader of the Jats, a mid-ranking caste of land owners in western Uttar Pradesh and Haryana, he served as a Congress minister in state governments from independence until 1967 and as opposition *chief minister* of Uttar Pradesh. Jailed during the *Emergency*, he served as finance minister in the national *Janata Party* government (1977–79). He split the Janata to become prime minister, in which post he served for six months in 1979, and he remained a powerful opposition leader until his death in 1986.

Singh, V. P. Prime minister of India since November 1989 and leader of the *Janata Dal*. Former finance and defense minister under Rajiv Gandhi, Singh ran into political difficulties in his April 1987 ouster from government because of his efforts to hunt down tax evaders and eliminate corruption from India's government arms deals. He was the principal architect of India's new liberal economic policy.

South Asian Association for Regional Cooperation (SAARC). Organization formed in 1985 to enhance regional cooperation in social, economic, and cultural development. The SAARC members are Bangladesh, Bhutan, India, the Maldives, Nepal, Pakistan, and Sri Lanka. The fourth SAARC summit was held in Pakistan in December 1988.

Sri Lanka Accord. Signed by Prime Minister Rajiv Gandhi and President J. R. Jayewardene on July 28, 1987, in Colombo, the accord provided for the ending of the guerrilla war by Indian armed forces, which were to disarm the *Liberation Tigers of Tamil Eelam (LTTE)* and other Tamil extremists, and for the holding of elections to newly empowered provincial assemblies in which Tamils would gain significant autonomy.

Telugu Desam. Ruling party in the state of Andhra Pradesh, 1983–1989. Formed in 1982 and led by *N. T. Rama Rao*, the party was badly defeated by the *Congress(I)* in the 1989 elections. It is a component of the *National Front*.

Vajpayee, Atal Behari. A leader of the *Bharatiya Janata Party*, he served as external affairs minister in the 1977–79 *Janata Party* government. He is seen as a "moderate" in the "Hindu nationalist" spectrum within the BJP.

Varanasi. Also Banaras, Kashi; names of the city on the banks of the Ganges that is considered the most holy by Hindus.

Venkataraman, R. *President* of India for the 1987–1992 term. A respected *Congress (I)* politician, who had most recently served in the cabinet as defense minister, he was vice-president of India for a brief period before his election as president.

Vishwa Hindu Parishad (VHP). A movement seeking to reinvigorate Hinduism; leader of Hindu sentiment and organizer of actions regarding the *Ramjanmabhoomi–Babri Masjid* controversy.

About the Contributors

John Adams is Professor of Economics at the University of Maryland. He is the author of *India: The Search for Unity, Democracy, and Progress*, second edition (1976), with Walter C. Neale, and *Exports, Politics, and Economic Development: Pakistan, 1970–1982* (1983), with Sabiha Igbal. His most recent book is *Economics as Social Science: An Evolutionary Approach* (1989), with Wendell Gordon. His research interests include long-term growth in South Asia, the economic history of the region in the 19th century, and patterns of rural and village development.

Vidya Dehejia is Associate Professor in the Department of Art History and Archaeology at Columbia University, where she teaches a wide range of courses on the art and architecture of India. Her many publications include *Yogini Cult and Temples: A Tantric Tradition* (1986), published by the National Museum in New Delhi.

Shekhar Gupta is currently Features Editor of *India Today* magazine. He has written extensively about social, political, and communal strife in India and adjoining countries and was the recipient of the INLAKS Foundation journalist-of-the-year award in 1986. The author of *Assam: A Valley Divided* (1984), he also contributed chapters to *The Punjab Story* (1984) and *The Assassination and After* (1985).

Alan Heston is Professor of Economics and South Asia and Chairman of the South Asia Department at the University of Pennsylvania. He is coauthor with I. B. Kravis and R. Summers of *World Product and Income* (1982), published by the United Nations International Cooperation Project, with which he has been associated since 1968.

Atul Kohli is Associate Professor of Politics and International Affairs at Princeton University. He is the author of *The State and Poverty in India: The Politics of Reform* (1987) and *Democracy and Disorder: India's Growing Crisis of Governability* (1990).

Leo E. Rose is Adjunct Professor of Political Science, University of California at Berkeley, and Editor of *Asian Survey*. He has been a consultant for the U.S. Department of State and was a member of the State Department's policy planning staff. His recent books are *War and Secession: Pakistan, India, and the Creation of Bangladesh* (1990), with Richard Sisson, and *Beyond Afghanistan: The Emerging U.S.–Pakistan Relations* (1989), with Kamal Matinuddin.

Index